Note from Frank Tapson, author of the first edition

This dictionary is written mainly for students in the 11 – 16 age group, but it should also be helpful to anyone seeking a basic knowledge of the vocabulary of mathematics that are outside the strict limits of a school curriculum.

This is not a dictionary of etymology, grammar or English usage. So, for instance, there is no attempt to list every possible noun, adjective or verb, or all singular and plural forms. The main purpose is to provide headwords in the form in which they are most often met in mathematics.

Any dictionary must use words to explain other words. There is no escape from this, and all users are assumed to have a grasp of non-mathematical English language. The real problem, which has been acknowledged since the time of Euclid, is that of defining the most basic words such as 'point', 'line, 'surface', and so on. These words are explained in this dictionary, but it has to be accepted that they are 'intuitive ideas' or 'common notions'. No matter where a start is made, understanding has to break in at some place.

Compared with the first edition, this new edition has been enlarged by over two hundred entries. Many extra formulas and symbols have also been provided. Thus, I have attempted to provide a wider, and in some cases deeper, coverage than was given by the first edition. It is hoped that this new edition will continue to provide a useful tool for the beginner while also giving support to the more advanced student.

How to use this dictionary

Headword:
is in alphabetical order, in blue

Other related words:
point you to other words that help you to explain this word or build more knowledge in this topic area

Definition:
shows what the word means and if a word has more than one meaning, then each meaning is numbered

FORMULA:

shows a mathematical formula and its component parts

Illustration:
helps to show the meaning of the word, often with extra labels and annotations

Derivative or phrase:
shows you an additional word or phrase from the same family as the headword

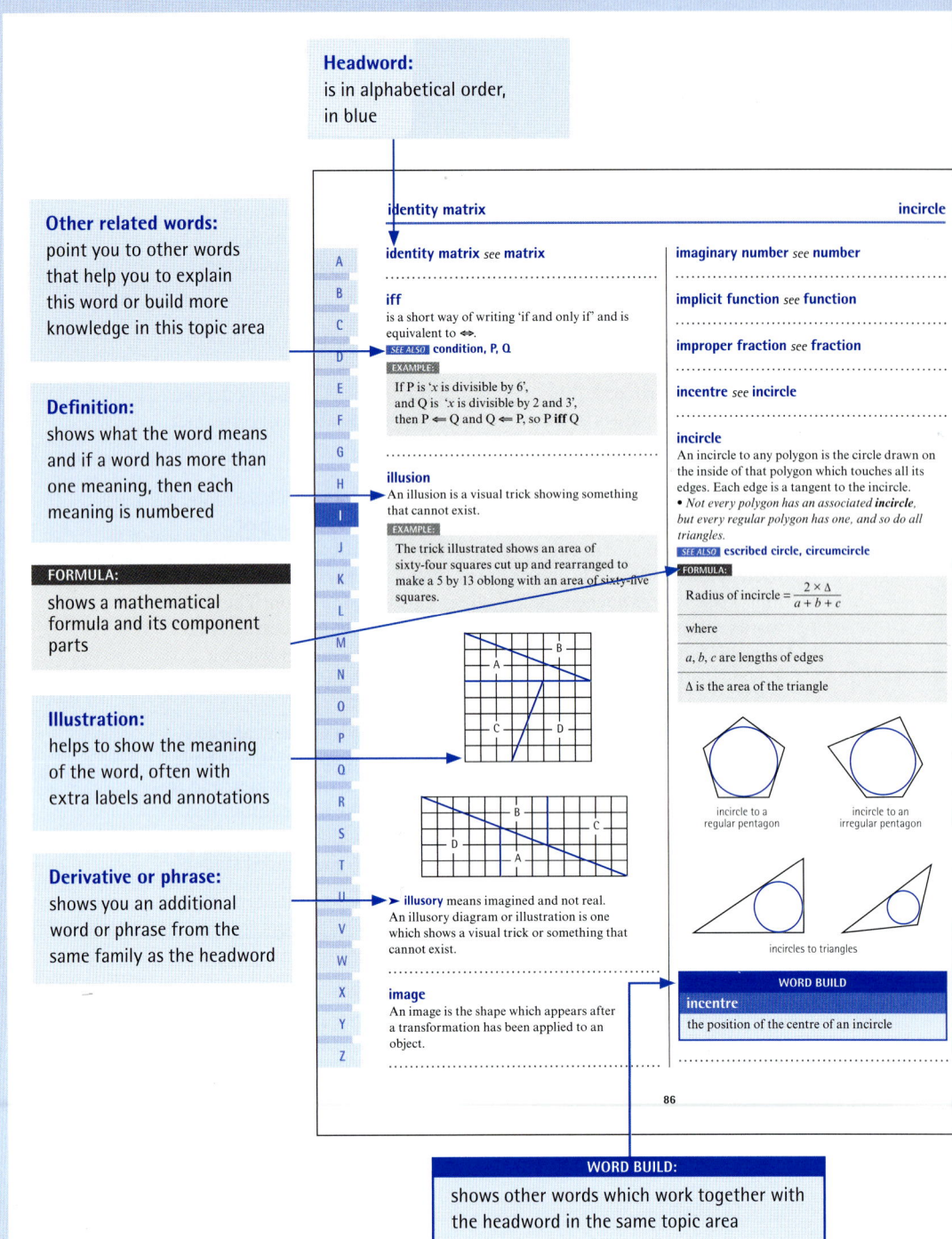

identity matrix   incircle

identity matrix *see* **matrix**

iff
is a short way of writing 'if and only if' and is equivalent to ⇔.
SEE ALSO **condition, P, Q**

EXAMPLE:
If P is '*x* is divisible by 6',
and Q is '*x* is divisible by 2 and 3',
then P ⇐ Q and Q ⇐ P, so P **iff** Q

illusion
An illusion is a visual trick showing something that cannot exist.
EXAMPLE:
The trick illustrated shows an area of sixty-four squares cut up and rearranged to make a 5 by 13 oblong with an area of sixty-five squares.

illusory means imagined and not real. An illusory diagram or illustration is one which shows a visual trick or something that cannot exist.

image
An image is the shape which appears after a transformation has been applied to an object.

imaginary number *see* **number**

implicit function *see* **function**

improper fraction *see* **fraction**

incentre *see* **incircle**

incircle
An incircle to any polygon is the circle drawn on the inside of that polygon which touches all its edges. Each edge is a tangent to the incircle.
• *Not every polygon has an associated **incircle**, but every regular polygon has one, and so do all triangles.*
SEE ALSO **escribed circle, circumcircle**

FORMULA:
Radius of incircle $= \dfrac{2 \times \Delta}{a + b + c}$

where

a, b, c are lengths of edges

Δ is the area of the triangle

incircle to a regular pentagon

incircle to an irregular pentagon

incircles to triangles

WORD BUILD
incentre
the position of the centre of an incircle

86

WORD BUILD:
shows other words which work together with the headword in the same topic area

6

OXFORD STUDENT'S Mathematics DICTIONARY

Frank Tapson

OXFORD

OXFORD
UNIVERSITY PRESS

Great Clarendon Street, Oxford OX2 6DP

Oxford University Press is a department of the University of Oxford.
It furthers the University's objective of excellence in research,
scholarship, and education by publishing worldwide.
Oxford is a registered trade mark of Oxford University Press
in the UK and in certain other countries

First published 1996
Second edition 1999
Third edition 2006
Fourth edition 2008
Fifth edition 2013
This edition 2020

All artworks © Oxford University Press

British Library Cataloguing in Publication Data

Data available

ISBN 978 0 19 277693 8
3 5 7 9 10 8 6 4 2

Printed in China

Paper used in the production of this book is a natural,
recyclable product made from wood grown in sustainable forests.
The manufacturing process conforms to the environmental
regulations of the country of origin.

The publishers would like to thank Rosalind Combley and Michael Heylings
for their contributions to this edition.

You can trust this dictionary
to be up to date, relevant
and engaging because
it is powered by the
Oxford Corpus, a unique
living database of children's
and adults' language.

Contents

Introduction

This new edition of the *Oxford Student's Mathematics Dictionary* contains over 1,000 words and phrases for students aged 11 – 16 years. It has been significantly updated and now uses alphabetical order to make a wide range of clearly defined mathematical terms and expressions accessible to young learners. It also brings together related terms in a way which builds connections and a deeper understanding of mathematical concepts.

With words from the curriculum and detailed vocabulary associated with number, algebra, ratio and proportion, geometry and measures, probability and statistics, and a 'Quick Reference' guide at the start with useful formulas, units of measurement, and handy lists of symbols, this book is designed to be a comprehensive tool for the classroom and for revision at home.

Where a word has several meanings, different meanings are numbered and often other related words are listed. This is a great way to build and extend vocabulary. Example sentences provide additional information about the headword and show its usage in a sentence. Example feature panels expand on this with further examples, often fully worked out, to support the meaning of information given by the definition.

Additional panels bring words that are related to, or can be used in connection with, the headword together in one place. Illustrations with appropriate annotations help to explain the meaning. 'Watch Out' feature panels also help to clarify the difference in meaning between similar-sounding words.

The book also provides additional help with revision and exam preparation by highlighting key topics such as circle theorem, graph, and vector, throughout the book. All of this makes the dictionary a key reference tool for use with textbooks, worksheets, revision guides, and tests.

Cross-reference:
points you to the main entry which gives you the definition of the word or phrase

Catch words:
show the first and last word on the page and guide you to the correct place to find the word you need

Related Words Panel
points you to other words that help to explain this word or build more knowledge in this topic area

Alternate form:
shows another name for the headword

Alphabet:
shows where the headword is in alphabetical order and the letter you are in is highlighted to help you find your way around easily

EXAMPLE:
shows a mathematical problem being worked through

Example sentence:
shows how you might use a word and helps you understand the meaning

WATCH OUT:
highlights commonly confused terms and helps you to avoid them

Other forms:
show you how to spell different forms of the word, such as plurals

---

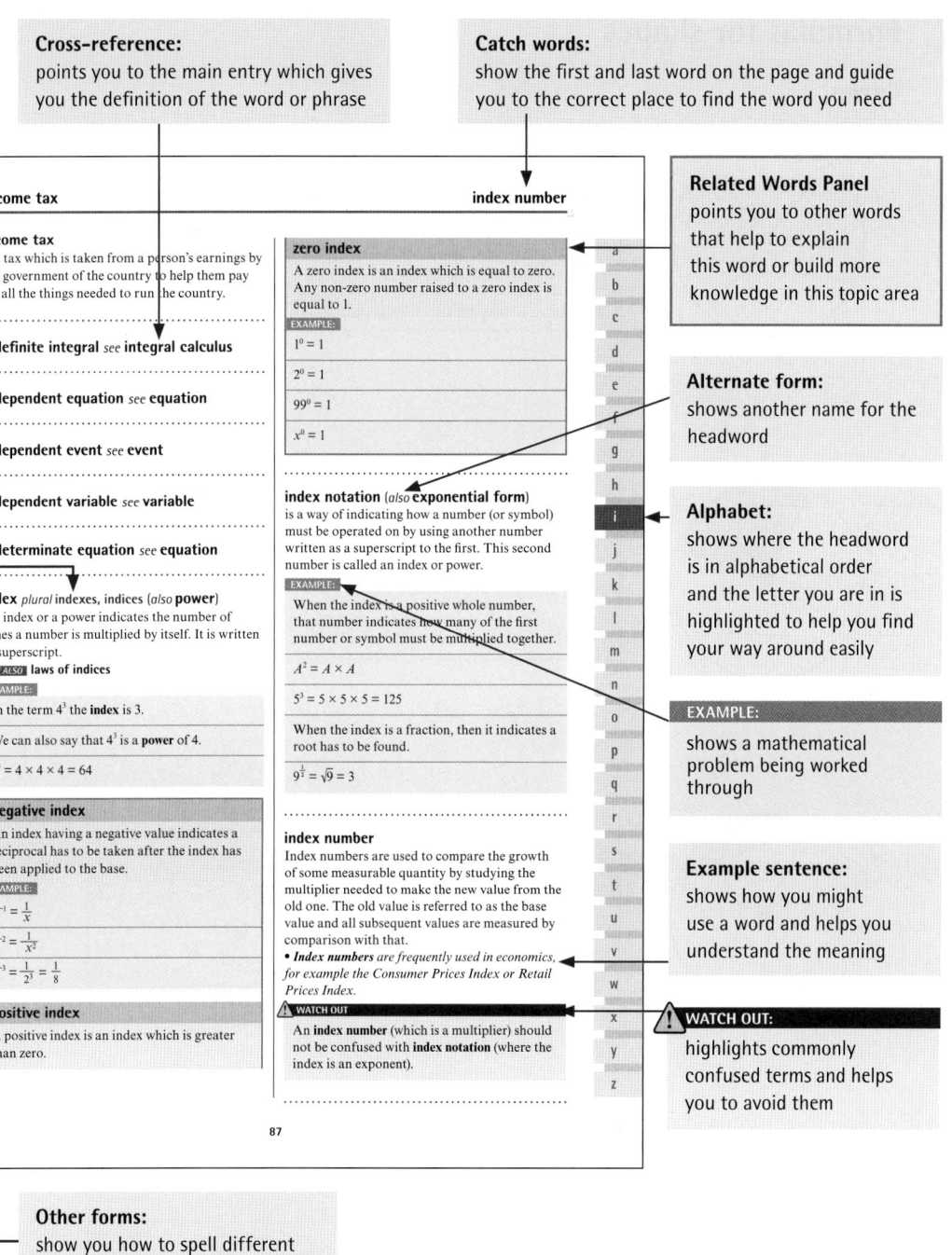

income tax   index number

income tax
is a tax which is taken from a person's earnings by the government of the country to help them pay for all the things needed to run the country.

indefinite integral *see* **integral calculus**

independent equation *see* **equation**

independent event *see* **event**

independent variable *see* **variable**

indeterminate equation *see* **equation**

index *plural* **indexes, indices** (*also* **power**)
An index or a power indicates the number of times a number is multiplied by itself. It is written in superscript.
SEE ALSO **laws of indices**
EXAMPLE:
In the term 4^3 the **index** is 3.

We can also say that 4^3 is a **power** of 4.

$4^3 = 4 \times 4 \times 4 = 64$

negative index
An index having a negative value indicates a reciprocal has to be taken after the index has been applied to the base.
EXAMPLE:
$x^{-1} = \frac{1}{x}$

$x^{-2} = \frac{1}{x^2}$

$2^{-3} = \frac{1}{2^3} = \frac{1}{8}$

positive index
A positive index is an index which is greater than zero.

zero index
A zero index is an index which is equal to zero. Any non-zero number raised to a zero index is equal to 1.
EXAMPLE:
$1^0 = 1$

$2^0 = 1$

$99^0 = 1$

$x^0 = 1$

index notation (*also* **exponential form**)
is a way of indicating how a number (or symbol) must be operated on by using another number written as a superscript to the first. This second number is called an index or power.
EXAMPLES:
When the index is a positive whole number, that number indicates how many of the first number or symbol must be multiplied together.

$A^2 = A \times A$

$5^3 = 5 \times 5 \times 5 = 125$

When the index is a fraction, then it indicates a root has to be found.

$9^{\frac{1}{2}} = \sqrt{9} = 3$

index number
Index numbers are used to compare the growth of some measurable quantity by studying the multiplier needed to make the new value from the old one. The old value is referred to as the base value and all subsequent values are measured by comparison with that.
• *Index numbers are frequently used in economics, for example the Consumer Prices Index or Retail Prices Index.*
⚠ WATCH OUT
An **index number** (which is a multiplier) should not be confused with **index notation** (where the index is an exponent).

a b c d e f g h i j k l m n o p q r s t u v w x y z

87

7

Formulas for shapes

Circles

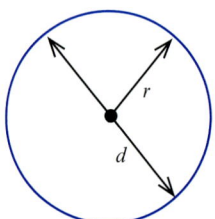

Area of a circle $= \pi r^2$
Circumference of a circle $= \pi d = 2\pi r$
where
r is the radius of the circle
d is the diameter of the circle

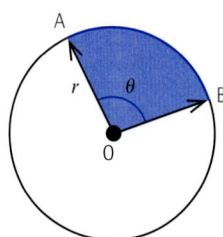

Length of arc AB $= \dfrac{\theta}{360} \times 2\pi r$
Area of sector OAB $= \dfrac{\theta}{360} \times \pi r^2$
If AB $= r$ then $\theta = 1$ radian

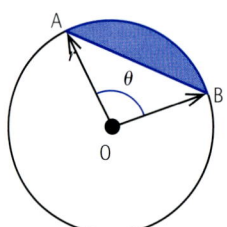

Length of chord AB $= 2r \sin\left(\dfrac{\theta}{2}\right)$
Area of sector OAB $= \left(\dfrac{\pi \theta}{360} - \dfrac{\sin \theta}{2}\right) \times \pi r^2$
If AB $= r$ then $\theta = 1$ radian

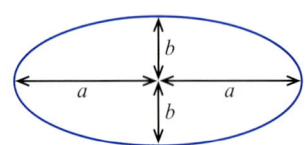

Area of an ellipse $= \pi ab$
where
a half the length of the major axis
b half the length of the minor axis

Triangles

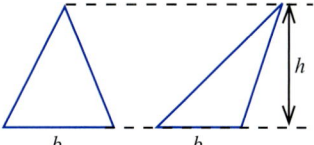

Area of a triangle = $(b \times h) \div 2$
where
b is the length of the base of the triangle
h is the perpendicular height of the triangle

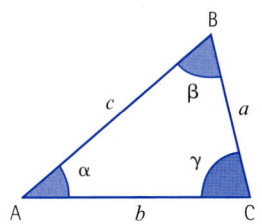

Area $= \frac{1}{2}\,ab\,\sin\gamma = \frac{1}{2}\,bc\,\sin\alpha = \frac{1}{2}\,ac\,\sin\beta$
or
Area $= \sqrt{s(s-a)(s-b)(s-c)}$
where
$s = (a + b + c) \div 2$

Sine rule:	Cosine rule:
$\dfrac{a}{\sin\alpha} = \dfrac{b}{\sin\beta} = \dfrac{c}{\sin\gamma}$	$a^2 = b^2 + c^2 - 2bc\,\cos\alpha$

Quadrilaterals

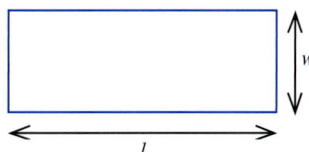

Area of rectangle = $l \times w$
Perimeter of a rectangle = $2l + 2w$
where
l is the length
w is the width

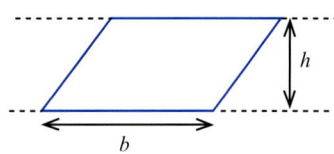

Area of a parallelogram = $b \times h$
where
b is the base
h is the perpendicular height

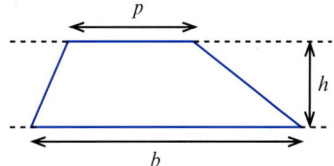

Area of a trapezium $= \dfrac{(b + p)}{2} \times h$
where
b is the base
p is the edge parallel to the base
h is the perpendicular height

3D shapes

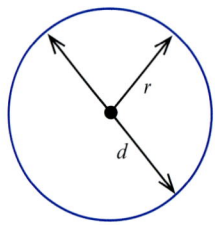

Volume of a sphere = $\dfrac{4\pi r^3}{3} \equiv \dfrac{\pi d^3}{6}$
surface area = $4\pi r^2 \equiv \pi d^2$
where
r is the radius of the sphere
d is the diameter of the sphere

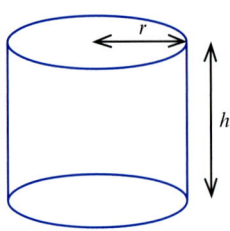

Volume of a cylinder = $\pi r^2 h$
Curved surface area = $2\pi rh$
Total surface area = $2\pi r(r + h)$
where
r is the radius of the cylinder
h is the height of the cylinder

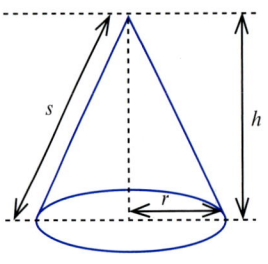

Volume of a cone = $\dfrac{\pi r^2 h}{3}$
Curved surface area = πrs
Slant height $s = \sqrt{r^2 + h^2}$
where
r is the base radius of the cone
h is the perpendicular height

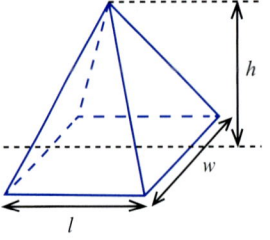

Volume of a pyramid = $\dfrac{lwh}{3}$
where
l is the length of the pyramid
w is the width of the pyramid
h is the perpendicular height

Units and conversions

Before the SI standardized units of measurement around the world with its **metric** units, every country had its own set of measurements. The tables below show how to convert between UK imperial and metric units.

Length

		1 inch	=	2.54 cm
12 inches	=	1 foot	=	30.48 cm
3 feet	=	1 yard	=	91.44 cm
1760 yards	=	1 mile	=	1609.344 m

Area

		1 square inch	=	6.4514 cm^2
144 square inches	=	1 square foot	=	929.0304 cm^2
9 square feet	=	1 square yard	=	0.8361 m^2
4840 square yards	=	1 acre	=	4046.8564 m^2 0.4046 hectares
640 acres	=	1 square mile	=	258.9988 hectares 2.589 km^2

Volume

		1 cubic inch	=	16.3871 cm^3
1728 cubic inches	=	1 cubic foot	=	28316.9088 cm^3 0.0283 m^3
27 cubic feet	=	1 cubic yard	=	0.7645 m^3

Capacity

		1 gill	=	142 ml
4 gills	=	1 pint	=	568 ml
2 pints	=	1 quart	=	1.136 litres
4 quarts	=	1 gallon	=	4.544 litres

Mass

437.5 grains	=	1 ounce	=	28.35 g
16 ounces	=	1 pound	=	453.6 g
14 pounds	=	1 stone	=	6.3504 kg
160 stones	=	1 ton	=	1016.064 kg 1.016 t (tonne)

Symbols

A symbol is a letter or sign used to represent instructions, or a number, in a more concise form.

Basic symbols

Symbol	Meaning	EXAMPLE
$=$	equals	$5 = 2 + 3$
$\neq$	does not equal	$5 \neq 4$
$\approx$	approximately equals	$\pi \approx 3.14$
$\equiv$	has the same value as	$£1 \equiv 100p$ $x^2 \equiv x * x$
$>$	greater than	$5 > 4$
$<$	less than	$4 < 5$
$\geqslant$	greater than or equal to	$5 \geqslant 4$
$\leqslant$	less than or equal to	$4 \leqslant 5$
$\propto$	is proportional to	$y \propto x$ means $y = \text{k}x$ where k is a constant
$+$	addition	$1 + 1 = 2$
$-$	subtraction	$2 - 5 = -3$
$\sim$	absolute difference of	$2 \sim 5 = 3$
$\pm$	both plus and minus	$3 \pm 5 = 8$ or -2
$*$ or $\times$	multiplication	$2 \times 3 = 6$
$\div$ or $/$	division	$6 \div 2 = 3$
$\%$	per cent	$1\% \equiv \frac{1}{100}$ 10% of $75 = 7.5$
$\%_0$	per mil	$1\%_0 \equiv \frac{1}{1,000}$ $10\%_0$ of $75 = 0.75$
x^n	x to the power of n	$x^2 \equiv x \times x$ $5^3 = 5 \times 5 \times 5 = 125$
$|x|$	absolute value of x	$|-5| \equiv |5| \equiv 5$
$\sqrt{x}$	square root of x	$\sqrt{25} = 5$
$\sqrt[3]{x}$	cube root of x	$\sqrt[3]{64} = 4$
$n!$	n factorial	$3! = 3 \times 2 \times 1 = 6$
π	pi	$\pi \approx 3.14159$
e	Euler's number	$e \approx 2.71828$
τ	golden ratio	$\tau \approx 1.61803$
∞	infinity	
$(\ )$	'do this first'	$7 + (1 \times 10) = 17$ but $(7 + 1) \times 10 = 80$
$[\ ]$	'do this first'	$3 * [5 + 6] = 33$ but $[3 * 5] + 6 = 21$

Geometric symbols

Symbol	Meaning	EXAMPLE
$\triangle$	triangle	$\triangle ABC$
$\angle$	angle	$\angle ABC = 45°$
∟	right angle	∟ABC = 90°
$\|\|$	is parallel to	AB $\|\|$ CD
$\perp$	is perpendicular to	AB $\perp$ CD
°	degree	one full turn = 360°
′	minute	1° = 60′
″	second	1° = 360″
$\overrightarrow{AB}$	line that starts from point A	
$\overline{AB}$	line from point A to point B	
$\overarc{AB}$	arc from point A to point B	

Set symbols

Symbol	Meaning	EXAMPLE
{}	a set	$\{1, 2, 3, A, B\}$
$\in$	is a member of	$A \in \{1, 2, 3, A, B\}$
$\notin$	is not a member of	$A \notin \{1, 2, 3, A, B\}$
$\subset$	is a subset of	$\{1, 2\} \subset \{1, 2, 3, A, B\}$
$\supset$	includes	$\{1, 2, 3, A, B\} \supset \{1, 2\}$
$\cup$	union of two sets	$\{1, 2\} \cup \{3, 4\} = \{1, 2, 3, 4\}$
$\cap$	intersection of two sets	$\{1, 2, 3\} \cap \{3, 4, 5\} = \{3\}$
$\varnothing$	null or empty set	$\{1, 2\} \cap \{7, 8\} = \varnothing$
$\mathbb{U}$	universal set of all possible values	
$\mathbb{N}$	set of all natural numbers	
$\mathbb{Z}$	set of all integers	
$\mathbb{Q}$	set of all rational numbers	
$\mathbb{R}$	set of all real numbers	
$\mathbb{C}$	set of all complex numbers	

Logic symbols

Symbol	Meaning	EXAMPLE
$\Rightarrow$	implies is a sufficient condition for	$P \Rightarrow Q$
$\Leftarrow$	is implied by is a necessary condition for	$P \Leftarrow Q$
$\Leftrightarrow$	implies and is implied by, iff, is a sufficient and necessary condition for	$P \Leftrightarrow Q$

Greek alphabet

The Greek alphabet is a rich source of symbols used in mathematics to the extent that almost all of them, both upper and lower case, are used in some way or another. Some are used in many ways.

Here is the full alphabet and the names of the letters, along with where some of them are commonly used.

Upper case	Lower case	Name	Used in
A	α	alpha	α and β are often used to identify angles
B	β	beta	$\dfrac{\alpha/\beta}{\beta/\alpha}\quad\dfrac{\alpha/\beta}{\beta/\alpha}\qquad \alpha + \beta = 180°$
Γ	γ	gamma	
Δ	δ	delta	Δ is used to represent change δ is used to mean 'a small amount of' e.g. δy
E	ε	epsilon	
Z	ζ	zeta	
H	η	eta	
Θ	θ	theta	θ is used to indicate the general angle in polar co-ordinates
I	ι	iota	
K	κ	kappa	
Λ	λ	lambda	λ is used to represent a scalar in vector work
M	μ	mu	μ is used to represent the prefix micro ($\times 10^{-6}$)
N	ν	nu	
Ξ	ξ	xi	ξ is sometimes used instead of $\mathbb{U}$ to represent the universal set
O	o	omicron	
Π	π	pi	Π is used to represent a continued product π is used to represent the number 3.14159 ....
P	ρ	rho	
Σ	σ	sigma	Σ is used to represent the sum of a series σ is used to represent the standard deviation of a population
T	τ	tau	τ is used to represent the value of the golden ratio 1.6180 ....
Y	υ	upsilon	
Φ	φ	phi	Φ is used incorrectly to represent the empty set $\varnothing$
X	χ	chi	
Ψ	ψ	psi	
Ω	ω	omega	

SI and its prefixes

SI stands for Système International (d'Unités) or International System (of Units). It is a set of seven base units of measurements—**metre, kilogram, second, kelvin, ampere, mole**, and **candela**—from which all other measurement units can be derived.

The SI allows other units to be created from the standard ones by using prefixes to act as multipliers. This list gives those prefixes, the symbol to be used for that prefix in abbreviated form, and the multiplying factor they represent. Note that these prefixes are case sensitive.

Prefix	Symbol	Multiplier	
yotta–	Y	$\times 10^{24}$	
zetta–	Z	$\times 10^{21}$	
exa–	E	$\times 10^{18}$	1,000,000,000,000,000,000
peta–	P	$\times 10^{15}$	1,000,000,000,000,000
tera–	T	$\times 10^{12}$	1,000,000,000,000
giga–	G	$\times 10^{9}$	1,000,000,000
mega–	M	$\times 10^{6}$	1,000,000
kilo–	k	$\times 10^{3}$	1,000
*hecto–	h	$\times 10^{2}$	100
*deca–	da	$\times 10^{1}$	10
		$\times 10^{0}$	1
*deci–	d	$\times 10^{-1}$	0.1
*centi–	c	$\times 10^{-2}$	0.01
milli–	m	$\times 10^{-3}$	0.001
micro–	μ	$\times 10^{-6}$	0.000 001
nano–	n	$\times 10^{-9}$	0.000 000 001
pico–	p	$\times 10^{-12}$	0.000 000 000 001
femto	f	$\times 10^{-15}$	0.000 000 000 000 001
atto–	a	$\times 10^{-18}$	0.000 000 000 000 000 001
zepto–	z	$\times 10^{-21}$	
yocto–	y	$\times 10^{-24}$	

* is a prefix not originally in the SI but was in the metric system and remained in use because it has proved so convenient for everyday units.

Examples of prefixes	
12 **mega**watts ≡ 12MW ≡ 12 millions of watts	25 **centi**metres ≡ 25 cm ≡ 25 hundredths of a metre

Aa

abacus

An abacus is a device that allows numbers to be shown physically and then manipulated so that calculations may be carried out.
• *An **abacus** can have various forms but is usually thought of as a frame holding wires along which beads can be moved. It is often seen as a child's toy.*

WORD BUILD

s'choty

A s'choty is the Russian form of a wire and bead abacus. In the most general type of s'choty, the wires are actually curved (upwards in the middle) so that the beads must go to one side or the other. The coloured beads are a visual aid to counting and the short row represents either fractions (quarters in the image) or a decimal comma.
• *The starting (zero) position is with all beads to the right so the beads to the left in the image of **s'choty** show the number 317.26.*

suan pan

The suan pan is the Chinese form of a wire and bead abacus. The frame is divided internally into two (unequal) sections; the smaller section holds two beads on each wire (each bead counting as a 5) while the larger section has five beads (each counting as a 1).
• *Only the beads touching the dividing bar count, so the number showing in the **suan pan** in the picture is 80,162.*

soroban

The soroban is a development of the suan pan and mainly used in Japan; it has only one bead on each wire in the smaller section and four in the other. Again it is only the beads touching the dividing bar which count, so the number showing is 40,925.
• *It is only the beads touching the dividing bar which count, so the number showing in the **soroban** is 40,925.*

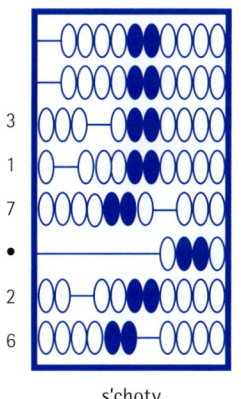

s'choty

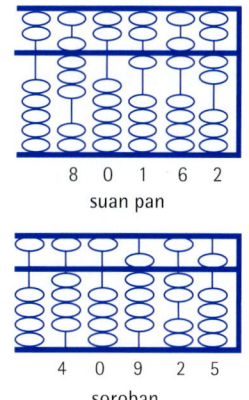

suan pan

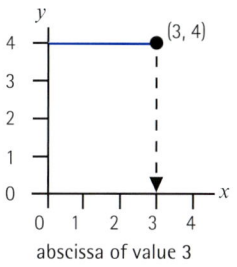

soroban

Abelian group *see* **commutative**

---

abscissa *plural* **abscissae**

The abscissa of a point in Cartesian coordinates is its distance from the y-axis, as measured on the x-axis. It is the value of the first number in the ordered pair for that point.

SEE ALSO **coordinate**

abscissa of value 3

---

absolute difference *see* **difference**

---

absolute error *see* **error**

---

absolute value

The absolute value of a vector is its size. Direction is ignored.

---

abundant number *see* **number**

---

acceleration

The acceleration of a moving object is a measure of how its velocity is changing in relation to time. It is a vector quantity, but its direction is often ignored and it is applied only to the speed component of the velocity. The SI unit of acceleration is metres per second squared, abbreviated to m/s^2 or $m\ s^{-2}$.   »

• *Acceleration may be positive (for speeding up) or negative (for slowing down).*

SEE ALSO **deceleration, gravitational acceleration, speed, velocity, velocity–time graph**

EXAMPLE:

Starting from rest, an object is given a steady **acceleration** of 3 m/s². What is its velocity after 10 seconds?

In this case the velocity will increase by 3 m/s after every second of its travel. So:

velocity after 1 second is 3 m/s

velocity after 2 seconds is 6 m/s

velocity after 3 seconds is 9 m/s

... velocity after 10 seconds is 30 m/s

accurate

An accurate number or measurement is exact, without any errors.

• *Very often in numerical work, and always when making measurements (unless counting distinct objects), the answer cannot be an exact one, so it is necessary to indicate just how **accurate** it is.*

SEE ALSO **approximation, estimation, tolerance**

➤ **accuracy** The accuracy of a number is an indication of how exact it is.

acute angle see angle

acute triangle see triangle

add see addition

addend

Each of the numbers in an addition sum is an addend.

• *In the sum 7 + 5 = 12, 7 and 5 are **addends**.*

SEE ALSO **augend**

addition

is the operation of combining numbers, each of which represents a separate measure of quantity, so as to produce a number representing the

measure of all those quantities together. If the number is to have any physical meaning, then the quantities must be of the same type.

• *Addition shows that nine people put with four people makes thirteen people.*

SEE ALSO **matrix, vector**

➤ **add** To add numbers is to combine them so as to produce a number representing the measure of all those quantities together.

complementary addition

is a method of subtracting two numbers using addition. It is a three step process.

EXAMPLE:

To solve 35,874 − 629:

1. Find the difference between each digit in the second number and 9, and then add 1.

   999 − 629 = 370. Add 1 to get 371.

2. Add the result of step 1 to the first number.

   35,874 + 371 = 36,245

3. Subtract 1 from the 'extra digits' on the left. That is, all the digits in the first number which go beyond the length of the second number. 36,245 has two extra digits, 3 and 6, over 629. So:
   36 − 1 = 35

   And that's how we have our answer:
   35,874 − 629 = 35,245.

equal addition

is a method of subtraction which adds the same amount to both numbers, where necessary, to allow the subtraction to take place. This is the method where the phrase 'borrow and pay back' occurs.

EXAMPLE:

$$\begin{array}{cc} 874 & 800 + 70 + 4 \\ -629 & \text{is} \quad 600 + 20 + 9 \end{array}$$

Add 10 to both numbers.

$$\begin{array}{ccc} 800 + 70 + 14 & & 8 \quad 7 \quad {}^1\!4 \\ -600 + 30 + \ 9 & \begin{array}{c}\text{written}\\\text{as}\end{array} & -6 \quad {}^3\!2 \quad 9 \\ \hline 200 + 40 + \ 5 & & 2 \quad 4 \quad 5 \end{array}$$

additive number system *see* number system

. . . .

adjacent

Adjacent means lying next to, or side by side.

SEE ALSO parallel

. . . .

adjacent angle *see* angle

. . . .

aggregate *see* total

. . . .

algebra

is the branch of mathematics that deals with generalized arithmetic by using letters or symbols to represent numbers. Any statement made in algebra is true for all numbers and not just specific cases.

• *In **algebra**, the convention is that letters for variables are taken from the end of the alphabet and are usually lower case (x, y, z), while those representing constants are taken from the beginning of the alphabet (A, B, C, a, b, c).*

EXAMPLE:

$9^2 - 6^2 = 81 - 36 = 45$ is true for those numbers.

But, $x^2 - y^2 = (x + y)(x - y)$ is true for all numbers.

$9^2 - 6^2 = (9 + 6)(9 - 6) = 45$ is just one example of many.

➤ **algebraic** related to or using algebra

. . . .

algebraic fraction *see* fraction

. . . .

algebraic number *see* number

. . . .

algorithm

An algorithm is a step-by-step procedure that produces an answer to a particular problem. Many algorithms are prepared ones which do the standard operations needed in an efficient or the most memorable way: multiplication, division, adding fractions, etc.

• *Algorithms are devised as they are needed, particularly for computers.*

. . . .

alidade

An alidade is an instrument like a ruler with sights fixed at each end and is used to copy a direction on to a piece of paper.

• *The observer rests the **alidade** on the paper, lines up the sights to give the direction of some distant object, and then draws a line on the paper.*

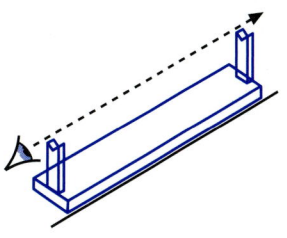

. . . .

aliquot part

One number (or quantity) is an aliquot part of another if it divides into it exactly. Usually this is applied only to whole numbers, and an aliquot part is the same as a proper fraction.

EXAMPLE:

3 is an **aliquot part** of 12.

10p, 20p, 25p and 50p are all **aliquot parts** of £1.

75p is not an **aliquot part** of £1.

WORD BUILD

aliquant part

is a number or quantity that is not an aliquot part. This term is rarely used.

• *7 is an **aliquant part** of 12.*

. . . .

alphametic *see* cryptarithm

. . . .

alternate angle *see* angle

. . . .

alternate segment *see* segment

. . . .

alternating series *see* series

. . . .

a
b
c
d
e
f
g
h
i
j
k
l
m
n
o
p
q
r
s
t
u
v
w
x
y
z

altitude see **perpendicular height**

....

ambiguous case

In solving a triangle for which the lengths of two edges are known, and also the size of an angle which is not between those two edges, it is sometimes possible to find two values for the length of the third edge.

EXAMPLE:

Triangle ABC has $AB = 30$; $BC = 21$; $\angle BAC = 40°$.

Use of the sine rule gives
$\sin C = 30 \sin 40° \div 21 = 0.918$.

This means $\angle ACB$ could be 66.7° or 113.3°.

Therefore $\angle ABC$ could be 73.3° or 26.7° and the corresponding lengths of AC could be 31.3 or 14.7.

This is shown by marking C' and C''.

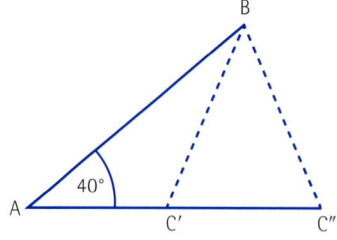

....

amicable pair

An amicable pair of numbers is two numbers with the property that the proper factors of each one add up to the value of the other.

EXAMPLE:

220 and 284 are an **amicable pair**.

220 gives $1 + 2 + 4 + 5 + 10 + 11 + 20 + 22 + 44 + 55 + 110 = 284$

284 gives $1 + 2 + 4 + 71 + 142 = 220$

....

angle

An angle is made when two straight lines cross or meet each other at a point, and its size is measured by the amount one line has been turned in relation to the other.

• *A full turn or revolution is a measure of the* ***angle*** *made when the line which is turning has moved right around and returned to its starting position.*

SEE ALSO dihedral angle, general angle, solid angle, subtended angle

acute angle

An acute angle is one which is less than a right angle.

adjacent angle

When two straight lines cross each other, four angles are made; any pair of these which touch each other along a line are adjacent angles. Adjacent angles add up to 180°.

alternate angle (also Z-angle)

When a transversal cuts two parallel lines, alternate angles or Z-angles are any pair of angles that lie on opposite sides of the transversal and on opposite relative sides of the parallel lines. Alternate angles are equal in size.

complementary angle

Complementary angles are a pair of angles which add together to make 90°.
• *Angles of 30° and 60° are* ***complementary***.

conjugate angle

Conjugate angles are a pair of angles which add together to make 360°.

corresponding angle

When a transversal cuts two parallel lines, corresponding angles are any pair of angles which lie on the same sides of the transversal and on the same relative sides of the parallel lines. Corresponding angles are equal in size.

negative angle

A negative angle is one measured in the clockwise direction. Whether an angle is positive or negative makes no difference to its actual size, which is the same in either direction, but is sometimes needed when a movement is being explained.

SEE ALSO **trigonometric ratio**

obtuse angle

An obtuse angle is one which is more than a right angle but less than a straight angle.

positive angle

A positive angle is one measured in the anticlockwise direction.

reflex angle

A reflex angle is one which is more than a straight angle but less than a full turn.

right angle

A right angle is the angle made by one-quarter of a full turn or 90°. It is usually shown on drawings by means of a small square in the corner.

round angle (*also* **perigon**)

A round angle or perigon is an angle of 360 degrees or one complete revolution.

straight angle

A straight angle is the angle made by one-half of a full turn and is equal to 180°. It looks exactly the same as a straight line.

supplementary angle

Supplementary angles are a pair of angles which add together to make 180°.
• *Angles of 30° and 150° are **supplementary**.*

vertically opposite angle

When two straight lines cross each other, four angles are made; any pair of these which touch each other only at the crossing point are vertically opposite angles. Vertically opposite angles are equal in size.

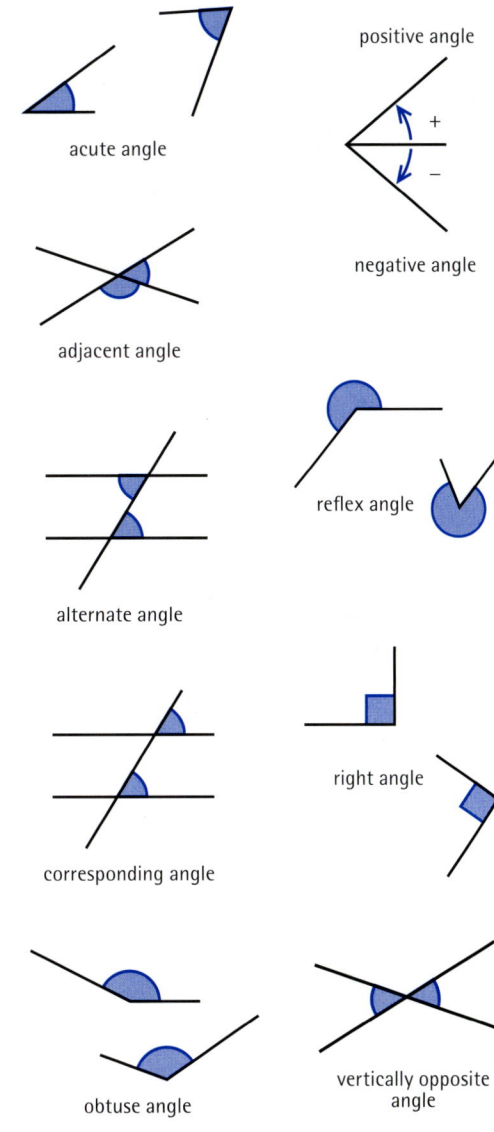

positive angle

acute angle

negative angle

adjacent angle

reflex angle

alternate angle

right angle

corresponding angle

obtuse angle

vertically opposite angle

⚠ **WATCH OUT**

Complementary angles and **supplementary angles** are both related to the right angle.

To complement something is to complete it, so **complementary angles** together make one complete right angle.

To supplement something is to add something extra, so **supplementary angles** together make two right angles or 180°.

angle of depression

The angle of depression of an object is the angle through which someone must look down from the horizontal plane to see that object.

• *The image shows a person standing on a cliff top looking at a small boat and seeing it at an **angle of depression** of 25°.*

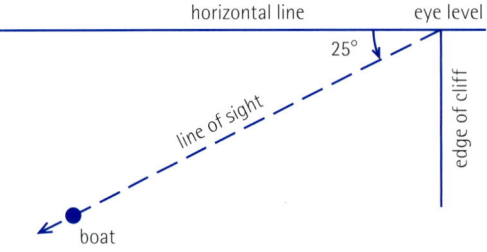

angle of elevation

The angle of elevation of an object is the angle through which someone must look up from the horizontal plane to see that object.

• *The image shows a person standing on level ground who sees the top of a mast at an **angle of elevation** of 25°.*

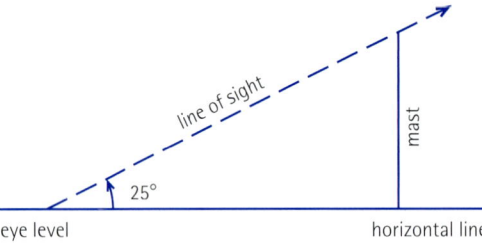

angle sum

The angle sum of a polygon is the total of all its interior angles added together.

FORMULA:

Angle sum of any polygon =
(180 × number of edges) − 360 degrees

EXAMPLE:

A triangle has 3 edges, so its **angle sum**
= (180 × 3) − 360 = 180°

A quadrilateral has 4 edges, so its **angle sum**
= (180 × 4) − 360 = 360°

annual percentage rate *see* APR

annuity

An annuity is a fixed amount of money paid yearly in return for a sum of money given to the business which is paying the annuity.

• *People often buy an **annuity** from an insurance company in order to have a regular income after they retire.*

EXAMPLE:

The size of an **annuity** is dependent not only upon the sum of money paid, but also upon the age and sex of the person (which is a guide to how long they might live).

A sum of £20,000 might produce an **annuity** of £2,300 for a 55-year-old man (a return of 11.5% per year) but only £2,150 for a 55-year-old woman (10.75%).

annulus

An annulus is a shape like a ring which is formed by the space enclosed between two concentric circles.

anticlockwise

An anticlockwise direction is one which is opposite to clockwise (the direction of the hands of a conventional clock).

SEE ALSO clockwise

antilogarithm

is the inverse function of the logarithm

SEE ALSO logarithm

antiprism

An antiprism is a polyhedron that has two faces identical and parallel to each other. All the other faces are identical triangles, with each vertex of every triangle touching a vertex of one of the end faces, so that four edges meet at every vertex. Unlike with a prism, its cross-section varies.

SEE ALSO **prism**

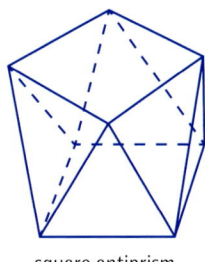

square antiprism

AP see **arithmetic progression**

aperiodic tiling see **tiling**

apex *plural* **apexes, apices**
The apex of a pyramid is the vertex at which the triangular faces meet.

Apollonius' circle see **circle**

apothem
An apothem is a line drawn from the centre of a regular polygon to an edge, and perpendicular to that edge. It is the perpendicular bisector of that edge, and also the radius of the inscribed circle to that polygon.
• *The diagram shows one **apothem** (out of the five possible) of a regular pentagon.*

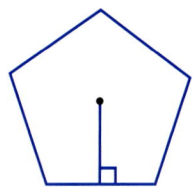

approximate
An approximate value is close to (but not equal to) the true value.
➤ **approximately** close to but not exactly
• *The symbol for 'approximately equal to' is ≈.*

EXAMPLE:

$\pi \approx 3.14$

approximation
An approximation is a stated value of a number that is close to (but not equal to) the true value of that number.

EXAMPLE:

3, 3.1 and 3.14 are all **approximations** to π (= 3.14159...).

Several reasonable **approximations** are always possible for any number. The one most suitable for the purpose in hand must be chosen.

⚠ WATCH OUT

Approximation and **estimation** are often used as being identical in meaning, but an approximation is not necessarily an estimation.

An **approximation** is applied to a number that already exists.

An **estimation** creates a number by making a judgement.

An **estimation** of the value of (23.7 × 19.1) ÷ 99.6 might be (20 × 20) ÷ 100 = 4, or (25 × 20) ÷ 100 = 5, or between 4 and 5.

Doing the arithmetic suggests that 4.54 is a good **approximation**.

APR
The APR is the Annual Percentage Rate, or interest rate calculated for one whole year, of a loan.

SEE ALSO **interest**
• *Organizations which lend money express their offers in various ways, but the law requires that the **APR** is also given so that comparisons can be made more easily. There are formulas for this.*

arc

❶ An arc is part of a curve. It must have two end points, though these might merely be marked to show the arc as part of a bigger curve.

❷ An arc of a circle is any piece of the curve which makes the circle.

FORMULA:

$$\text{Length of arc} = \frac{\text{Angle (in degrees) of arc at centre}}{360} \times \text{Circumference of full circle}$$

❸ In topology, an arc is another word for an edge.

major arc

When an arc is made in a circle, the remainder of the circle makes another arc. The larger of the two is the major arc.

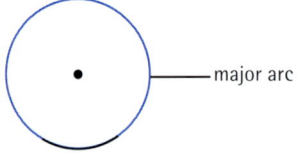
major arc

minor arc

When an arc is made in a circle, the remainder of the circle makes another arc. The smaller of the two is the minor arc.

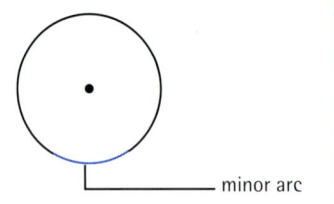
minor arc

arccos see **trigonometric ratio**

Archimedean solid

A semi-regular polyhedron which is not a prism or antiprism is known as an Archimedean solid. There are only 13 possible solids like this.

Archimedes' spiral see **spiral**

arcsin see **trigonometric ratio**

arctan see **trigonometric ratio**

area

The area of a surface is a measure of how much two-dimensional space is covered by that surface. The surface may be flat or curved.

• *Area is usually measured in terms of how many squares of some unit size (square inches, square metres, etc.) would cover an equivalent amount of space.*

SEE ALSO **polygon, curve, triangle**

Argand diagram

An Argand diagram allows complex numbers to be shown in a way that is not possible on a simple real number line.

EXAMPLE:

An **Argand diagram** uses a number line as one axis to plot the real part of the complex number, and a second number line to form an axis at right angles to the first, on which the imaginary part of the same complex number can be plotted.

With these two points as a coordinate pair, a single point can be plotted to represent the complex number.

The illustration shows the complex number 4 + 3i on an **Argand diagram**.

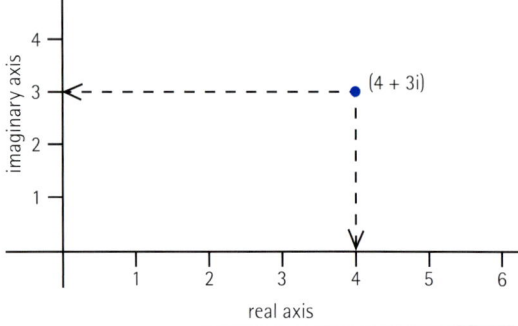

argument

An argument is a set of one or more statements which uses a system of logic to show how one particular statement is arrived at.

arithmetic

is a part of mathematics that deals with the properties and handling of numbers, and their use in counting and calculating.

➤ **the four rules of arithmetic** are the operations of addition, subtraction, multiplication and division.

➤ **fundamental theorem of arithmetic** Any composite number can be made by multiplying together a set of prime numbers, and this can be done in only one way. The reordering of the prime numbers is not considered as different.

EXAMPLE:

$12 = 2 \times 2 \times 3$ or $2^2 \times 3$

$126 = 2 \times 3 \times 3 \times 7$ or $2 \times 3^2 \times 7$

arithmetic mean *see* **mean**

arithmetic progression (*also* **AP**)

An arithmetic progression or AP is a sequence where each new term after the first is made by adding on a constant amount to the previous term.

• *3, 7, 11, 15, 19, ... is an **AP** with a first term of 3 and a constant of 4.*

SEE ALSO **geometric progression**

WORD BUILD

arithmetic series

An arithmetic series is an AP with addition or subtraction signs inserted between the various terms.

• *Using the AP above, the **arithmetic series** is 3 + 7 + 11 + 15 + 19 + ...*

EXAMPLE:

To find the sum (S_n) of an **arithmetic series** over *n* terms, use the formula

$S_n = [2a + (n - 1)d]$

where

a is the first value of the term

n is the number of terms

d is the constant added to each term

array

An array is an orderly display of data arranged in a rectangular shape.

arrowhead (*also* **dart, deltoid**)

An arrowhead, dart or deltoid is a quadrilateral which has two pairs of adjacent edges of the same length and one interior angle which is bigger than 180 degrees. It has one line of symmetry and its diagonals do not cross.

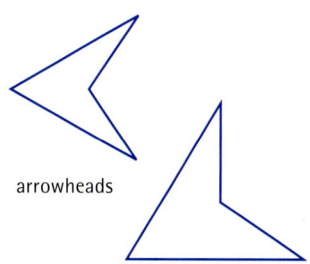

arrowheads

associative

A binary operation (one that combines two objects to produce a third) is said to be associative if, when it is being applied repetitively, the result does not depend on how the pairs are grouped (whether by working or by the insertion of brackets).

SEE ALSO **commutative**

EXAMPLE:

Addition is **associative** since
$1 + 2 + 3 = (1 + 2) + 3$ or $1 + (2 + 3) = 6$.

Subtraction is not **associative** since $5 - 4 - 2$ might be either $5 - (4 - 2) = 3$ or $(5 - 4) - 2 = -1$, producing two different results.

assumption (*also* **premise**)

An assumption or a premise is a statement (true or false) which is to be taken as true for the purpose of the argument which follows.

asterithm *see* **cryptarithm**

astroid *see* cycloid

....

asymmetric

An asymmetric shape has no symmetry at all.

• *These are all examples of shapes that are **asymmetric**.*

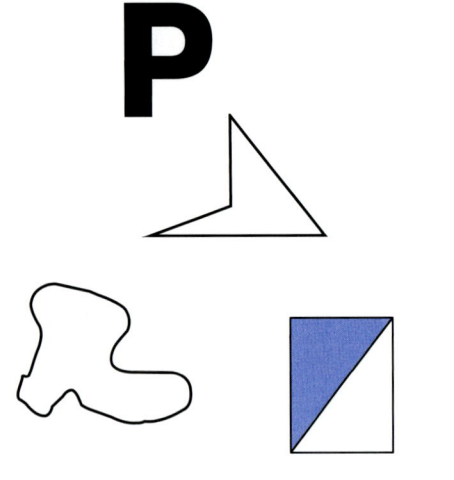

....

asymptote

An asymptote to a curve is a straight line to which the curve continuously draws nearer but without ever touching it.

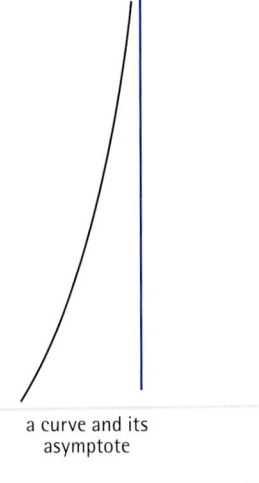

a curve and its
asymptote

....

attribute

An attribute is a property such as colour, shape, size, number of sides or type of angle.

SEE ALSO property

....

augend

In an addition sum, the first of the numbers being added together is the augend.

• *In the sum 8 + 6 = 14, 8 is the **augend**.*

SEE ALSO addend

....

automorphic number

a number whose last digits are unchanged after the number has been squared

• *76 and 625 are **automorphic** since $76^2 = 5,776$ and $625^2 = 390,625$.*

....

auxiliary circle *see* ellipse

....

average

An average of a set of data is any measure of central tendency. Usually it is taken to be the same as the arithmetic mean.

SEE ALSO measure of central tendency

moving average

A moving average is used to smooth out the fluctuations in value of a set of data which varies widely over time. It is made by re-evaluating the mean of the last few pieces of data whenever a new piece of data is added to the list.

EXAMPLE:

A **moving average** is used to give a clearer idea of the underlying trend.

For example, a shop's recorded weekly sales of pencils might be:

8	10	6	11	4	9	9	6	5	10

Taking 3-weekly **moving averages** gives this smoother looking set:

8	9	7	8	7.3	8	6.7	7

Notice that each value of the moving average is placed at the middle of the group of three pieces of data for which it has been calculated.

The effect is most marked when the data is plotted onto a graph. This is shown here with the black line for the raw data, and the red line showing the **moving average**.

There is a clear indication that sales are decreasing.

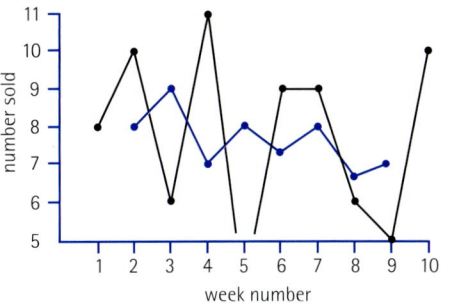

Mean, **median** and **mode** are all kinds of average.

The **mean** or **arithmetic mean** of a set of data is the numerical value found by adding together all the separate values and dividing by how many pieces of data there are.

The **median** is the numerical value of the piece of data in the middle of the set, after arranging the set in size order.

The **mode** of a set of data is the piece of data found most often.

average speed see **speed**

axiom

An axiom is a statement which is assumed to be true, and is used as a basis for developing a system. Any system of logic starts by saying clearly what axioms it uses.

axis *plural* axes

The axes are the two fixed lines in the Cartesian coordinate system. They are usually identified as the x-axis and the y-axis and are placed at right angles to each other.

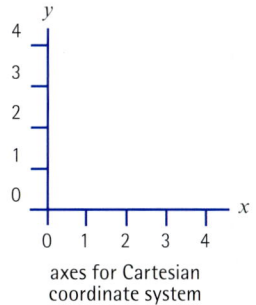

axes for Cartesian coordinate system

SEE ALSO **coordinate, ellipse**

polar axis

A polar axis is a fixed line, one end of which is a pole.

x-axis

The x-axis is the horizontal axis of a graph in the Cartesian coordinate system.

y-axis

The y-axis is the vertical axis of a graph in the Cartesian coordinate system.

axis of rotation see **rotation**

axis of symmetry

An axis of symmetry is a line about which a shape can be rotated, by an amount which is less than a whole turn, so that the total effect is to leave the shape unchanged. A shape can have more than one axis of symmetry.

• *In the case of a shape having rotational symmetry, the axis of symmetry is a line passing through the centre of symmetry and perpendicular to the plane of the shape.*

SEE ALSO **symmetry**

Bb

Babylonian number system *see* **number system**

....

back bearing *see* **bearing**

....

bar chart *see* **chart**

....

barrel

A barrel, of the traditional type and made of wood, is roughly cylindrical in shape having two circular ends of the same diameter, but bulging outwards in the middle of its height (or length) to a bigger diameter.

EXAMPLE:

It is difficult to calculate the capacity of a **barrel** exactly, but a very good approximation can be found using:

$$\frac{\pi h}{360}\,(39D^2 + 26Dd + 25d^2)$$

where

d is the diameter of one end

D is the diameter in the middle

h is the height of the barrel

....

base

❶ The base of a triangle is any edge chosen to serve that purpose. Usually it is the edge which is at the 'bottom' when the triangle is in a given position.

base

base

base

❷ The base of a cone is the simple closed curve used in making it.

❸ The base of a pyramid is the polygonal face which names the pyramid.

❹ The base of a place-value number system controls the relationship between the places.

❺ In index notation, the base is the number (or symbol) upon which the index is to operate.

• *In $A^2 y^{-1} 3^4 10^x$, A, y, 3, and 10 are all **bases**.*

SEE ALSO **number base**

....

base line (*also* chaining line)

A base line or chaining line is a line forming part of a survey (whose length may be known) from which other lines, and their measurements, are taken.

....

beam compass *see* compass

....

bearing

The bearing of position B from position A is the direction (usually given as a compass angle) in which someone travelling in a straight line from A to B must go.

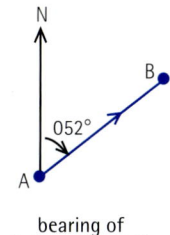

bearing of
B from A = 052°

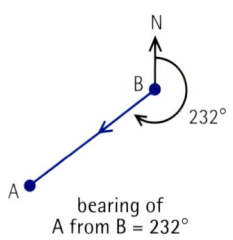

bearing of
A from B = 232°

---

reciprocal bearing (*also* back bearing)

A reciprocal bearing or back bearing is the direction which is the reverse of the given bearing.

EXAMPLE:

If the given bearing is from A to B, the **reciprocal bearing** is the bearing from B to A.

If bearing is less than 180°, add 180° to get the **reciprocal bearing**.

If bearing is more than 180°, subtract 180° to get the **reciprocal bearing**.

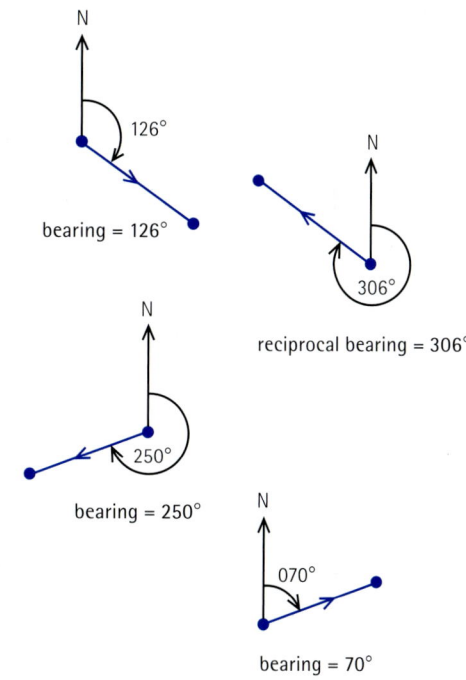

bearing = 126°

reciprocal bearing = 306°

bearing = 250°

bearing = 70°

....

benchmark

A benchmark is a mark cut into the walls of bridges, churches, etc which gives the height of that point above (rarely below) the national datum.

• *The drawing shows a **benchmark**.*

....

biased

A biased item is one in which all outcomes are not equally likely.

....

bicimal (also bicimal fraction)

A bicimal or bicimal fraction is similar in structure to a decimal fraction but the numbers are written in base 2 or binary form.

EXAMPLE:

The **bicimal** 0.101_2 is equivalent to the following common fraction (when both the top and bottom numbers are in binary):

$$\frac{101}{1,000}$$

Changing to base 10:$101_2 \rightarrow 5$ and $1,000_2 \rightarrow 8$ so

$$\frac{101}{1,000} \rightarrow \frac{5}{8} \text{ or } 0.625$$

WORD BUILD
tercimal
a fraction similar in structure to a decimal fraction but the bers are written in base 3 or ternary form

....

BIDMAS

is an aid to remembering the order of operations.

EXAMPLE:

BIDMAS stands for:
Brackets
Indices
Division
Multiplication
Addition
Subtraction

SEE ALSO order of operations

....

bilateral symmetry see **symmetry**

....

bimodal

A set of grouped data is said to be bimodal when the distribution (shown graphically) has two separate and distinct peaks.

• *The drawing shows a distribution which is* **bimodal**.

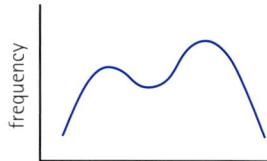

....

binary see **number base**

....

binary operation see **operation**

....

binomial see **multinomial**

....

binomial distribution

A probability distribution of a set of discrete events which can have only one of two outcomes. It has a symmetrical frequency diagram.

SEE ALSO distribution

....

binomial theorem

a formula for finding any power of a binomial without doing the series of multiplications

....

biquadratic see **quartic**

....

bisect

To bisect an object, usually a line, a shape or an angle, is to cut or divide it into two parts which are equal in size and shape.

....

bisector

A bisector is a line which divides another line into two parts of equal size and shape.

perpendicular bisector

The perpendicular bisector of a line is another line which bisects it and is at right angles to it. Any point on the perpendicular bisector is at the same distance from either end of the line it bisects.

• *The diagram shows the* **perpendicular bisector** *of the line* AB. *It cuts* AB *at O so* AO *must be equal to* OB *in length.*

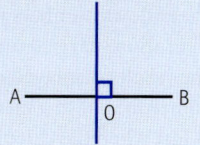

---

block graph see graph, frequency diagram

---

border pattern see pattern

---

bound

Bounds are two limits that values of a particular function cannot be greater or less than.

• *It is usual to make the* **bounds** *as tight as possible.*
• *It may, or it may not, be possible for values to actually touch the stated* **bounds**.

lower bound

a limit below which the function can produce no lower values

upper bound

a limit above which the function can produce no higher values

EXAMPLE:

Given $f(x) \equiv 2(\sin x + 1)$, then

$f(x)$ has an **upper bound** of 4 and a **lower bound** of 0 since its value cannot go above or below those limits.

---

bow compass see compass

---

box and whisker diagram (*also* box plot)

a diagram which displays five measures relating to one set of data. The diagram must be matched to a relevant number line, which is usually the 'horizontal' axis of the associated frequency diagram. The numerical values of the measures may, or may not, be written in as well. Two other measures, the range and the interquartile range, can be calculated from the diagram.

• *A* **box and whisker diagram** *or* **box plot** *is a useful pictorial summary when comparing sets of data, for example the summary of data concerning the heights of a group of people.*

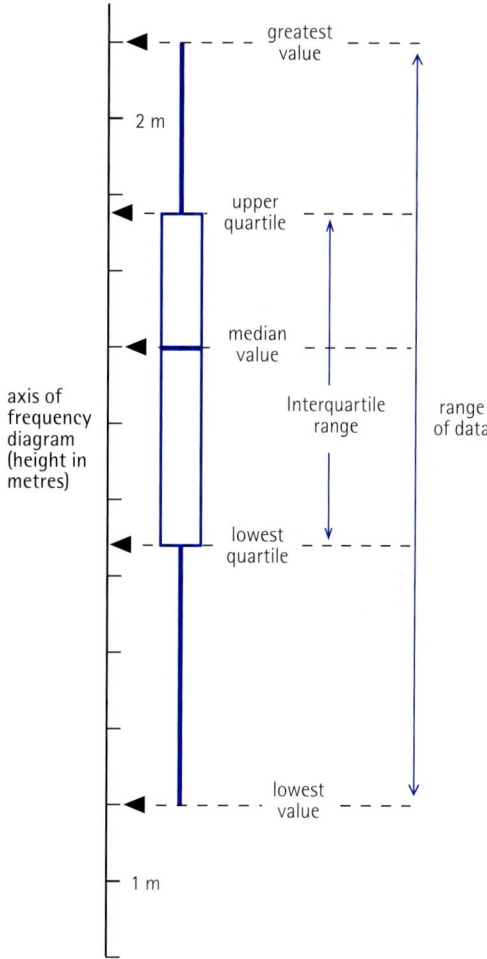

---

breadth see dimension

A
B
C
D
E
F
G
H
I
J
K
L
M
N
O
P
Q
R
S
T
U
V
W
X
Y
Z

bridges of Königsberg

This problem relates to the city of Königsberg (now called Kaliningrad) whose buildings were spread over the banks of a river and an island, with all the four principal areas of land connected by seven bridges. The problem was to devise a route, starting anywhere, that would cross each bridge once and once only. It was generally believed to be impossible, but no one could prove it could not be done. In 1736 Euler proved no answer was possible and, in doing so, started the branch of mathematics now known as topology.

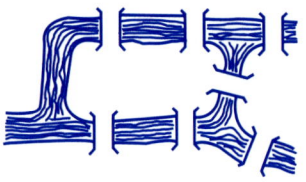

bureau de change

A bureau de change is a place where currencies of different countries can be exchanged.

buying price *see* **cost price**

Cc

calculator

A calculator is a device or an app on a device that allows numbers to be entered, mathematical operations carried out electronically, and the results displayed on a screen. Calculators sometimes have a memory facility, but all data is lost when the calculator is switched off or no longer in use.

• *A basic **calculator** is usually restricted to the operations* $+ - \times \div \sqrt{}$ *and the display shows eight digits.*

graphics calculator

a programmable calculator that has a larger display screen, so that graphs, text and numbers can be shown.

programmable calculator

a scientific calculator in which small programs can be keyed in, so it serves as a simple computer. It also has a memory which does not lose its contents when switched off.

scientific calculator

a calculator that can carry out many more operations (in trigonometry, statistics, etc.). It has a slightly bigger display so that it can show large numbers in scientific notation.

calculus

Calculus is the branch of mathematics studying the rate of change of quantities (differentiation) and the length, area, and volume of objects (integration).

WORD BUILD

differentiation (*also* **differential calculus**)

Differentiation is the act of calculating the derivatives of a curve or function.

• *If the function is shown as a graph, **differentiation** allows the gradient of the graph at any particular point to be calculated.*

> **integration** (*also* **integral calculus**)
> Integration is the act of calculating the integral of a function.

....

cancel

To cancel a fraction is to find an equivalent fraction by dividing both the numerator and denominator of the fraction by a common factor. This process is called cancelling.

....

cap

A cap is a segment of a sphere which is smaller than a hemisphere.

....

capacity

The capacity of a three-dimensional space is a measure of how much it can hold.

⚠ **WATCH OUT**

Mathematically, **capacity** and **volume** both measure the size of a 3-dimensional space and use the same units. But they are used differently.

Capacity refers to a containing space and the room available to hold something.

Volume is the space actually occupied by an object or the bulk of some substance.

If a bucket has a **capacity** of 20 litres, the **volume** of water needed to fill the bucket is 20 litres.

....

cardinal number *see* **number**

....

cardioid *see* **cycloid**

....

Cartesian coordinates *see* **coordinate**

....

cash discount *see* **discount**

....

casting out nines

is a method of checking on the accuracy of some arithmetic processes. For the processes of addition, subtraction, or multiplication of numbers, if the same process is applied to the digital roots of those numbers, then the digital root of that answer should be the same as the digital root of the actual answer obtained from the full numbers.

• *If there is an error, **casting out nines** will not identify where it is, only that there is one.*

SEE ALSO **digital root**

EXAMPLE:

In these sums (x) is the digital root of the preceding number.

$806_{(5)} + 57_{(3)} = 863_{(8)}$	$[5 + 3 = 8]$ ✓
$806_{(5)} - 57_{(3)} = 749_{(2)}$	$[5 - 3 = 2]$ ✓
$806_{(5)} \times 57_{(3)} = 45{,}942_{(6)}$	$[5 \times 3 = 15 \rightarrow 1 + 5 = 6]$ ✓

....

categorical data *see* **data**

....

catenary

A catenary is the curve formed by a heavy uniform string or cable which is hanging freely from two end points.

• *A **catenary** is most commonly seen in overhead electricity cables.*

....

Celsius scale *see* **temperature**

....

centigrade

❶ Centigrade is another name for Celsius, a scale used to measure temperature.

SEE ALSO **temperature**

❷ A centigrade is the angle made by $\frac{1}{100}$ part of a grade.

• *Grades and **centigrades** are now little used for angle measurement, though they are found on calculators under the label GRA.*

SEE ALSO **grade**

....

a
b
c
d
e
f
g
h
i
j
k
l
m
n
o
p
q
r
s
t
u
v
w
x
y
z

centred polygon number *see* polygon number

centre of enlargement *see* enlargement

centre of rotation *see* rotation

centre of symmetry *see* rotational symmetry

centroid

The centroid of any triangle is the point at which the three medians cross. The point is situated two-thirds of the length of each median from the corresponding vertex.
• *If the triangle is made of some material of uniform thickness and density, the **centroid** is also the centre of mass.*

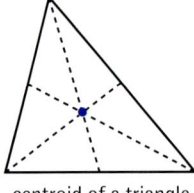

centroid of a triangle

chaining line *see* base line

chance

The chance of an outcome is the probability of that outcome.
• *The **chance** of getting heads when you toss a coin is one-half.*
SEE ALSO **probability**

changing the subject *see* subject

chart

A chart is an orderly or graphical way of showing data.
SEE ALSO **frequency diagram**

bar chart

A bar chart is a frequency diagram using rectangles of equal width whose heights or lengths are proportional to the frequency. The rectangles or bars may be of any width and sometimes are no more than lines.
• *Usually adjacent rectangles or bars in a **bar chart** only touch each other if the data is continuous; for discrete data a space is left between the bars.*
SEE ALSO **histogram**

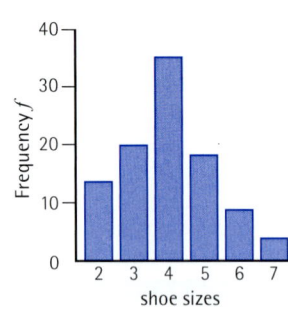

pie chart

A pie chart is a circular frequency diagram using sectors whose angles at the centre are proportional to the frequency.

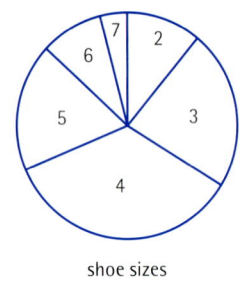

shoe sizes

chord

A chord of a circle is any straight line drawn across a circle, beginning and ending on the curve making the circle.
• *A **chord** which passes through the centre of a circle is also its diameter.* • *A **chord** extending beyond the circle is a secant.*

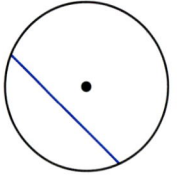

intersecting chord

Intersecting chords are two chords drawn in the same circle which cross at some point. The crossing point may be outside the circle and require the lines of the chords to be extended.

EXAMPLE:

If **two intersecting chords** are labelled as AB and CD and they cross at O, then $OA \times OB = OC \times OD$.

If the point O falls outside the circle, then the lines OAB and OCD are secants.

In the particular case where O is outside the circle, with OT a tangent and OAB a secant to that circle, then $OA \times OB = OT^2$.

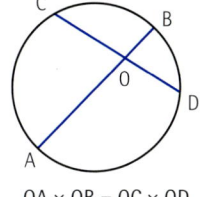

$OA \times OB = OC \times OD$

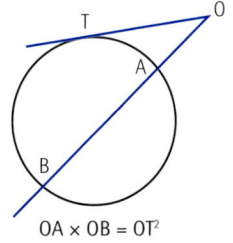

$OA \times OB = OT^2$

chronological

Items or events in chronological order are put in order of time, starting with the earliest.

EXAMPLE:

These Summer Olympic years are in **chronological** order:

Beijing 2008
London 2012
Rio 2016
Tokyo 2020

➤ **chronology** Chronology is the order of time in which events happen, starting with the earliest time.

circle

A circle is a shape formed by a line which curves around and joins up with itself in a closed curve on a plane or flat surface.

SEE ALSO **circumcircle, ellipse, escribed circle, great circle, incircle, quadrature, semicircle, transformation**

Apollonius' circle

Given two fixed points A and B then the locus of a point P moving in the plane of A and B, in such a way that the value of $AP \div BP$ is constant, is a circle.

SEE ALSO **locus**

EXAMPLE:

In the drawing shown the distance AB is 15 mm and $AP \div BP = 2$.

concentric circle

Concentric circles are two or more circles which have been drawn using the same position for their centres.

eccentric circle

Eccentric circles are two or more circles which have been drawn using different positions for their centres.
• *Usually, for two **eccentric circles**, one is completely inside the other, or else there is some area which is common to all the circles.*

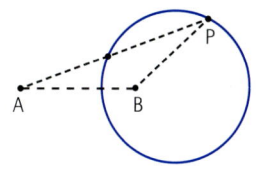

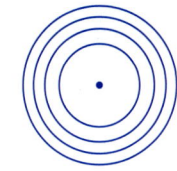

Apollonius' circle   concentric circles

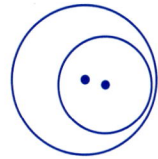

eccentric circles

circle projection *see* **ellipse**

circle theorem

Circle theorems are a collection of theorems which state the relationships between various parts of a circle (chord, segment, etc.) and the angles associated with them.

SEE ALSO **chord**

circle theorem 1: angle at the centre

The angle subtended by an arc at the centre is twice the angle subtended at the circumference.

SEE ALSO **subtended angle**

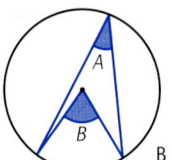

B = A × 2

circle theorem 2: angles in a semicircle

The angle at the circumference in a semicircle is a right angle.

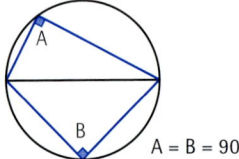

A = B = 90°

circle theorem 3: angles in the same segment

Angles in the same segment subtended by the same arc are equal.

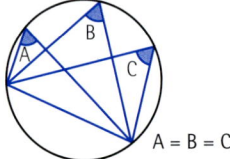

A = B = C

circle theorem 4: cyclic quadrilateral

Opposite angles in a cyclic quadrilateral add up to 180°.

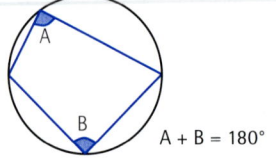

A + B = 180°

SEE ALSO **quadrilateral**

circle theorem 5: radius to a tangent

The radius is perpendicular to the tangent at the point at which they meet, so the angle between them is always a right angle.

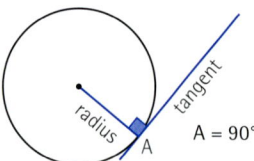

A = 90°

circle theorem 6: tangents from a point to a circle

The tangents drawn from the same point to different parts of a circle are equal in length.

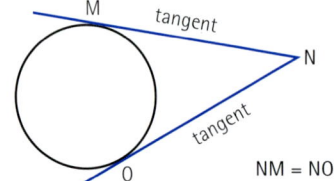

NM = NO

circle theorem 7: radius through a chord

The radius through the mid-point of a chord, will bisect the chord at a right angle.

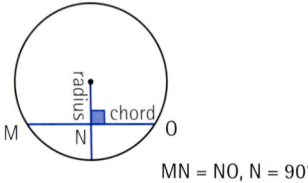

MN = NO, N = 90°

alternate segment theorem

The angle between the tangent and a chord is equal to the angle in the alternate segment or the opposite interior angle.

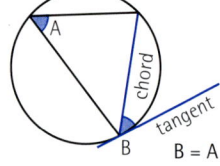

B = A

circular cone *see* cone

circular paraboloid *see* paraboloid

circumcentre
The circumcentre of a circumcircle is the position of its centre.

circumcircle
A circumcircle to any polygon is the circle drawn around the outside of that polygon which touches all of its vertices.

• *Since it is necessary for the circle to touch every vertex of the polygon, it is not possible to draw a **circumcircle** for every polygon, but it is always possible for regular polygons and for any triangle.*

SEE ALSO **escribed circle, incircle**

FORMULA:

Radius of circumcircle for any triangle = $\dfrac{abc}{4 \times \Delta}$

where

a, b, c are the lengths of the triangle's edges

Δ is the area of the triangle

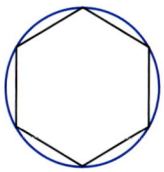 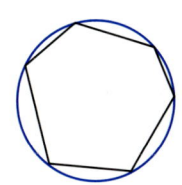

circumcircle to a regular hexagon   circumcircle to an irregular hexagon

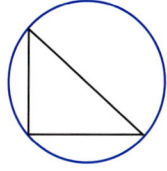 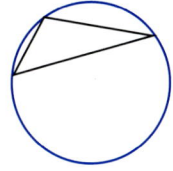

circumcircle to triangles

circumference
❶ The circumference of a circle is the distance measured around the curve which makes the circle.

FORMULA:

circumference of a circle = $\pi \times$ diameter = πd

❷ The circumference of an ellipse is another word for its perimeter.

SEE ALSO **ellipse**

circumscribe
A second shape is said to circumscribe a first shape if the second completely encloses the first, generally touching it at several points, but not cutting it. It is usual to require the circumscribing shape to be the smallest possible under the conditions given. The most common examples are the circumcircle to a polygon and the circumsphere to a polyhedron.

• *The image shows a regular hexagon **circumscribing** an irregular quadrilateral.*

SEE ALSO **inscribe**

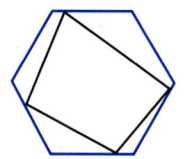

circumsphere
A circumsphere is the sphere which can be drawn around the outside of a polyhedron so as to pass through all its vertices.

• *It is always possible to draw a **circumsphere** for a regular convex polyhedron, and for any Archimedean solid, but it may not be possible for others.*

class
A class of data is one of the groups in a collection of grouped data.

➤ **class interval** The class interval is the width of a class as measured by the difference between the class limits.

• *In any collection of grouped data the **class intervals** are very often all the same but do not have to be. Common exceptions are the classes at each end when arranged in size order.* **»**

EXAMPLE:

When recording data about the heights of many people, you might group them as follows (in cm):

less than 100; 100–120; 120–140; 140–160; 160–180; 180–200; over 200.

This uses definite **class intervals** of 20 cm except for the first and last classes (or groups), which are open.

➤ **class limit** Class limits are the two values which define the two ends of a class and between which the data must lie.

....

clinometer
A clinometer is a hand-held instrument used to measure the angle of elevation of some point, in relation to the horizontal plane of the observer.
• *A clinometer has either a built-in plumb line or a level, and the angle through which the instrument has to be tilted out of the horizontal so as to be aligned with the point being looked at is shown on a suitable scale.*

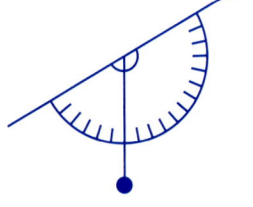

....

clockwise
The direction of a movement around a circular arc is described as being clockwise if it moves in the same direction, relative to the centre, as that of the hands of a conventional clock.
SEE ALSO **anticlockwise**

....

closed
An operation on a particular set is said to be closed if the operation always produces a result that is also in the set.

EXAMPLE:

Addition on numbers is **closed** since:
number + number = number.

Multiplication is also **closed**.

Subtraction on positive numbers is not **closed** as it is possible to get a negative result which is not in the set.

Division on integers is not **closed** because fractions are excluded.

....

closed curve *see* **curve**

....

codomain *see* **domain**

....

coefficient
A coefficient is a constant attached in front of a variable, or a group of variables, where it is understood that once the value of the variable(s) has been worked out, then the result is to be multiplied by the coefficient.
• *The absence of a coefficient is equivalent to a 1 being present.*
SEE ALSO **derivative, Pearson's product-moment correlation coefficient, Spearman's rank-order correlation coefficient**

EXAMPLE:

In $3x$ the **coefficient** is 3.

In $7xy$ the **coefficient** is 7.

In $Ax^2 y$ the **coefficient** is A.

In y^2 the **coefficient** is 1.

....

collinear
Three, or more, points are said to be collinear if one straight line can be drawn which passes through all of them.

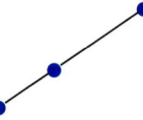

....

column

A column of a matrix is the set of elements making up one complete line, reading down the matrix from top to bottom.

- *The matrix* $\begin{pmatrix} 4 & 6 & 9 \\ 1 & 0 & 7 \end{pmatrix}$ *has 3* **columns**.

SEE ALSO **row**

---

column matrix *see* **matrix**

---

column vector *see* **vector**

---

combination

A combination of objects is an unordered arrangement of those objects.

- *The fact that a* **combination** *is unordered means that ABC is considered to be the same as BCA or CAB or CBA, etc.*

EXAMPLE:

$^{n}C_r$ is the symbol for the total number of **combinations** possible when, from a set of n objects, r are chosen at a time.

It is said as 'From n choose r'.

SEE ALSO **permutation**

FORMULA:

When the objects are all distinguishably different then:

$$^{n}C_r = \frac{n!}{r!(n-r)!}$$

EXAMPLE:

When $r = n$ then $^{n}C_r = 1$

$$^{49}C_6 = \frac{49!}{6! \times 43!} = 13{,}983{,}816$$

(which is almost 14 million)

Some values of $^{n}C_r$ for various values of n and r											
n =	2	3	4	5	6	7	8	9	10	11	12
r = 2	1	3	6	10	15	21	28	36	45	55	66
3		1	4	10	20	35	56	84	120	165	220
4			1	5	15	35	70	126	210	330	495
5				1	6	21	56	126	252	462	792
6					1	7	28	84	210	462	924
7						1	8	36	120	330	792
8							1	9	45	165	495

---

combined event *see* **event**

---

common factor *see* **factor**

---

common fraction *see* **fraction**

---

common logarithm *see* **logarithm**

---

common tangent *see* **tangent**

---

commutative

A commutative operation is one in which the order of combining the two objects does not matter.

- *Addition is* **commutative** *since* $3 + 5 = 5 + 3$.
- *Subtraction is not* **commutative** *since since* $6 - 4 \neq 4 - 6$.

SEE ALSO **associative**

> **WORD BUILD**
>
> ### commutative group (*also* Abelian group)
>
> A commutative group is a group of objects such that the group operation, when applied to any two of the group's members, is commutative.

---

compass

❶ A compass is an instrument used to find direction. The needle of a compass always points to a position called North.

➤ **points of the compass** The points of the compass are those directions defined (relative to North) by dividing a circle into four, eight, sixteen or thirty-two equal parts. The principal points are North, South, East, and West, and the next four are the points between those: North East (NE), etc.

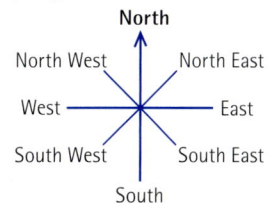

North, North West, North East, West, East, South West, South East, South

»

➤ **compass angle** A compass angle is the angle (in degrees) measured clockwise from the North-line to the line of the required direction. This allows a direction to be given to any (reasonable) accuracy between 0° and 360°.

• *Compass angles are always written with three digits, so 57° becomes 057° and 6° is 006°.*

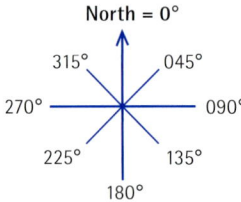

North = 0°

315°   045°

270° —————— 090°

225°   135°

180°

❷ Compass or compasses are shortened ways of saying a pair of compasses, which is an instrument consisting of two legs hinged together, with one leg having a sharp point at the end and the other a pen or pencil. Their principal use is for drawing circles or parts of a circle.

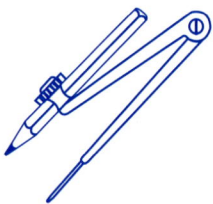

beam compass (*also* trammel compass)

A beam compass is a pair of compasses in which the two legs are not hinged together but are held on a single horizontal bar, along which they can be moved and then locked into position.

• *A **beam compass** is especially suitable for drawing larger circles because the drawing implement is always perpendicular to the surface over which it moves.*

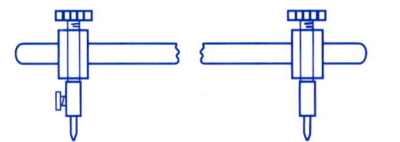

bow compass

A bow compass is a pair of small compasses which are intended for use in drawing small circles. Because of their small size they are easy to manipulate, and circles can be drawn with a simple twisting action between finger and thumb.

• *Bow compasses usually have a device to allow very fine adjustments to be made.*

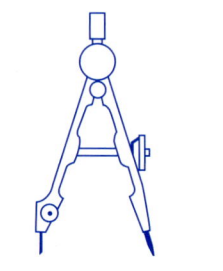

compass and traverse

is a method of fixing the shape and size of the boundary to a shape by considering the boundary as a series of traverses and measuring the length and direction (by taking a compass bearing) of each one.

• *Compass and traverse measurements allow an accurate drawing to be made. Bearings are taken at both ends of each traverse as a check.*

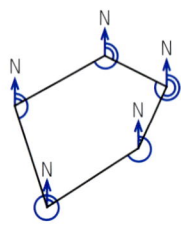

complement

❶ The complement of an acute angle is the amount needed to be added on to make 90°.

• *The **complement** of 70° is 20°.*

SEE ALSO **supplement**

❷ The complement of a set is all those members which are not in that set, but which are in the universal set originally given.

• *The symbol for the **complement** of a set is '(the apostrophe).*

SEE ALSO **set**

EXAMPLE:

Suppose the universal set is {odd numbers less than 30} and the set A is {all prime numbers}.

Then the **complement** of A is shown by A' and is {1, 9, 15, 21, 25, 27}.

complementary addition *see* **addition**

complementary angle *see* **angle**

complementary ratio

Complementary ratios are trigonometric ratios which are connected by their complementary angles.

FORMULA:

The three most important complementary ratios are:

$\sin \theta = \cos (90 - \theta)$

$\cos \theta = \sin (90 - \theta)$

$\tan \theta = \cot (90 - \theta)$

complex conjugate

The complex conjugate of the complex number $a + bi$ is $a - bi$ (and vice versa). Their real parts are equal. Their imaginary parts have the same magnitude but are opposite in sign.

SEE ALSO **number, complex number**

complex number *see* **number**

composite number *see* **number**

composite shape *see* **shape**

compound event *see* **event**

compound interest *see* **interest**

compound measure

A compound measure is a measure that requires more than one unit to give its value.

• *Speed is measured in metres per second (m/s). This is a **compound measure** as it combines the unit measure for distance (metres) and the unit measure for time (seconds) to define it.*

To change x into y	mph	km/h
miles per hour (mph)	1	1.6093
kilometers per hour (km/h)	0.62137	1
metres per second (m/s)	2.2369	3.6
feet per second (ft/s or ft/sec or fps)	0.68182	1.0973

To change x into y	m/s	ft/s
miles per hour (mph)	0.44704	1.4667
kilometers per hour (km/h)	0.27778	0.91134
metres per second (m/s)	1	3.2808
feet per second (ft/s or ft/sec or fps)	0.3048	1

concave polygon *see* **polygon**

concentric circle *see* **circle**

concrete objects

Concrete objects are any items that can be picked up and manipulated to help understand a concept or idea.

concurrent

Two, or more, lines are said to be concurrent if they have one point in common, through which all the lines pass.

a
b
c
d
e
f
g
h
i
j
k
l
m
n
o
p
q
r
s
t
u
v
w
x
y
z

condition

a statement that must be true in order for another statement to be true

SEE ALSO P, Q

necessary condition

A necessary condition for a statement Q to be true is another statement P which must be true whenever statement Q is true; then statement P is said to be a necessary condition. When P is true, then Q may be true or false, but when P is false, then Q must also be false.

EXAMPLE:

A **necessary condition** for the statement (Q) 'x is divisible by 6' is statement (P) 'x is even', but condition (P) by itself allows values such as 2, 4, 8, etc. which are clearly not divisible by 6.

sufficient condition

A sufficient condition for a statement Q to be true is another statement P which, when P is true, guarantees that statement Q must also be true. When statement P is false then statement Q may be true or false.

EXAMPLE:

A **sufficient condition** for the statement (Q) 'x is divisible by 6' is statement (P) 'x is divisible by 12', but condition (P) by itself excludes values such as 6, 18, 30, etc. which are also divisible by 6.

necessary and sufficient condition

A necessary and sufficient condition for a statement to be true is a second statement such that both the first and the second statement must be true at the same time. Both statements will be false together as well, but it cannot be that one is true and one is false.

EXAMPLE:

A **necessary and sufficient condition** for the statement 'x is divisible by 6' is that 'x is even and divisible by 3'.

conditional equation *see* equation

conditional probability *see* probability

cone

A cone is the three-dimensional shape formed by a straight line when one end is moved around a simple closed curve, while the other end of the line is kept fixed at a point, which is not in the plane of the curve.

• The word *cone* is often used to mean *right circular cone*.

SEE ALSO conic section

➤ **curved surface of a cone** The curved surface of a right circular cone is the sector which could be bent around until the edges meet to form the cone. When opened out and laid flat, the curved surface of a right circular cone forms the sector of a circle.

FORMULA:

Radius of circle to make sector = slant height of cone

Angle of sector (in degrees) = 360 × base radius ÷ slant height of cone

Area of sector = π × base radius × slant height of cone

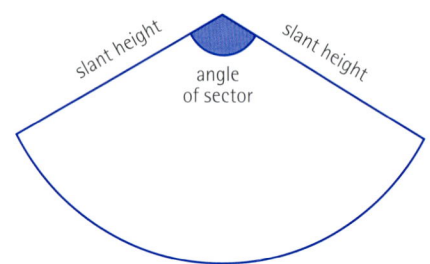

➤ **perpendicular height of a cone**
The perpendicular height of a cone is the distance of its vertex above the plane of its base.

FORMULA:

Volume of any cone = area of base × perpendicular height ÷ 3

➤ **slant height of a cone** The slant height of a right circular cone is the length of any straight line from the circumference of its base to the vertex.

FORMULA:

Slant height $= \sqrt{r^2 + h^2}$ where r is radius of base h is perpendicular height

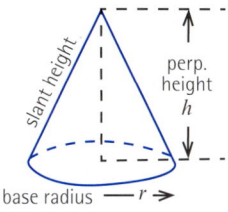

circular cone

A circular cone is a cone made using a circle as its base.

oblique circular cone

An oblique circular cone is a non-right circular cone. The vertex is not placed over the centre of the base.

right circular cone

A right circular cone is a cone made using a circle as its base and with its vertex placed on a line passing through the centre of the base and perpendicular to the plane of the base. It is what is usually meant when only the word 'cone' is used.

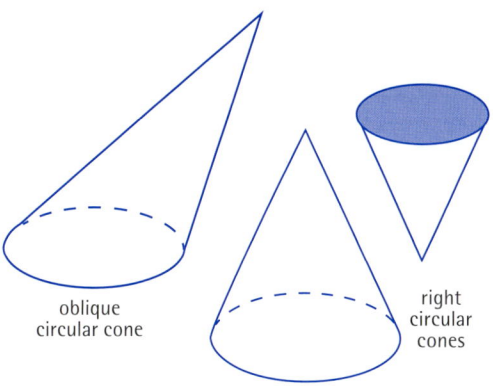

oblique circular cone

right circular cones

conformable matrix

A conformable matrix is one which has dimensions which are suitable for a particular operation.

• *If A is an m × n matrix, then B is a conformable matrix for the multiplication AB provided that B is an n × k matrix.*

SEE ALSO matrix

congruent

❶ Geometrical figures are said to be congruent if they are the same in shape and size. Such shapes are also described as being identical or equal.

• *One **congruent** shape can be fitted exactly over another, being turned around and/or over as necessary.* • *These four triangles are all **congruent**.*

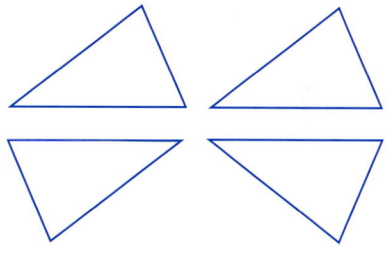

⚠ **WATCH OUT**

Congruent and **similar** are both used to compare geometrical shapes. **Congruent** shapes must be identical to each other in every way, except that one may be turned around, or over. **Similar** only requires the two shapes to be identical in their shape, and one may be bigger than the other. Given one large and one small square, they are **similar** but not **congruent**.

❷ Two numbers are said to be congruent to each other if they both have the same residue when using the same modulus.

• ≡ *is the symbol for 'is **congruent** to'.*

SEE ALSO modulus, residue

EXAMPLE:

7 and 15 both have a residue of 3 after division by 4; so 7 is **congruent** to 15 (mod 4).

$7 \equiv 3 \pmod 4$; $7 \equiv 15 \pmod 4$.

conic section (*also* conic curve)

is the general name given to the four types of curve that can be produced by the section of a cone as it is sliced through by a straight cut at various angles.

• *As the angle at which the cut is made changes, the four types of curve produced by the **conic sections**, are the circle, ellipse, hyperbola, and parabola.*

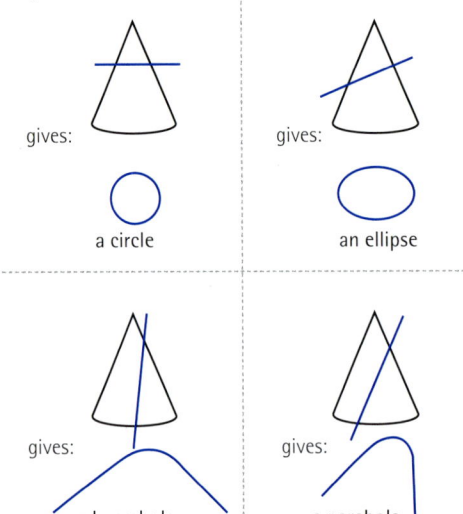

gives: a circle

gives: an ellipse

gives: a hyperbola

gives: a parabola

conjecture

A conjecture is a statement which, although much evidence can be found to support it, has not been proved to be either true or false.

⚠ **WATCH OUT**

A **conjecture** and a **hypothesis** are both unproven statements for which, usually, a lot of supporting evidence can be found.

Conjectures are generally about numbers and allow no exceptions.

Hypotheses generally occur in statistics, are usually set up before carrying out a search for supporting evidence, often involve a probability as to their correctness, and are sometimes put in a negative form as it is then easier to search for evidence that they are wrong.

conjugate angle *see* angle

consecutive number *see* number

constant

❶ A constant is a value that is unchanged whenever it is used for the particular purpose for which it was defined.

• *Usually a **constant** is given as a number, but in some cases a letter might be used to indicate that a constant of the correct value must be put in that place.*

SEE ALSO term

❷ (*also* uniform) When a property does not change during the period of time being considered, that property is described as constant or uniform.

• *For example, one can have **constant** speed, **constant** velocity, and **constant** acceleration.*

Consumer Price Index *see* Retail Prices Index

continued product *see* product

continuous data *see* data

contradiction *see* proof

contrapositive

The contrapositive of a statement is formed by taking the conclusion as the starting-point and the starting-point as the conclusion and then changing each from positive to negative and vice versa. If the original statement was true, then the contrapositive must also be true.

• *The statement 'If a number is even, it can be divided by two' has the **contrapositive**: 'If a number cannot be divided by two, then it is not even'.*

SEE ALSO converse

convergent series *see* series

converse

The converse of a theorem (or statement) is formed by taking the conclusion as the starting-point and having the starting-point as the conclusion. Though any theorem can be

re-formed in this way, the result may or may not be true and it needs its own proof.
• *One theorem states that if a triangle has two edges of equal length then the angles opposite to those edges are also equal in size. The **converse** is that if a triangle has two angles of equal size, then the edges opposite to those angles must be equal in length— and that can also be proved.*

SEE ALSO **contrapositive**

conversion factor

Conversion factors are multipliers (or dividers) which can be used to change a numerical measure in one type of unit into its equivalent measure in another type of unit.

conversion graph

A conversion graph is used to show the corresponding values between two quantities, which have a fixed relationship between them, by means of a line drawn on a squared grid. In making a conversion graph, the two quantities which are related are marked on a squared grid, using any suitable scales and putting one along each axis. A line is then plotted and drawn which shows the relationship between the two quantities so that intermediate values can be read off.
• *The **conversion graph** shown can be used to change temperatures between the Celsius and Fahrenheit scales. The blue dotted lines in the graph show that the readings of 35°C and 95°F are measuring the same temperature.*

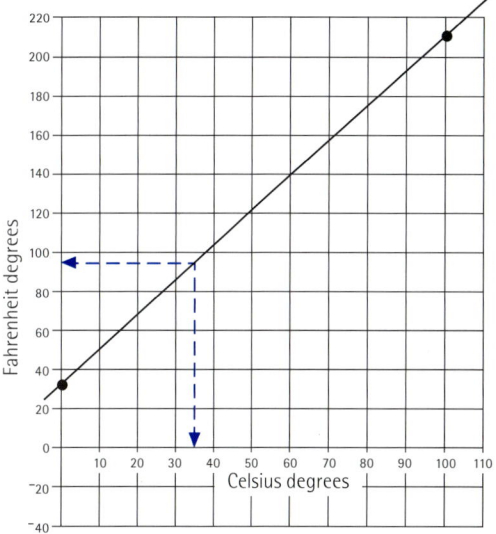

---

conversion scale

A conversion scale serves the same purpose as a conversion graph, but the two scales are matched directly side by side. It is more difficult to draw, since both scales have to be matched along their entire lengths, but it is easier to use.
• *A **conversion scale** for changing between °F and °C is shown.*

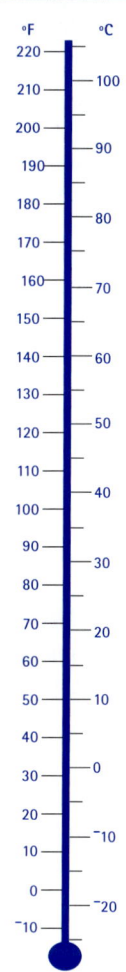

---

convex polygon see **polygon**

---

convex polyhedron see **polyhedron**

---

coordinate

Coordinates are numbers or letters that describe the position of a point in relation to some other fixed positions. The fixed positions might be points, lines or planes, depending on the coordinate system used.

Cartesian coordinates (*also* rectangular coordinates)

give the position of a point in two-dimensional space by stating its shortest distances from two fixed reference lines, or axes, set at right angles to each other. The distances may be given as positive or negative values.

polar coordinates

give the position of a point in two-dimensional space by stating its distance from a pole and the size of the angle between the polar axis and a line drawn from the point to the pole.

- *(r, θ) is the symbol for showing **polar coordinates**, where r is the length of the radius vector and θ is the angle (in radians or degrees) between the polar axis and the radius vector.*

FORMULA:

To change polar coordinates (r, θ) into Cartesian coordinates (x, y) use the following formulae:

$x = r \cos \theta$

$y = r \sin \theta$

three-dimensional coordinates

give the position of a point in three-dimensional space by using three fixed reference lines. The third axis, identified as the z-axis, is at right angles to both the x- and y-axes.

world coordinate system

Positions on the face of the Earth are given by reference to an imaginary coordinate system based on lines of longitude and lines of latitude. Longitude corresponds to the x-numbers, and latitude to the y-numbers in the Cartesian coordinate system.

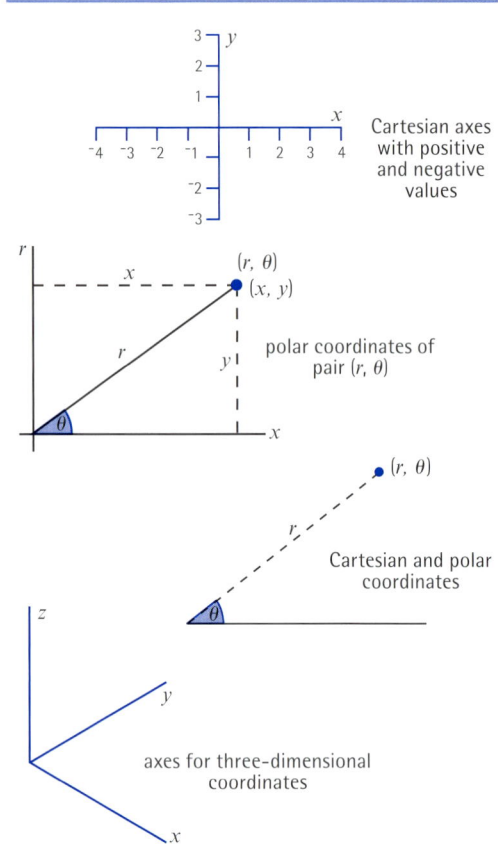

Cartesian axes with positive and negative values

polar coordinates of pair (r, θ)

Cartesian and polar coordinates

axes for three-dimensional coordinates

coprime (*also* relatively prime)

Two or more whole numbers are said to be coprime, or relatively prime, to each other if they have no factors (other than 1) in common.

EXAMPLE:

12 and 25 are **coprime**.

8, 9 and 11 are also **coprime**.

corollary

A corollary follows after a theorem and is a proposition which must be true because of that theorem.

- *It can be proved that the three interior angles of a triangle add up to 180° (a theorem). A **corollary** of this is that the exterior angle at one vertex must equal the sum of the interior angles of the other two vertices.*

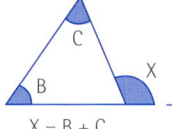

X = B + C

correlation

is an assessment of how strongly two pieces of data appear to be connected to the extent that a change in one of them must produce a change in the other. A correlation can vary from being non-existent through weak to very strong.

• *A correlation is usually made after a scatter graph has been drawn.* • *Sometimes, as in this illustration, the scatter graph can show no correlation.*

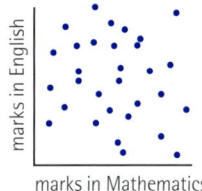

negative correlation

is a correlation in which an increase in the value of one piece of data tends to be matched by a decrease in the other.

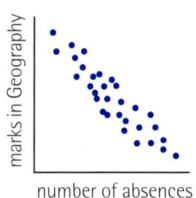

positive correlation

is a correlation in which an increase in the value of one piece of data tends to be matched by an increase in the other.

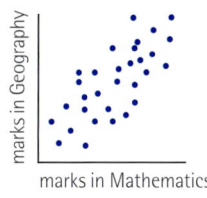

....

correlation coefficient *see* **Pearson's product-moment correlation coefficient, Spearman's rank-order correlation coefficient**

....

correspondence

A correspondence occurs when a mapping matches one or more elements in the domain with one or more elements in the codomain.

SEE ALSO **mapping diagram**

many-to-one correspondence

A many-to-one correspondence occurs when a mapping matches more than one element in the domain with the same element in the codomain.

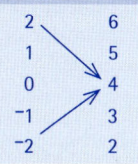

EXAMPLE:

The rule 'is the number whose square is' would match both −2 and 2 from the domain with 4 in the codomain.

The rule 'is the child whose mother is' could match more than one child to one woman.

one-to-many correspondence

A one-to-many correspondence occurs when a mapping matches one element in the domain with more than one element in the codomain.

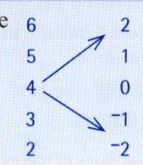

EXAMPLE:

The rule 'is the number whose square root is' would match 4 from the domain with both 2 and −2 from the codomain.

The rule 'is the mother of' could match one woman to more than one child.

one-to-one correspondence

A one-to-one correspondence occurs when a mapping between two sets of the same size pairs all the elements of each set without using any element twice.

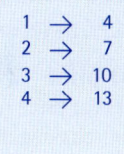

....

corresponding angle *see* **angle**

....

cos⁻¹ *see* **trigonometric ratio**

....

cosecant (*also* **cosec**) *see* **trigonometric ratio**

....

cosine (*also* **cos**) *see* **trigonometric ratio**

....

cosine curve

A cosine curve is the graph showing how the value of the cosine of an angle changes with the size of the angle.

• *The* **cosine curve** *is the sine curve shifted left by 90°.* • *The values have an upper bound of 1 and a lower bound of −1.*

SEE ALSO sine curve, tangent curve

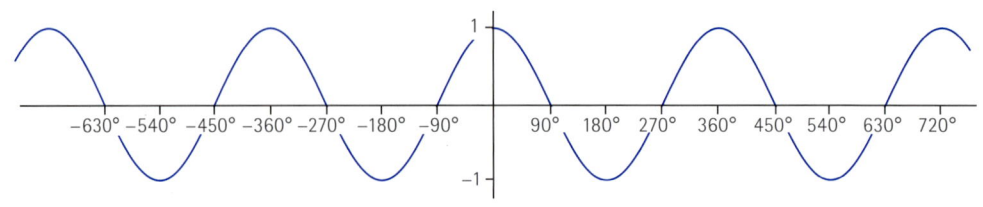

cosine rule

The cosine rule is an extension of Pythagoras' theorem, which allows it to be applied to any triangle.

SEE ALSO sine rule

FORMULA:

$$a^2 = b^2 + c^2 - 2bc \cos A$$

$$b^2 = c^2 + a^2 - 2ca \cos B$$

$$c^2 = a^2 + b^2 - 2ab \cos C$$

$$\cos A = \frac{b^2 + c^2 - a^2}{2bc}$$

Cost of Living Index see Retail Prices Index

cost price

The cost price of an article is the cost of making or purchasing that article. In the process of buying and selling, say from A to B, the selling price for A is the cost price for B.

SEE ALSO selling price

WORD BUILD

buying price

The buying price is the cost of purchasing an article which has simply been bought, and not made.

---

cotangent (*also* cot) see trigonometric ratio

counter-example

A counter-example to a statement is a particular instance of where that statement is not true. This makes the statement invalid.

• *For the statement 'All prime numbers are odd', a* **counter-example** *is 2.* • *It only requires one* **counter-example** *to make a statement invalid.*

counting number see number

counting on

is a method of subtraction which finds the difference between two numbers by counting on from the smaller to the larger and then adding up all the 'steps' needed. The steps can be of any convenient size that can be handled mentally.

• **Counting on** *is sometimes called the 'shopkeeper's method' from the way change used to be given.*

counting-out problem

Counting-out problems are based on the idea that a set of objects (or people) are arranged in a circle and then, after counting up to some number n while moving around the circle, the nth object is removed; this being continued until only one object is left. Problems are based on a requirement to predetermine where in the circle an object should be placed to ensure it is selected.

• **Counting-out problems** *are often seen in games where someone or something is chosen by counting using a rhyme.*

EXAMPLE:

Twelve playing cards (Ace to Queen) are arranged in a circle and then, starting the count at the first position with the Ace, every seventh card is removed until none are left. How must they be arranged so that the cards removed are in their correct numerical order, from the Ace to the Queen?

Answer: In clockwise order: Ace, 8, 3, 10, 5, Queen, 7, 2, 9, 4, Jack, 6

crescent *see* **lune**

cross–multiplication

is a method of simplifying an equation involving fractions based on the fact that:

$$\frac{a}{b} = \frac{c}{d} \Leftrightarrow ad = bc.$$

EXAMPLE:

$$\frac{2}{5} = \frac{4}{x} \Leftrightarrow 2x = 5 \times 4 \text{ so } x = 10$$

cross–section

A cross-section of any 3D shape is the 2D figure shown when that shape is cut across, in some specified place and direction, by a plane.

cross–staff

A cross-staff is a simple, easily made instrument to measure the subtended angle of two distant points at the observer's position.

EXAMPLE:

There are two parts to the **cross-staff** in the image: the main shaft EF and the crossbar AB which is free to slide along EF.

The observer's eye is put close to *E* while looking at the two distant points being considered. Cross-bar *AB* is then slid along EF until one of the distant points is coincident with A and the other is coincident with B.

The angle subtended by those two points at *E* can then be read off where *AB* cuts across a scale marked on *EF*.

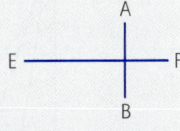

cryptarithm

Cryptarithms are sums in arithmetic in which some (or all) of the original digits have been hidden in some way, and it is required to find them.

WORD BUILD

alphametic

Alphametics are cryptarithms in which all of the digits have been replaced by letters (each letter always representing the same digit, and each digit always represented by the same letter) and with the arrangement forming real words.

EXAMPLE:

SEND + MORE = MONEY

Answer: 9567 + 1085 = 10652

asterithm

Asterithms are cryptarithms in which some of the digits have been replaced by asterisks, and the puzzle is to find the correct values of the missing digits.

EXAMPLE:

46 + 28 = 4*1

Answer: 146 + 285 = 431

cube

❶ A cube is a regular hexahedron and all its faces are squares.

❷ The cube of a number is the result of multiplying it by itself and then multiplying the result of that by the original number.

• *The* **cube** *of 1 is 1.* • x^3 *is the symbol meaning* '**cube** *the number that appears in the place of* x'.

EXAMPLE:

To **cube** 4, work out $4 \times 4 \times 4 = 64$

To **cube** −4, work out $-4 \times -4 \times -4 = -64$

When $x = 1.7$ then x^3 means $1.7 \times 1.7 \times 1.7 = 4.913$

»

WORD BUILD

cube root

The cube root of a number is another number which, when cubed, will equal the first number.
• $\sqrt[3]{\ }$ is the symbol meaning 'find the cube root of the number given'.

EXAMPLE:

The **cube root** of 1 is 1.

The **cube root** of 8 is 2 or
$\sqrt[3]{8} = 2$ since $2 \times 2 \times 2 = 8$

$\sqrt[3]{4.096} = 1.6$ since $1.6 \times 1.6 \times 1.6 = 4.096$

cubic

❶ A cubic equation, expression or function is one of degree 3.
• $2x^3 + 4x^2 - 8 = 0$ is a **cubic equation**.

SEE ALSO quartic, quintic

❷ A cubic graph is a graph in which the relationship between the variables involves an expression of degree 3.
• The **cubic graph** of $y = x^3 - 4x^2 - 15x + 18$ is shown. Its roots are −3, 1 and 6.

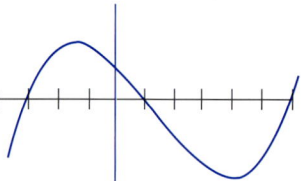

cuboid

A cuboid is a hexahedron whose faces are all rectangles.

cumulative frequency see frequency

cumulative frequency diagram see frequency

curve

In most cases 'curve' is used to describe a line which is not straight. However, in mathematics it also includes straight lines.
• 'Join the points with a **curve**' allows a straight line to be drawn if that is appropriate.

SEE ALSO cosine curve, curve of pursuit, French curve, sine curve, tangent curve

➤ **area under a curve** The area under a curve is the area enclosed between a curve drawn on a coordinate grid, two limiting ordinates and the x-axis. Three methods of finding an approximate value for this area (apart from counting squares) are the mid-ordinate rule, Simpson's rule, and the trapezium rule.

SEE ALSO mid-ordinate rule, Simpson's rule

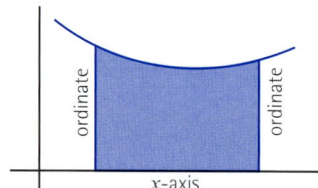

closed curve

A closed curve is a curve which joins up with itself and has no end points. No beginning or ending can be identified.

plane curve

A plane curve is a curve whose entire length lies within a single flat surface or plane.

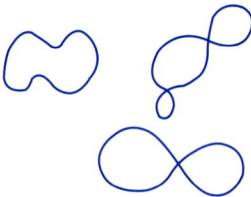

ruled curve

A ruled curve is a recognizable curve which is produced by drawing only straight lines. The smoothness of the curve depends upon the arrangement and number of lines drawn.

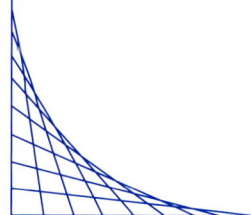

simple closed curve (*also* **Jordan curve**)

A simple closed curve is a closed curve which does not cross itself at any point.

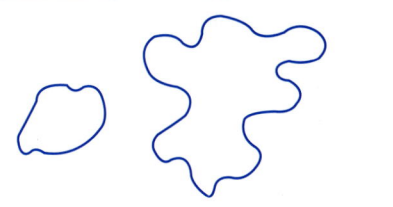

....

curve of constant width *see* **Reuleaux polygon**

....

curve of pursuit

A curve of pursuit is the line followed by one object moving directly towards another object which is also moving.

• *The simplest case of a **curve of pursuit**, when both objects are moving along the same straight line, is not usually considered.*

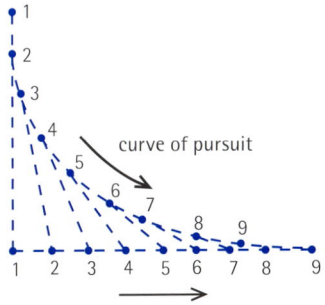

....

cusp

A cusp is a point on a curve where the curve makes a complete reversal of direction.

• *At the **cusp** the two parts of the curve share the same tangent.*

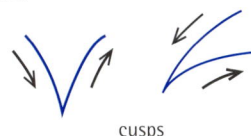

cusps

....

cutting number *see* **number**

....

cycle

Cycles using numbers are found by first making a rule by which one number is used to produce another number and then, by continuous use of that rule, seeing if a loop or chain is made when a previous number is repeated.

EXAMPLE:

By using this rule for making happy numbers, some **cycles** will be found:

A number has all its digits squared and added together to make a new number. This process is repeated until a 1 is obtained, when the original number is described as happy.

....

cyclical variation *see* **variation**

....

cyclic formula

Cyclic formulas are formulas in which the letters identifying the various quantities can be systematically exchanged and keep the formula correct.

SEE ALSO **cosine rule**

EXAMPLE:

In the cosine rule, the three formulas for a^2, b^2 and c^2 are really the same formula with a, b, c changed around and the angle (A, B or C) altered to match.

The formula for cos A in the cosine rule is a transposition of the formula for a^2 and is also cyclic.

Note that the formula statement for Pythagoras's theorem is not cyclic since c must be the hypotenuse.

In using **cyclic formulas**, it is important to match the letters in the formula to the data for the triangle.

....

cyclic quadrilateral *see* **quadrilateral**

....

cycloid

A cycloid is the locus of a single point on a circle when that circle is rolled along a straight line. A complete turn of the circle makes one arch.

• *The diagram shows a **cycloid** traced out by a point on a circle rolling along a straight line.*

SEE ALSO **cusp, parametric equation**

FORMULA:

Area between one arch and the line = $3\pi a^2$

Length of one arch = $8a$ where a = radius of the circle being rolled along on a separate line after a rule.

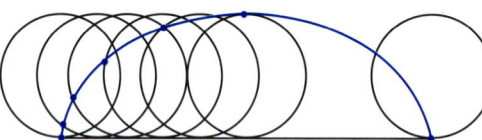

WORD BUILD

epicycloid

An epicycloid is the locus of a single point on a circle when that circle is rolled around the oustide of another circle known as the base circle.

• *The exact shape of an **epicycloid** or a **hypocycloid**, and the number of cusps it has, will be determined by the relative sizes of the rolling circle and the base circle.*

FORMULA:

The x, y coordinates needed to plot an epicycloid are given by the parametric equations:

$x = a(n \cos \theta + \cos n\theta)$

$y = a(n \sin \theta - \sin n\theta)$

θ may take any values (normally in the range $0°$ to $360°$)

If n is a whole number, then there will be $(n - 1)$ cusps. In the image, the epicycloid has 5 cusps, so $n = 6$.

The value of a changes the size of the curve.

hypocycloid

A hypocycloid is the locus of a single point on a circle when that circle is rolled around the inside of another circle known as the base circle.

FORMULA:

The x, y coordinates needed to plot a hypocycloid are given by the parametric equations:

$x = a(n \cos \theta + \cos n\theta)$

$y = a(n \sin \theta - \sin n\theta)$

The same remarks apply as for the epicycloid equations except that in this case there will be $(n + 1)$ cusps.

In the image, the hypocycloid has 5 cusps, so $n = 4$.

astroid

An astroid is a hypocycloid having only four cusps.

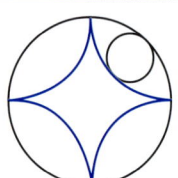

EXAMPLE:

For an **astroid**, in the equations for the hypocycloid, $n = 3$. The equations can be rewritten more simply as:

$x = 4a \cos^3 \theta$

$y = 4a \sin^3 \theta$

Area enclosed by astroid = $\dfrac{3}{8}\pi a^2$

Perimeter length = $6a$

cardioid

A cardioid is an epicycloid having only one cusp. It is the locus drawn when the rolling circle and the base circle are the same size.

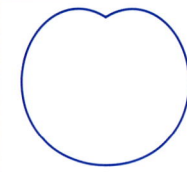

EXAMPLE:

For a **cardioid**, in the equations for the epicycloid, $n = 2$.

Area enclosed by cardioid $= 6\pi a^2$

Perimeter length $= 16a$

deltoid

A deltoid is a hypocycloid having only three cusps. The rolling circle is $\frac{1}{3}$ the size of the base circle.

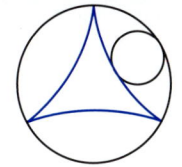

EXAMPLE:

For a **deltoid**, in the equations for the hypocycloid, $n = 2$.

Area enclosed by deltoid $= 2\pi a$

Perimeter length $= 16a$

nephroid

A nephroid is an epicycloid having only two cusps. The rolling circle is half the size of the base circle.

EXAMPLE:

For a **nephroid**, in the equations for the epicycloid, $n = 3$.

Area enclosed by nephroid $= 12\pi a$

Perimeter length $= 24a$

cyclotomy

is the topic concerned with dividing the circumference of a circle into equal parts, using only geometrical constructions.

EXAMPLE:

Early Greek mathematicians knew this was possible for all cases where the number of divisions was 2^n, 3, or 5 and all other numbers obtained by multiplying any two of those together. So it was possible for 2, 3, 4, 5, 6, 8, 10, 12, 15, ... divisions.

The German mathematician Gauss (1777–1855) proved that it was possible to construct $2^{2^n} + 1$ divisions provided only that the expression yielded a prime. That added 17, 257 and 65,537 ($n = 2$, 3, and 4) to the list.

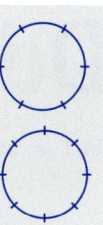

cylinder

A cylinder is formed by using two identical simple closed plane curves that are parallel to each other and joining up corresponding points on each of the curves with straight lines. The word cylinder is often used to mean right circular cylinder.

➤ **curved surface of a cylinder** The curved surface of a right circular cylinder is the rectangle which could be bent around (until two opposite edges meet) to fit the two circular ends and so form the complete cylinder.

FORMULA:

Curved surface area $= 2\pi rh$

where

r is the radius of the circular end of the cylinder

h is the height of the cylinder

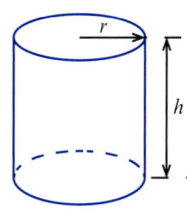

right circular cylinder

A right circular cylinder is a cylinder in which the ends are circles and the line joining their centres is an axis of symmetry of the cylinder.

FORMULA

Volume of right circular cylinder $= \pi r^2 h$

where

r is the radius of the circular end of the cylinder

h is the height of the cylinder

a
b
c
d
e
f
g
h
i
j
k
l
m
n
o
p
q
r
s
t
u
v
w
x
y
z

Dd

dart *see* **arrowhead**

....

data *singular* **datum**
is the complete set of individual pieces of information being used in any of the processes connected with statistics.

• *In statistics and computing, **data** is increasingly used only as a singular collective noun: we say 'the **data** is' rather than 'the **data** are'.*

continuous data

is data which can take any value within certain restrictions. If the data is grouped, these restrictions might be the bounds of the groups. If the data is measured, the restrictions might be defined by the accuracy of the measuring device.

• *A survey of the lengths of people's feet involves **continuous data**. They can be of any length, but the usual measuring instruments do not record beyond three decimal places, and common sense dictates that there are both upper and lower limits to what we might expect to find.*

discrete data

is data which can only be of certain definite values.

• *A survey of shoe sizes being worn by a group of people would use **discrete data**, since there are only a limited amount of values for the sizes in which shoes are made and sold.*

grouped data

is data that has been put into groups according to some particular rules to make it easier to handle. It is most often grouped according to size.

EXAMPLE:

Collecting data about the heights of 100 people could result in 100 different measurements. **Grouped data** is easier to handle.

Suitable groups might be: less than 100; 100–120; 120–140; 140–160; 160–180; 180–200; over 200 (all in cm).

With these groups, decisions are needed as to where a piece of data at the end of a group goes. For instance, to which group does a person of height 160 cm belong?

For greater precision this is done by writing the class interval as falling between two inequalities such as '140 < height ≤ 160 cm'.

In this case the first and last groups would be 'height ≤ 100 cm' and 'height > 200 cm'.

primary data

is data which has been collected at first hand, usually by the individual(s) actually doing the statistics with that data.

qualitative data (*also* categorical data)

is data which is described by a quality that it possesses. For example, type and colour. A survey of cars might separate them by colour.

• *The statistical measures of mean and median cannot be applied to **qualitative data**, but the mode can.*

quantitative data (*also* quantitive data, numerical data)

is data which is described by means of a measurement of some kind. The measurements most commonly used are those of length and weight.

• *Most statistics is concerned with **quantitative data**.*

raw data

is the data as it was originally collected, before any processing at all has been done.

secondary data

is data which has been taken from an existing source.

....

datum

In measuring heights it is necessary to have a fixed horizontal line (or plane) from which all measurements up or down can be taken. This fixed line is known as the datum.

• *In order that heights can be compared over an entire country, there has to be one overall recognized **datum** and, for Great Britain, this is the Mean Sea level measured at Newlyn in Cornwall.*

deceleration (*also* **retardation**)

If the velocity of a moving object is decreasing, then its acceleration is negative and is often described as deceleration.

SEE ALSO **acceleration**

decimal fraction (*also* **decimal**)

A decimal fraction or decimal is a way of expressing values of fractions less than 1 using the normal decimal place-value system extended to the right of the units column so as to give values of $\frac{1}{10}$, $\frac{1}{100}$, etc.

• *The **decimal fraction** 0.376 means*

$$\frac{3}{10} + \frac{7}{10} + \frac{6}{1,000} = \frac{376}{1,000}$$

SEE ALSO **bicimal**

WORD BUILD

recurring decimal (*also* **periodic decimal**)

A recurring decimal or periodic decimal is a decimal fraction which goes on repeating itself without end.

SEE ALSO **period**

EXAMPLE:

These are some **recurring decimals**.

0.3333333 ... is usually written $0.\dot{3}$ recurring

0.14285714285714285714 ... is usually written $0.\dot{1}4285\dot{7}$

The dot or dots above the number show what is to be repeated; it may be either a single digit or a block of digits.

terminating decimal

A terminating decimal is a decimal fraction that ends after a definite number of digits have been given.

EXAMPLE:

These are some **terminating decimals**.

0.5

0.123

0.67

0.747474

decimal place (*also* **dp**)

is the number of digits after the decimal point.

• *12.56 has 2 **decimal places**.*

➤ to '...' decimal places (*also* to '...' dp) indicates an approximation has been made by rounding to leave only the number of digits after the decimal point stated in '...'.

EXAMPLE:

π = 3.14 to 2 decimal places

π = 3.14159 to 5 decimal places

It is correct to use the = sign rather than ≈.

decimal point

A decimal point is a dot used to show that the values which follow make up a decimal fraction.

• *In some countries, as well as in the metric and SI systems, a comma is used to represent a **decimal point**.*

decimal system *see* **number base**

decomposition

is a method of subtraction which breaks down the first number in the operation, where necessary, to allow the subtraction to take place.

EXAMPLE:

| 874 | is | 800 + 70 + 4 |
| −629 | | 600 + 20 + 9 |

which becomes	800 + 60 + 14	written as	$8\ \ ^{6}\not{7}\ \ ^{1}4$
	600 + 20 + 9		6 2 9
	200 + 40 + 5		2 4 5

➤ decompose In a subtraction, to break down the first number in the operation to allow the subtraction to take place.

a b c d e f g h i j k l m n o p q r s t u v w x y z

deficient number *see* **number**

. . . .

degree

❶ A degree is the angle made by $\frac{1}{360}$ part of a full turn. A degree has 60 minutes and each minute has 60 seconds.

• *Degrees and decimal fractions are most often used for angles, except in navigation, when minutes and seconds are used.* • ° *is the symbol for* **degree**, ´ *is the symbol for minute, and* ´´ *is the symbol for second.*

EXAMPLE:

There are 360 **degrees** in a circle or in a full turn.

103° 26´ 47´´ is 103 **degrees**, 26 minutes and 47 seconds. In decimal form this is about 103.446°.

❷ A degree is a unit used to measure temperature.
SEE ALSO **temperature**

❸ The degree of an algebraic term is found by adding together all the indices of the variables in that term.

EXAMPLE:

$2x^3$ has **degree** 3

$4x^3y^2$ has **degree** 5

$3xy$ has **degree** 2

❹ The degree of an expression is given by the highest value found among the degrees of all the terms in that expression.

EXAMPLE:

$x^4 - 4x^3y^2 + 6y^2$ is an expression of **degree** 5 (the middle term).

. . . .

Delian problem (*also* **duplication of a cube**)
The Delian problem says that starting with a cube whose length of edge is e, use a geometrical construction to construct a second cube with length of edge k whose volume is twice that of the original one. In this case, $k^3 = 2e^3$ or $k = e \times \sqrt[3]{2}$.

EXAMPLE:

In two dimensions the equivalent problem is to draw a square which is twice the area of a given square. In that case $k = e \times \sqrt{2}$ and k is easily constructed as shown.

It was not proved until the 19th century that there was no possible geometrical construction for $k = e \times \sqrt[3]{2}$.

. . . .

deltahedron
a polyhedron whose every face is an equilateral triangle

EXAMPLE:

There are only eight possible convex **deltahedrons**.

Three are regular tetra-, octa-, and icosahedrons.

The other five possible convex **deltahedrons** are irregular and have six, ten, twelve, fourteen, or sixteen faces.

SEE ALSO **polyhedron**

. . . .

deltoid *see* **arrowhead, cycloid**

. . . .

denary *see* **number base**

. . . .

denominator
The denominator is the bottom number in a common fraction.
• *In the fraction* $\frac{8}{9}$, *8 is the numerator, 9 is the* **denominator**.
SEE ALSO **numerator**

. . . .

denumerable set *see* **set**

. . . .

dependent event *see* **event**

. . . .

dependent variable *see* **variable**

. . . .

depreciation
The depreciation of the value of an object is the amount by which that value has fallen.
• *Depreciation is similar to compound interest, except that the value is decreasing.*

FORMULA:

If the rate of depreciation (as a % per period) is known, then the new value can be worked out from this formula:

$$new = original \times (1 - r/100)^n$$

where

new is the new value after *n* periods

original is the original value

r is the rate of depreciation as a % per period

---

depth *see* **dimension**

---

derangement

Given *n* different objects to be put into *n* boxes then there are *n*! (factorial *n*) ways of doing it. However, if each object has to be matched to a particular box (say objects and boxes are numbered) then there can only be one way of doing it correctly. If every object is in a wrong box then that is known as a derangement of the objects. Some right and some wrong is not a derangement.

• *For any value of n the number of all possible* **derangements** *is shown by !n.*

EXAMPLE:

Given 1, 2, 3 as the objects, then 2, 3, 1 and 3, 1, 2 are the only 2 possible **derangements** (1, 3, 2;   2,1,3;   3,2,1 are not) and so !3 is 2.

Some values of !*n* (also known as subfactorial *n*) are given in the table.

n	!*n*
1	0
2	1
3	2
4	9
5	44
6	265
7	1,854
8	14,833

---

derivative (*also* **differential coefficient**)

The derivative or the differential coefficient of a function for some particular value is a measure of either the rate at which the function is changing at that value, or the gradient of the graph of the function at that point.

• *For f(x) $\equiv$ x² + 4x −7 the* **derivative** *when x = 3 is 10*

SEE ALSO **calculus**

---

derived function *see* **function**

---

determinant

The determinant of a square matrix is a single number obtained by applying a particular set of rules to the elements of that matrix.

EXAMPLE:

In $\begin{vmatrix} a & b \\ c & d \end{vmatrix}$ the two ruled lines are a symbol that the **determinant** of the matrix $\begin{pmatrix} a & b \\ c & d \end{pmatrix}$ has to be found.

For a 2 by 2 matrix, the rule is $ad - bc$.

$\begin{pmatrix} 2 & 3 \\ 4 & 7 \end{pmatrix}$ is $(2 \times 7) - (3 \times 4) = 14 - 12 = 2$

---

deviation

The deviation of a value is the difference between that value and some other value, usually the mean or median of the data.

SEE ALSO **mean deviation, standard deviation**

---

diagonal

❶ A diagonal of a shape is a straight line which joins one vertex to another vertex and which is not an edge of that shape.

❷ A diagonal of a polygon is a straight line drawn between two vertices that are not adjacent to each other.

❸ In a square matrix, a diagonal is a set of elements making up a complete line from a top corner to the opposite bottom corner.

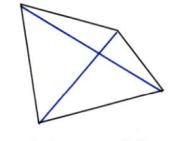
diagonals in a quadrilateral

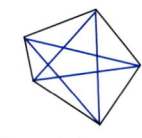
diagonals in a pentagon

»

face diagonal

A face diagonal of a three-dimensional shape is a diagonal which lies entirely in one face of the shape.

main diagonal (*also* leading diagonal, principal diagonal)

the set of elements making up one complete line reading from the top left corner to the bottom right corner of a square matrix

• *In matrix* $\begin{pmatrix} 7 & 2 \\ 4 & -9 \end{pmatrix}$ *the main diagonal is 7 −9 and the trailing diagonal is 2 4.*

secondary diagonal (*also* trailing diagonal)

the set of elements making up one complete line from top right to bottom left of a square matrix

space diagonal

A space diagonal of a three-dimensional shape is a diagonal which is not a face diagonal.

diagonal matrix *see* matrix

diagonal scale

A diagonal scale is used to increase the accuracy with which readings can be taken from a scaled ruler by giving markings of one-hundredths of the unit being used.

EXAMPLE:

In the drawing the diagonal lines on the left divide each tenth into ten equal parts.

The length of the line between the two black dots is 1.26 units.

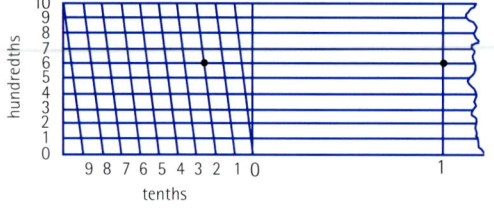

diameter

A diameter of a circle is a straight line passing through the centre and which touches the curve forming the circle at each of its ends.

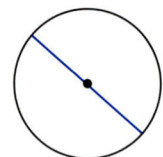

diamond (*also* lozenge)

A diamond or lozenge is a rhombus (a quadrilateral whose edges are all the same length and whose diagonals bisect each other at right angles) with no interior angle being a right angle.

difference

In arithmetic, a difference is the result of subtracting one number from another.

• *Arithmetically, the difference between 4 and 6 is 2.*

SEE ALSO square

absolute difference

The absolute difference is the difference between two numbers ignoring any negative sign in the answer. It is a measure of the 'distance' between the two numbers when placed on a number line.

• *~ is the symbol meaning that the absolute difference is needed. For example, 3 ~ 5 = 2.*

EXAMPLE:

The **absolute difference** of 2 and 5 is 3.

The **absolute difference** of −2 and 5 is 7.

differential calculus *see* calculus

differential coefficient *see* derivative

differential equation

Is an equation which expresses a relationship between a function and at least one of its derivatives.

SEE ALSO calculus

a b c d e f g h i j k l m n o p q r s t u v w x y z

EXAMPLE:

$$\frac{dy}{dx} = 2x - 1 \qquad \frac{d^2y}{dx^2} + \frac{dy}{dx} - 6y = 0$$

are two **differential equations** of the first and second order respectively.

. . . .

differentiate
To differentiate is to calculate the derivative of a function.

SEE ALSO **derivative**

. . . .

differentiation see calculus

. . . .

digit (also numeral)
Digits or numerals are the single symbols 0, 1, 2, 3, 4, 5, 6, 7, 8, and 9 as used in everyday arithmetic. They are also numbers but, more importantly, they are put together to make numbers.
• *2167 is a number made of four **digits**.*

. . . .

digital invariant
Digital invariants have been defined as those numbers which are equal to the sum of all their separate digits when raised to the same power.
• *153 is a **digital invariant** since $1^3 + 5^3 + 3^3 = 1 + 125 + 27 = 153$.*

. . . .

digital root
The digital root of a positive whole number is made by finding its digit sum to make a new number and repeating this process on each new number made until only a single digit remains. This is the digital root of the original number.
• *$8,579 \rightarrow 8 + 5 + 7 + 9 = 29 \rightarrow 2 + 9 = 11 \rightarrow 1 + 1 = 2$, so 2 is the **digital root** of 8,579.*

. . . .

digit sum
The digit sum of a number is found by adding all its digits together.
• *The **digit sum** of 742 is $7 + 4 + 2 = 13$.*

. . . .

dihedral angle
When two planes intersect in a common straight line, the dihedral angle between the planes is the one measured between two lines, one in each plane, drawn from the same point on that common line and perpendicular to it.
• ***Dihedral angles** are most often met with as the angle between two adjacent faces of a polyhedron.*

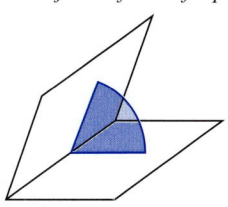

. . . .

dimension
❶ A dimension of a shape is one measurement taken between two specific points on the outline of the shape or, in some cases, inside the shape. Usually several dimensions are needed to fix the size of a shape.
• *The three main **dimensions** of a cupboard are generally referred to as its width, depth, and height.*
❷ The dimension of a vector is a measure of how many numbers are needed to express it, or the dimension of the space needed to show it.
• *(1, 7, −5) is a vector of **dimension** 3.*

. . . .

Diophantine equation see equation

. . . .

Diophantine problem
Diophantine problems are ones that seem at first to have insufficient information for their solution but, because the objects involved can only be counted using whole numbers (such as live animals), at least one solution can be found.

EXAMPLE:

In the market, ducks cost £5 each, hens cost £1 each and baby chickens were twenty for £1.

Kim bought at least one of each, 100 birds altogether, for a total of £100. How many of each did Kim buy?

One possible solution is : Kim bought 19 ducks, 1 hen, and 80 baby chickens.

. . . .

direct common tangent see tangent

. . . .

directed number see number

. . . .

direction

For movement over the surface of the Earth, the direction of a line is measured relative to another line pointing to a position called North.

SEE ALSO **compass**

EXAMPLE:

There are two positions known as North.

The North Pole is fixed and known as True North.

A magnetic compass points at Magnetic North.

The difference between True North and Magnetic North varies and can be as much as 20°.

....

direct isometry *see* isometry

....

direct proof *see* proof

....

direct proportion *see* proportion

....

directrix *plural* directrices

A directrix is a fixed straight line used in drawing the conic curves.

SEE ALSO **conic section**

....

direct variation *see* proportion

....

discount

A discount is an amount which is taken off the price of something. Discounts are usually stated as percentages.
• *If a price of £12 has a* **discount** *of 10%, £1.20 is taken off.*

cash discount

A cash discount is a discount which is sometimes given if the amount owing is paid in cash, usually within a certain time.

....

discrete data *see* data

....

discriminant *(also* Δ*)*

The discriminant of the quadratic equation $ax^2 + bx + c = 0$ is $\sqrt{b^2 - 4ac}$. Its value helps to determine the nature of the solutions of the equation.

SEE ALSO **quadratic equation**

....

disjoint set *see* set

....

dispersion *(also* spread*)*

The dispersion or spread of a set of data is a measure of the way in which the distribution is spread out.
• *There are various ways* **dispersion** *can be measured but the one most often used is the standard deviation.*

SEE ALSO **distribution, standard deviation**

....

displacement

The displacement of an object in motion is the distance and direction from its starting position to its finishing position. It is a vector.

....

dissection

Dissection puzzles require one shape to be cut up into a number of pieces and these pieces then re-assembled to make some other shape.

EXAMPLE:

The illustration shows the **dissection** of an equilateral triangle into the smallest possible number of pieces that can be rearranged to make a square.

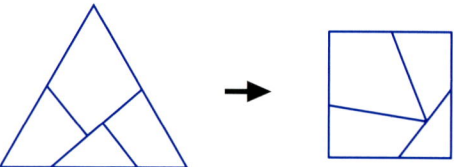

➤ **dissect** To dissect a shape is to cut it up into a number of pieces.

....

distance-time graph *(also* travel graph*)*

A distance-time graph is a graph that shows the relationship between the distance moved by an object in relation to time.

SEE ALSO **velocity-time graph**

The gradient of a line drawn on the **distance-time graph** is a measure of velocity.

If the line of the relationship is curved, the particular velocity at some moment in time can only be found by drawing a tangent to the curve at that point and measuring its gradient.

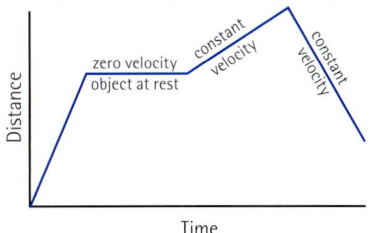

distribution
The distribution of a set of data is a graph or table showing the frequency of the data in each class, or of each type.
• *This table shows the **distribution** of shoe sizes among 100 people.*

Shoe size	2	3	4	5	6	7
Frequency	14	20	35	18	9	4

normal distribution
A normal distribution is one in which the frequency diagram is symmetrical about a line through the mean value (which is also the median and the mode), and has a shape like that shown in the picture.

The curve of a **normal distribution** (known as a 'bell-curve') is derived from a particular formula for continuous data.

It needs a lot of data to produce something that approximates to a curve, but the phrase is loosely used for frequency diagrams that seem to have that rough general shape.

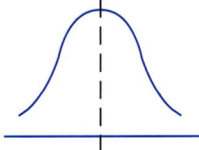

skewed distribution
A skewed distribution is one in which the frequency diagram, whilst having a single mode, is not symmetrical about the mean.

distributive law
The distributive law describes how two operators may be used together when linked in a particular way.
• *The **distributive law** of arithmetic says that multiplication is distributed over addition as in $(a \times b) + (a \times c)$.*

divergent series *see* **series**

divide *see* **division**

dividend
The dividend is the amount in a division operation which is to be shared out, or the number which must be divided into parts.
• *In $21 \div 3 = 7$ the **dividend** is 21.*

dividers (*also* **pair of dividers**)
are an instrument similar in appearance to compasses but with both legs having a sharp point at the end. They are used for measuring, or marking off, the distance between two points on a drawing, a ruler or a scale.

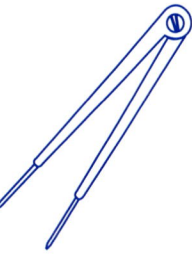

a b c d e f g h i j k l m n o p q r s t u v w x y z

A
B
C
D
E
F
G
H
I
J
K
L
M
N
O
P
Q
R
S
T
U
V
W
X
Y
Z

division

is the operation between two numbers which measures how many times bigger one number is than the other. With whole numbers, division can be seen as equivalent to the sharing out of a quantity into a number of equal-sized portions; the general case for all numbers is an extension of that.

EXAMPLE:

÷ and **/** are two symbols which both mean that **division** is to be done.

$18 \div 6 = 3$ and $18 / 6 = 3$

➤ **divide** To divide one number by another is to measure how many times bigger it is than the other.

long division

is an algorithm to deal with division for those cases where the numbers are too difficult to work with mentally.

short division

is the description used when division is done mentally. Numbers may be written down, but none of the processes are.

divisor

The divisor is the amount in a division operation which must do the dividing, or among which the dividend must be shared.
• *In $18 \div 9 = 2$ the **divisor** is 9.*
SEE ALSO **dividend**

domain

In a mapping, the domain is the set that the mapping is coming from.

WORD BUILD

codomain

The codomain is the set that the mapping is going to.

dot product *see* **scalar product**

doubling sequence *see* **sequence**

dp *see* **decimal place**

duodecimal *see* **number base**

Ee

e

e is an irrational number and, like π, it cannot be written as a simple fraction. It is the base of natural logarithms which were invented by the Scotsman John Napier.

eccentric circle *see* circle

eccentricity

The eccentricity of an ellipse is a measure of how much it varies from a circle.

• *The **eccentricity** of a circle is zero.*

SEE ALSO **ellipse**

FORMULA:

The value of the eccentricity of an ellipse is given by the formula:

$$\sqrt{1-\frac{b^2}{a^2}}$$

where

a is half the length of the ellipse's major axis

b is half the length of the ellipse's minor axis

edge

❶ An edge of a shape is the line, or one of the lines, defining the outline of that shape.
❷ An edge of a polyhedron is a straight line formed where two faces meet.
❸ An edge in a topological graph is one of the lines which make the graph, and which must have a vertex at each end.

Egyptian number system *see* number system

eigenvector

An eigenvector is a vector which undergoes a transformation and is stretched so that it changes its length without any rotation. The length scale factor of the transformation is called the eigenvalue.

element

❶ An element of an array is one complete piece of the data in the array.

EXAMPLE:

Consider this array of four numbers:

3.8   4.2   6.1   7.9

In this array, 3.8 is an **element** but 8 is not as it is not the complete piece of data.

❷ An element of a set is a member.

elevation

An elevation drawing of an object is the two-dimensional vertical view seen when the object is looked at from a position to one side of the object and looking straight at it.

• *Usually **elevations** are drawn to scale so that measurements can be taken from them, and are further identified as 'front', 'side', or 'end' elevations.*

SEE ALSO **angle of elevation, isometric drawing, plan**

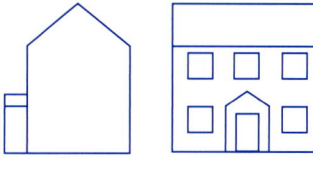

side elevation   front elevation

elimination

The elimination of a variable from an expression is the removal of that variable and is usually done by substitution.

SEE ALSO **substitution**

EXAMPLE:

If $4y + 3x = 22$ and $y = 2x$

Then $4(2x) + 3x = 22$ by substituting $2x$ for y, eliminating y.

This simplifies to $11x = 22$ or $x = 2$.

➤ **eliminate** To eliminate a variable from an expression is to remove it.

ellipse

An ellipse is the locus of a point which moves in such a way that its distances from two foci add together to a constant amount. Once the two foci

a b c d e f g h i j k l m n o p q r s t u v w x y z

are fixed and the constant amount is decided then only one ellipse is possible.

• *A circle is a special case of **ellipse**. It has only one focus and its major and minor axes are the same length.*

FORMULA:

An ellipse may be drawn as a graph using the equation $\frac{x^2}{a^2} + \frac{y^2}{b^2} = 1$

where

a is half the length of the ellipse's major axis

b is half the length of the ellipse's minor axis

Area of an ellipse = πab

A circle may be drawn as a graph using the equation $x^2 + y^2 = a^2$

The perimeter of an ellipse is difficult to calculate exactly, but Ramanujan's formula gives a very accurate approximation:

$\pi \left[3(a + b) - \sqrt{(a + 3b)(3a + b)}\right]$

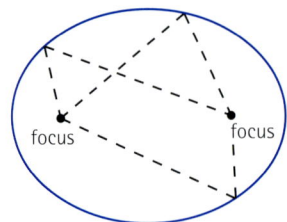

ellipse as a locus

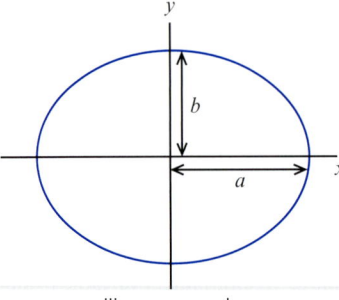

ellipse as a graph

➤ **elliptic** having the shape of an ellipse
➤ **auxiliary circle of an ellipse** a circle with a diameter equal to that of the major axis of the ellipse

➤ **major axis of an ellipse** the straight line drawn through the two foci with each end of the line touching the ellipse. It is a line of symmetry.

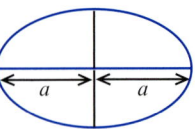

➤ **minor axis of an ellipse** the longest straight line that can be drawn at right angles to the major axis with each end of the line touching the ellipse. It is a line of symmetry.

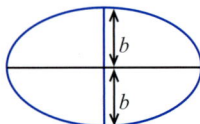

WORD BUILD

circle projection

A circle projection describes the shape of a circle's shadow on a surface behind it. If the surface is parallel to the circle, the shadow will also be a circle. If the surface is not parallel, it will be an ellipse whose major axis will have the same length as the circle's diameter. However, the length of the ellipse's minor axis will depend on the angle θ between the plane of the circle and the plane of the ellipse.

FORMULA:

Length of minor axis = diameter of circle × cos θ

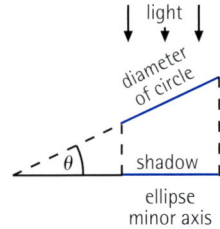

ellipsoid

An ellipsoid is a three-dimensional shape having three mutually perpendicular axes of symmetry and, of the three different cross-sections, at least one that is elliptic. The others may be elliptic or circular. If all the cross-sections were circular it would be a sphere.

• *The ball used in rugby football is approximately an **ellipsoid**.*

Volume of an ellipsoid $= \frac{4}{3}\pi abc$

where

a is the radius of the ellipsoid on the x-axis

b is the radius of the ellipsoid on the y-axis

c is the radius of the ellipsoid on the z-axis

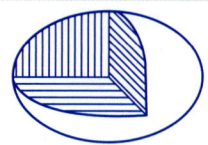

elliptic paraboloid *see* **paraboloid**

empty set *see* **set**

end
The ends of a cylinder are the two simple closed curves used to make it.

enlargement
An enlargement is a transformation in which the distances between every pair of points in the object are multiplied by the same amount to produce the image. The multiplier can take any value—a whole number or a fraction—but not zero.

object   image =   image =
object × 2   object × 3

centre of enlargement
When the object and image of an enlargement have their corresponding points joined by straight lines, then all those lines will cross at a common point called the centre of enlargement.

enumerate
To enumerate a set or subset is to list all its members.

envelope
An envelope is the curve which appears as the outline resulting from drawing whole families of other curves.
• *In this image, the **envelope** of this set of circles is an ellipse.*

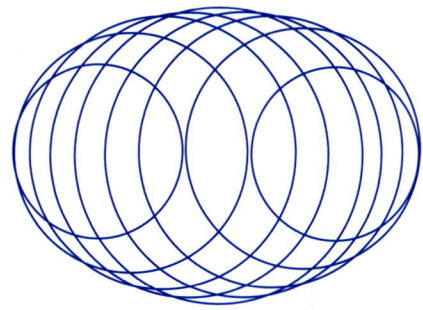

epicycloid *see* **cycloid**

equal
the same in size, amount, or value
• *10 mm is **equal** to 1 cm.*
SEE ALSO **congruent**

EXAMPLE:

= is the symbol for 'is equal to': 10 mm = 1 cm

≈ is the symbol for 'is approximately equal to': $\pi \approx 3.14$

equal addition *see* **addition**

equally likely *see* **likely**

equation
An equation is a statement that two expressions (one of which may be a constant) have the same value separated by an equals sign (=).
• *$2x + 7 = 15$ and $3(x + 5) = 3x + 15$ are both equations.* »

conditional equation

A conditional equation is an equation which is only true for a particular value, or a number of values, of the variable(s).
- *$2x + 7 = 15$ is only true when $x = 4$*

Diophantine equation

Diophantine equations are indeterminate equations having only whole numbers for coefficients and having only whole numbers as acceptable solutions.
- *If the indeterminate equation $x + 2y = 3$ were a **Diophantine equation**, it could only have solutions such as (1, 1) (3, 0) (5, −1) ...*

independent equation

A set of equations is independent if no single equation in the set can be made from some combination of the others.

EXAMPLE:

These 3 equations are not **independent** since the 3rd can be made by adding the first two:

$x + y = 7$

$2x − z = 6$

$3x + y − z = 13$

Changing the 3rd to $3x + y + z = 13$ would make an independent set.

indeterminate equation

An indeterminate equation is an equation (or a set of equations) for which any number of solutions can be found.
- *$x + 2y = 3$ has many solutions including: (x, y) (1, 1) (2, 0.5) (3, 0) (4, −0.5) ...*

linear equation

A linear equation is an equation involving only an expression, or expressions, of degree 1. Such an equation can be represented graphically by a straight line.

EXAMPLE:

These are all **linear equations**:

$y = 3x + 2$

$y = 4$

$x = 3y − 5$

quadratic equation

A quadratic equation is an equation involving an expression, or expressions, containing a single variable, of degree 2.

EXAMPLE:

These are all **quadratic equations**:

$x^2 + 3x − 5 = 0$

$3(x + 1)^2 = 0$

$4x^2 − 3x + 4 = 0$

simultaneous equation

A set of simultaneous equations consists of two or more equations whose variables all take the same value at the same time. Provided all the equations are independent, and a solution is possible, then n simultaneous equations containing n variables will have a unique solution.
- *There are several ways of solving **simultaneous equations**, the most common being by a combination of substitution and elimination.*

· ·

equator *see* **great circle**

· ·

equiangular polygon *see* **polygon**

· ·

equiangular spiral *see* **spiral**

· ·

equilateral polygon *see* **polygon**

· ·

equilateral triangle *see* **triangle**

....

equivalent

Two things are said to be equivalent to one another if they have the same value, or produce the same effect in use, but have different forms.
• *£1 is **equivalent** (in value) to 100 pence.*

....

equivalent fraction *see* **fraction**

....

Eratosthenes' sieve

is an algorithm for finding prime numbers.

EXAMPLE:

First write down as many numbers as required to be searched, in order, starting with 1 and not missing any out.

Cross out 1. Leave 2 and cross out every second number (4, 6, 8, etc.).

Leave 3 and cross out every third number (6, 9, 12, etc.).

4 is already crossed out, so leave 5 and cross out every fifth number (10, 15, etc.).

When complete the numbers left are the prime numbers.

1	2	3	4	5	6
7	8	9	10	11	12
13	14	15	16	17	18
19	20	21	22	23	24
25	26	27	28	29	30
31	32	33	34	35	36
37	38	39	40	41	42
43	44	45	46	47	48
49	50	51			

error

The error is the difference between the value of an approximation, or an estimation, and the true value. It may or may not have a plus (+) or minus (−) sign attached indicating whether it is too big or too small.

SEE ALSO **sampling error**

absolute error

The absolute error is the actual size of the error with no sign.

EXAMPLE:

An approximate value for π is 3.14

The true value of π is 3.1415926535...

The **absolute error** of this approximation is therefore 0.0015926535...

percentage error

The percentage error is the relative error as a percentage.
• *π = 3.14 gives a **percentage error** of about 0.05%.*

relative error

The relative error measures the size of the error as a fraction of the true value.

EXAMPLE:

An approximate value for π is 3.14

The true value of π is 3.14159...

The **relative error** of this approximation is the absolute error divided by the true value:

0.00159... ÷ 3.14159... = 0.000506957...

rounding error

A rounding error is an error introduced by rounding a number.

truncation error

A truncation error is an error introduced by truncating a number.

....

escribed circle

An escribed circle to any polygon is the circle which touches the outside of one edge of the polygon and also the two adjacent edges extended as necessary.
• ***Escribed circles** can be drawn on any polygon, but they are most commonly associated with triangles.*

SEE ALSO **circumcircle, incircle**   »

a
b
c
d
e
f
g
h
i
j
k
l
m
n
o
p
q
r
s
t
u
v
w
x
y
z

FORMULA:

The three escribed circles for a triangle with edges of length a, b, and c have radii r_a, r_b, and r_c respectively where:

$$r_a = \frac{\Delta}{s - a}$$

$$r_b = \frac{\Delta}{s - b}$$

$$r_c = \frac{\Delta}{s - c}$$

Δ is the area of the triangle

$$s = \frac{a + b + c}{2}$$

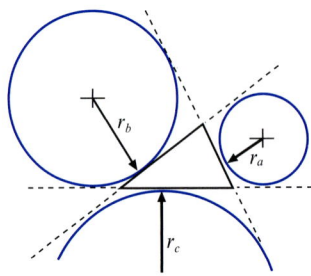

estimation

An estimation is an approximation of a quantity which has been decided by judgement rather than by carrying out the process (such as measuring or doing a sum) needed to produce a more accurate answer.

SEE ALSO approximation

EXAMPLE:

An **estimation** of the number of people in a room might be thirty, when actual measurement (i.e. counting) shows it is twenty-seven.

An **estimation** of the value of $(23.7 \times 19.1) \div 99.6$ might be $(20 \times 20) \div 100 = 4$, or $(25 \times 20) \div 100 = 5$, or between 4 and 5.

Doing the arithmetic suggests that 4.54 is a good approximation.

Euclidean geometry

is the geometry that keeps within the rules as laid down by Euclid. It is what is usually meant when the word geometry is used without any other descriptor. It is also the geometry which is most often used in the ordinary, everyday world.

Euclid's algorithm

is a method to find if two numbers have a common factor (other than 1), and its value if there is.

FORMULA:

Consider two numbers M and N with $M > N$

1. Let $P = M$ and $Q = N$

2. Divide P by Q and find the remainder R

3. If $R = 0$ then Q is a factor of M and N

4. If $R = 1$ then M and N have only 1 as a common factor

5. If $R > 1$ then put $P = Q$ and $Q = R$ and go to step 2

Euler point

The Euler points of a triangle are the mid-points of the lines joining each vertex A, B, and C of the triangle to its orthocentre O.

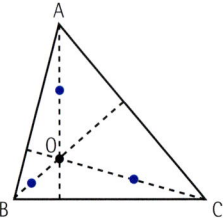

Euler points of a triangle

Euler square see Latin square

evaluate

To evaluate something is to work out its numerical value.

• *'Evaluate* $x^2 + 5$ when $x = 3$' requires the answer 14.

even number *see* **number**

....

evens

When the odds are 1 to 1 they are even odds or evens. The probability for evens is $\frac{1}{2}$.

....

event

❶ An event is an activity.

❷ An event is some specific result of an activity.

> ⚠ **WATCH OUT**
>
> Rolling a single die is an **event** (first meaning), and a result of that activity (getting a 1, 2, 3, 4, 5, or 6) is also an **event** (second meaning).
>
> When talking about probability, it is better to use the word **outcome** for the second meaning.

combined event (*also* **compound event**)

Combined events or compound events describe the putting together of two or more separate events or outcomes to be considered as one single event or outcome. This is usually done in order to find the probability of a final single outcome. The separate outcomes might be independent of, or dependent upon, each other.

dependent event (*also* **dependent outcome**)

Two events or outcomes are dependent if a statement or probability for one of them affects a statement or probability for the other.

• *Taking two counters from a bag of mixed colours without replacing the first is combining two dependent outcomes.*

independent event (*also* **independent outcome**)

Two or more events or outcomes are independent if the happening of one of them has no effect on the other.

• *When two dice are rolled there are two independent outcomes, since the number showing on one does not influence the number on the other.*

mutually exclusive events (*also* **mutually exclusive outcomes**)

are sets of events or outcomes for which the happening of one of them means that none of the others can happen.

• *When rolling a die the outcomes are **mutually exclusive events**, since when one number comes to the top it must mean that none of the others can.*

....

even vertex *see* **vertex**

....

exchange rate *see* **rate of exchange**

....

exhaustion *see* **proof**

....

expansion

The expansion of an expression is carried out by doing as much as possible to make it into a collection of terms connected only by + and − signs.

• *Expansion usually entails doing as much multiplication as can be done, and removing all the brackets.*

> **EXAMPLE:**
>
> $(3x + 1)(x − 2) + 4(x − 5)$ expands to
>
> $3x^2 + x − 6x − 2 + 4x − 20$

....

experimental probability *see* **frequency**

....

explicit function *see* **function**

....

exponent

Exponent is the name we give to the number 2 in the expression 5^2. We say the exponent of 5 is 2. This is also known as an index.

SEE ALSO **index, index notation**

> **EXAMPLE:**
>
> $5^2 = 5 \times 5 = 25$

....

a b c d e f g h i j k l m n o p q r s t u v w x y z

exponential

Of or expressed by a mathematical exponent.
• An **exponential** curve might be described by
the equation $y = 2^x$ • $y = 2^x$ is an **exponential**
relationship.

....

exponential form *see* **index notation**

....

expression

An expression in algebra is most often a
collection of quantities, made up of constants
and variables, linked by signs for operations
and not including a relationship sign, such as
=, <, or >.

EXAMPLE:

These are all **expressions**:

$x + y$

$3 + x^2 - y$

$4(x - y)$

$3x^2 + 5y$

literal expression

A literal expression is an expression in which
the constants are represented by letters as well
as the variables.
• $Ax^2 + Bx + C$ and $ax + b$ are **literal**
expressions.

....

exterior angle *see* **polygon**

....

extrapolation

An extrapolation is an estimation of the likely
value of an unknown piece of data, falling outside
the range of some known data and based on the
evidence provided by that known data.
• **Extrapolation** usually involves using the
trend line.
SEE ALSO **interpolation, trend line**
➤ **extrapolate** to estimate the likely value of an
unknown piece of data using extrapolation

EXAMPLE:

In the graph shown, the values of the known
data are shown by black dots, and the
extrapolated value by a blue dot.

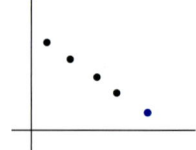

Ff

face

❶ A face is a plane surface enclosed by an edge or edges.

❷ (also **region**) A face or region in a topological graph is any single space completely enclosed by edges. The space surrounding the graph, outside its boundary edges, is considered as one of the faces of that graph.

....

face diagonal see **diagonal**

....

factor

❶ A factor is a number which divides exactly into another number. A number can have several factors.

SEE ALSO **conversion factor, scale factor, multiple**

EXAMPLE:

1 is a **factor** of every number and every number is a **factor** of itself.

3 is a **factor** of 6

4 is a **factor** of 12

7 is a **factor** of 7

2 and 17 are **factors** of 68

❷ The factors of an expression in algebra are two, or more, other expressions which can be multiplied together to produce the original expression.

EXAMPLE:

$(x + 1)$ and $(x - 2)$ are **factors** of $x^2 - x - 2$ since $(x + 1)(x - 2) \equiv x^2 - x - 2$

common factor

Common factors are those factors shared by two or more numbers.

EXAMPLE:

12 has 1, 2, 3, 4, 6, 12 as factors.

18 has 1, 2, 3, 6, 9, 18 as factors.

So the **common factors** of 12 and 18 are 1, 2, 3 and 6.

highest common factor (also HCF)

The highest common factor of two or more numbers is the common factor of all those numbers which has the greatest value.

EXAMPLE:

In some cases the **HCF** may be 1 or one of the actual numbers.

The **HCF** of 12 and 18 is 6.

The **HCF** of 12 and 17 is 1.

The **HCF** of 5, 15, and 30 is 5.

prime factor

The prime factors of a number are all those factors of the number which are themselves prime numbers. A prime number has only one prime factor: itself.

EXAMPLE:

All the factors of 12 are 1, 2, 3, 4, 6 and 12 but its only **prime factors** are 2 and 3.

proper factor (also proper divisor)

The proper factors of a number are all of its factors except for the number itself.

EXAMPLE:

The factors of 12 are 1, 2, 3, 4, 6 and 12, but its **proper factors** are only 1, 2, 3, 4 and 6.

The **proper factors** of 20 are 1, 2, 4, 5 and 10.

....

factorial

The value of factorial n is found by multiplying together all the whole numbers from 1 up to, and including, n. A special case is $0! = 1$

EXAMPLE:

The symbol for **factorial** n is ! written after the number n.

$5! = 5 \times 4 \times 3 \times 2 \times 1 = 120$.

$7! = 7 \times 6 \times 5! = 5,040$

The table shows all the values of factorial n for numbers from 0 to 10.   »

Values of factorial *n* for 0 to 10		
0!	=	1
1!	=	1
2!	=	2
3!	=	6
4!	=	24
5!	=	120
6!	=	720
7!	=	5,040
8!	=	40,320
9!	=	362,880
10!	=	3,628,800

factorize

To factorize a number is to find its factors or to express it in factors.

• *Finding ways to **factorize** numbers has always fascinated mathematicians. The problem has become of practical interest because of modern encryption methods which use very large numbers that have only two prime factors.*

EXAMPLE:

2,001 can be **factorized** into $3 \times 23 \times 29$.

factor pair

A pair of numbers that give a particular product when multiplied together.

SEE ALSO factor, product

EXAMPLE:

The **factor pairs** of 12 are:

1 and 12
2 and 6
3 and 4

Fahrenheit scale *see* temperature

fair

A fair item, such as a dice, is one for which all outcomes are equally likely.

fallacy

A fallacy is an argument which seems to be correct but which contains at least one error and, as a consequence, produces a final statement which is clearly wrong.

EXAMPLE:

Let $x = y$

Then $x^2 = xy$ and $x^2 - y^2 = xy - y^2$

This gives $(x + y)(x - y) = y(x - y)$ so that dividing both sides by $(x - y)$ leaves $x + y = y$

From this result, putting $x = y = 1$ means $2 = 1$

Or, subtracting y from both sides means x (= any number) = 0

The error is in dividing by $(x - y)$ which is zero.

false

Within a system, a statement is said to be false when it is contrary to a statement known to be true.

Fermat's last theorem

Fermat's last theorem is one of the most famous theorems in mathematics. It states that the equation $x^n + y^n = z^n$ has no solutions in whole numbers for x, y and z if $n > 2$ and x, y, $z > 1$.

• *Fermat's last theorem was really a conjecture since, although Fermat claimed to have a proof, it was not properly proved until 1994 by Andrew Wiles.*

Fermat's problem

Fermat's problem is to find a point in an acute triangle ABC whose distances from A, B, and C have the smallest possible sum.

ferry problem (*also* river crossing problem)

A ferry problem describes a situation in which there are a number of objects that need transporting across a river but they can only be taken over the river one at a time and each of the objects has rules on how it interacts with the other objects. The puzzle is to find the fewest number of trips across the river to get all the objects across.

EXAMPLE:

You need to transport a fox, a chicken and a sack of corn across the river.

The fox will eat the chicken if left alone.

The chicken will eat the corn if left alone.

What is the fewest number of trips from one side of the river to the other you need to take all three across uneaten?

Answer : seven

Fibonacci sequence see **sequence**

---

figurate number see **polygon number**

---

figure
A figure may be either a digit or a number.
• *Both 6 and 76 are figures.*
SEE ALSO **significant figure**

---

finite
A quantity is said to be finite if it can be counted or measured in some way.
• *As long as it is known or believed that it does not go on endlessly, then a quantity is finite.*
• *For example, the number of leaves on all the trees in the world, and the number of the atoms in the Universe are both finite quantities.*
SEE ALSO **infinite**

---

finite set see **set**

---

first quadrant see **quadrant**

---

flow diagram (*also* **function machine**)
A flow diagram is a drawing intended to make clear the order in which operations have to be done so as to produce a result. While they can be used to explain any production process, they are most commonly used in mathematics as an aid to working out values of functions, formulas, etc.

EXAMPLE:

This **flow diagram** shows $y = 3x^2 + 5$.

Enter x → Square it → × 3 → + 5 → gives y

---

focus *plural* **focuses, foci**
A focus is a fixed point used in the drawing of any conic section.

---

foot see **perpendicular**

---

formula *plural* **formulas, formulae**
A formula is a statement, usually written as an equation, giving the exact relationship between certain quantities, so that, when one or more values are known, the value of one particular quantity can be found.
• *In a formula, the convention is to use letters which best serve as reminders of the quantities being handled.*
SEE ALSO **cyclic formula, polyhedral formula**

EXAMPLE:

For a sphere of diameter d, the volume V can be found from the **formula** $V = \pi d^3 \div 6$.

---

four 4s
This type of problem, which originated in 1871, requires as many whole numbers as possible to be represented by the use of four 4s joined by mathematical operations.
• *There are many variations of the four 4s including using four of any other digits besides 4 or using any four digits but keeping them in order. For example 2021 could yield $20 + 21 = 41$. In all of this work it is particularly important to be aware of the order of operations.*

EXAMPLE:

$1 = (4 + 4) \div (4 + 4)$
$2 = (4 \div 4) + (4 \div 4)$
$3 = (4 + 4 + 4) \div 4$
$4 = 4 + 4 - \sqrt{4} - \sqrt{4}$
$15 = 44 \div 4 + 4$
$17 = 4 \times 4 + 4 \div 4$
$27 = 4! + \sqrt{4} + (4 \div 4)$

four-colour problem

This is a problem which can be stated simply as: for any map that might be drawn on a flat surface, what is the least number of colours that are needed to colour it in such a way that no two countries which touch along a common border have the same colour?

• *In 1976, a proof was found that the least number of colours needed is four. The problem was then called the* **four-colour theorem**.

....

four rules of arithmetic *see* arithmetic

....

fourth quadrant *see* quadrant

....

fraction

A fraction is a measure of how something is to be divided up or shared out. There are three principal ways of expressing fractions: common, decimal, percentage.

SEE ALSO **decimal fraction**

algebraic fraction

An algebraic fraction is like a common fraction in its form but uses algebraic expressions for its numerator and/or denominator.

EXAMPLE:

These are **algebraic fractions**:

$$\frac{a}{b} \qquad \frac{x+y}{3x-y} \qquad \frac{3(x+y)(x-y)}{8(x^2+y)}$$

common fraction (*also* vulgar fraction)

A common fraction or vulgar fraction is a fraction written in the form of two whole numbers, one above the other, separated by a line. The bottom number must not be a 1 or zero.

EXAMPLE:

These are all **common fractions**:

$$\frac{1}{2} \qquad \frac{3}{4} \qquad \frac{2}{3} \qquad \frac{99}{150} \qquad \frac{-1}{4}$$

SEE ALSO **denominator, numerator**

equivalent fraction

Equivalent fractions are two or more fractions that have the same value but are different in form. Common fractions, decimal fractions, and percentages can be converted into each other so they remain equivalent.

EXAMPLE:

These are equivalent fractions:

$$\frac{3}{4} \qquad \frac{6}{8} \qquad \frac{63}{84} \qquad 75\% \qquad 0.75$$

To change a common fraction into a decimal fraction, divide the top number by the bottom.

To change $\frac{3}{7}$ work out $3 \div 7 = 0.428571...$

To change a decimal fraction into a percentage, multiply it by 100.

To change 0.428571 work out $0.428571 \times 100 = 42.8571\%$

To change a common fraction into a percentage, do both the above in that order.

To change $\frac{3}{7}$ work out $3 \div 7 \times 100 = 42.8571\%$

improper fraction

An improper fraction is a common fraction in which the numerator (the top number) is bigger than the denominator (the bottom number).

EXAMPLE:

These are all **improper fractions**:

$$\frac{9}{8} \qquad \frac{4}{3} \qquad \frac{100}{17}$$

proper fraction

A proper fraction is a common fraction in which the numerator (the top number) is smaller than the denominator (the bottom number).

reduced fraction

A reduced fraction is a common fraction in its simplest possible form.

SEE ALSO **reduce**

Table of values of some equivalent fractions		
%	common fraction	decimal fraction
5	$\frac{1}{20}$	0.05
10	$\frac{1}{10}$	0.1
20	$\frac{2}{10}$ $\frac{1}{5}$	0.2
25	$\frac{1}{4}$	0.25
30	$\frac{3}{10}$	0.3
$33\frac{1}{3}$	$\frac{1}{3}$	0.333 ...
40	$\frac{4}{10}$ $\frac{2}{5}$	0.4
50	$\frac{5}{10}$ $\frac{1}{2}$	0.5
60	$\frac{6}{10}$ $\frac{3}{5}$	0.6
$66\frac{2}{3}$	$\frac{2}{3}$	0.666 ...
70	$\frac{7}{10}$	0.7
75	$\frac{3}{4}$	0.75
80	$\frac{8}{10}$ $\frac{4}{5}$	0.8
90	$\frac{9}{10}$	0.9

....

free vector *see* **vector**

....

French curve

French curves are templates which are formed from a variety of curves to provide a firm edge and allow a good quality curved line to be drawn. They are mainly used by technical illustrators.

EXAMPLE:

The drawing shows one **French curve** from a commercially produced set of three.

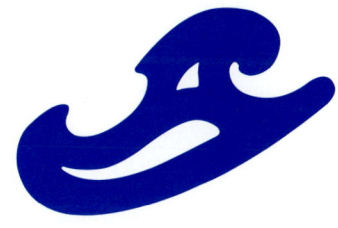

frequency

❶ In statistics, the frequency of data is the number of times each piece of that data is found.
• *f is the symbol for **frequency**.*
❷ In probability, the frequency of an outcome is the number of times it happens.

cumulative frequency

is the total of all the frequencies of a set of data up to any particular piece or group of data.

relative frequency (*also* experimental probability)

The relative frequency of an outcome is the value found after an activity has been done several times.
• *A biased die might be rolled many times to determine the **relative frequency** of getting a 5.*
• *A drawing pin might be thrown several times to determine the **relative frequency** of whether it landed 'point up' or 'point down'.*

FORMULA:

The relative frequency is found by:

$$\frac{\text{Number of times that named outcome(s) did happen}}{\text{Number of times activity was done}}$$

WORD BUILD

cumulative frequency diagram (*also* cumulative frequency polygon)

A cumulative frequency diagram is a diagram on which cumulative frequencies are plotted, each against the data value for which it has been calculated. The points may be joined by straight lines (when it is usually called a polygon) or, if there are sufficient points to define it, by a curve.

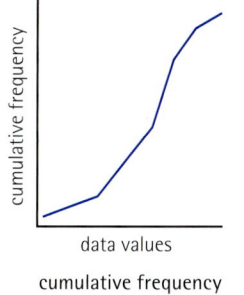

cumulative frequency polygon

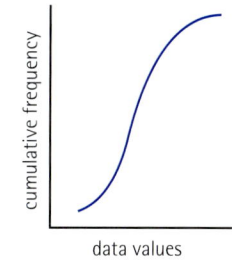

cumulative frequency curve

....

frequency density

When a set of (usually continuous) data is grouped into classes, the frequency density of a particular class is the frequency of that class divided by the width of that class. On a histogram, the heights of the columns give the frequency densities and the areas of the columns give the frequencies.

frequency diagram (also frequency polygon)

A frequency diagram is a graphical way of showing the amount of data found in each of the groups or types being counted.

SEE ALSO chart, frequency

frieze pattern *see* pattern

frustum *plural* frusta, frustums

❶ The frustum of a cone is the part of the cone cut off between the base and a plane which is parallel to the base.

frustum of a cone

❷ A frustum of a pyramid is the part of a pyramid cut off between the base and a plane which is parallel to the base.

FORMULA:

Volume of frustum $= (A + B + \sqrt{A \times B}) \times h \div 3$

where

A and B are the areas of the top and bottom faces of the frustum

h is the distance between the faces

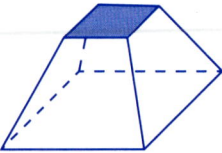

frustum of a pyramid

function

A function is a mapping which involves either a one-to-one correspondence or a many-to-one correspondence. The sets to be used for the domain and codomain must be defined; they can be the same.

• *For positive numbers the mapping 'is the square of' is a **function**.* • *$f(x)$ is the symbol for a **function** involving a single variable x.* • *$y = f(x)$ and $f:x \rightarrow y$ are equivalent ways of saying that there is a **function** of x that defines how x-numbers maps to y-numbers.*

SEE ALSO symmetric expression, trigonometric function

EXAMPLE:

Given $f(x) \equiv 2x + 3$, then $y = f(x)$ is the same as $y = 2x + 3$ or $f:x \rightarrow 2x + 3$ and both produce the same mapping (or table of values).

$f(x) \equiv 3x + 1$

$f(x) \equiv 4x^2 + 3x - 7$

$f(x) \equiv 2x(x - 8)$

composite function

A composite function is formed when the output of one function is used as the input of a second function. It can be thought of as two flow diagrams, one following after the other.

EXAMPLE:

If $f(x) = 3x - 4$ and $g(x) = x^2$, then $f(g(x)) = 3x^2 - 4$ and $g(f(x)) = (3x - 4)^2$.

derived function

From a given function $f(x)$ the rules of calculus allow another function to be made, known as the derived function and shown as $f'(x)$, which allows a derivative of the given function to be calculated for any particular value of x.

• *The **derived function** is sometimes referred to as the derivative but this should be avoided.*

SEE ALSO calculus, derivative

EXAMPLE:

Given $f(x) \equiv x^2 + 4x - 7$ then $f'(x) \equiv 2x + 4$.

If $x = 3$ the value of $f'(x)$ is 10 which is the derivative of $f(x)$ when $x = 3$.

explicit function

An explicit function is a function that is given entirely in terms of the independent variable.

EXAMPLE:

These are all **explicit functions**:

$f(x) \equiv 2x + 5$

$y = x^2 + 3$

$f{:}x \to x(x - 1)$

implicit function

An implicit function is a function that is given in terms of both the independent and the dependent variables.

EXAMPLE:

Implicit functions are usually written in a way that equates them to zero:

$x^2 + 2xy - y^2 = 0$

$f(x, y)$ is the symbol for an **implicit function** involving two variables, identified in this case as x and y.

inverse function

An inverse function is a second function that reverses the direction of the mapping produced by a first function. For an **inverse function** to exist, the first function must produce a one-to-one correspondence.
• $f^{-1}(x)$ is the symbol for the **inverse function** of $f(x)$.

EXAMPLE:

Sometimes a function can be forced into being of the one-to-one type by restricting the numbers to be used in the domain and codomain.

$f(x) \equiv x^2$ is a function of x producing a many-to-one correspondence since x or x will both produce the same value of $f(x)$.

This means that, though the mapping can be reversed (using square roots), the reverse mapping is one-to-many and therefore not a function.

If the restriction is made that only positive numbers are allowed, then $f(x)$ is a one-to-one correspondence and an **inverse function** exists.

. . . .

function machine *see* **flow diagram**

. . . .

functions of general angles
Each of the trigonometric ratios (sine, cosine, tangent) can have infinite values for any single value. The functions of general angles define formulas to determine those angles for any given value.

FORMULA:

If $\sin A = \sin \alpha$ then $A = 180n + (-1)^n \alpha$

If $\cos A = \cos \alpha$ then $A = 360n \pm \alpha$

If $\tan A = \tan \alpha$ then $A = 180n + \alpha$

where n is an integer

EXAMPLE:

For example, $\sin A = 0.5$ (which is $\sin 30°$) so $A = 180 \times n + (-1)^n \times 30$

Then A can be 30° or 150° or 390° or 510° or 750° or 870° ...

. . . .

a
b
c
d
e
f
g
h
i
j
k
l
m
n
o
p
q
r
s
t
u
v
w
x
y
z

Gg

Gaussian integer *see* **number**

....

gelosia multiplication

A gelosia is a grid used as the basis of a method of multiplication, which was then named after it.

EXAMPLE:

The diagram shows 635 × 724.

Each separate pair of digits is multiplied together and the answer written in the appropriate square in the way shown, with a split between the tens and the units.

All these answers are then added up diagonally, remembering to 'carry' a figure where necessary from top right to bottom left, to produce a final answer of 459,740.

	6	3	5	×
4	4/2	2/1	3/5	7
5	1/2	.6	1/0	2
9	2/4	1/2	2/0	4
	7	4	0	

....

geodesic line

A geodesic line between two points on the surface of a three-dimensional shape is the line which also lies entirely on the surface of the shape and is of the shortest possible length.
• *On a sphere a **geodesic line** is an arc of the great circle which passes through the two given points. This fact is important in finding the shortest distance between two places on the Earth's surface.*

....

geodetic surveying *see* **surveying**

....

geometrical construction

A geometrical construction is an accurate diagram drawn as an answer to a problem, using only a pair of compasses and a straight-edge.
• *The Italian mathematician Mascheroni (1750–1800) proved that any **geometrical** construction which was possible with compasses and a straight-edge could also be done using only a pair of compasses.*

....

geometric mean *see* **mean**

....

geometric progression (*also* GP)

A geometric progression or GP is a sequence where each new term after the first is made by multiplying the previous term by a constant amount.

SEE ALSO **arithmetic progression**

EXAMPLE:

2   6   18   54   162 ...
is a GP with a first term of 2 and a constant of 3.

14   7   3   5   1.75   0.875 ...
is a GP with a first term of 14 and a constant of 0.5.

WORD BUILD

geometric series

A geometric series is a GP with addition or subtraction signs inserted between the various terms.

FORMULA:

To find the sum S_n of a geometric series over n terms, use the formula:

$$S_n = \frac{a(r^n - 1)}{r - 1}$$

where

a is the value of the first term

n is the number of terms

r is the constant multiplier ($r \neq 1$)

....

geometry

is the study of the properties and relationships, of points, lines, and surfaces in space.

SEE ALSO **transformation geometry**

plane geometry

is geometry confined to two-dimensional space only.

....

glide reflection *see* **reflection**

global maximum *see* **maximum**

global minimum *see* **minimum**

Goldbach's conjecture
is that every even number from 4 onwards can be made by adding two prime numbers.

EXAMPLE:

$6 = 3 + 3$
$10 = 3 + 7$ or $5 + 5$
$22 = 3 + 19$ or $5 + 17$ or $11 + 11$

golden ratio
The golden ratio is used to divide an object into two parts so that the ratio of the larger to the smaller part is the same as the ratio of the whole object to the larger part. Its value is the irrational number $(\sqrt{5} + 1) \div 2$ which is 1.6180 (to four decimal places).
• *The **golden ratio** often appears in architectural design; it is believed to be particularly pleasing to look at.*

WORD BUILD

golden rectangle
A golden rectangle is an oblong with its two edge-lengths sized in the proportions of the golden ratio ($\approx$1.618: 1).

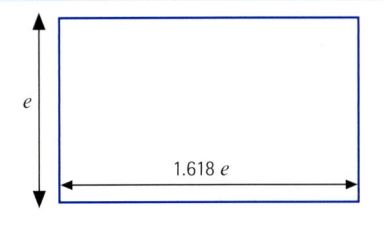

e

1.618 e

googol
A googol is 10^{100} which is 1 followed by 100 zeros.

googolplex
A googolplex is 10^{googol} which is 1 followed by a googol of zeros.

GP *see* **geometric progression**

grade (*also* **grad**)
A grade or grad is the angle made by $\frac{1}{100}$ part of a right angle.

gradient
The gradient of a line drawn on a graph is a measure of its slope relative to the x-axis. This is expressed as the ratio of its vertical change to its horizontal change, both changes being measured on the scales of their respective axes.

EXAMPLE:

In the diagram the **gradient** is given by $a \div b$ and is positive since y increases as x increases.

$y = mx + c$ is the equation of a straight line which has a **gradient** of value m and an intercept (where it crosses the y-axis) at c.

$y = 3x - 4$ has a **gradient** of 3 and an intercept of -4.

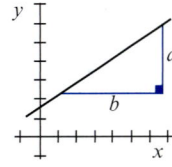

negative gradient
A negative gradient is a gradient which shows that y decreases as x increases. It is measured as for gradient but has a negative sign in front of the value.

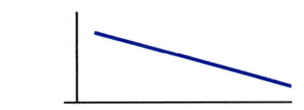

Graeco-Latin square *see* **Latin square**

graph

A graph is a diagram showing the relationship between some variable quantities, usually by means of points plotted on a coordinate system.

SEE ALSO **chart, distance–time graph, velocity–time graph**

block graph

A block graph is a bar chart where, usually, the bars themselves are divided to mark off each individual piece of data.

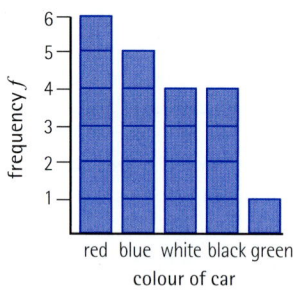

conversion graph

A conversion graph is used to show the corresponding values between two quantities, which have a fixed relationship between them, by means of a line drawn on a squared grid.

• *The **conversion graph** shown can be used to change temperatures between the Celsius and Fahrenheit scales. The line of blue dashes show that the readings of 35°C and 95°F are measuring the same temperature.*

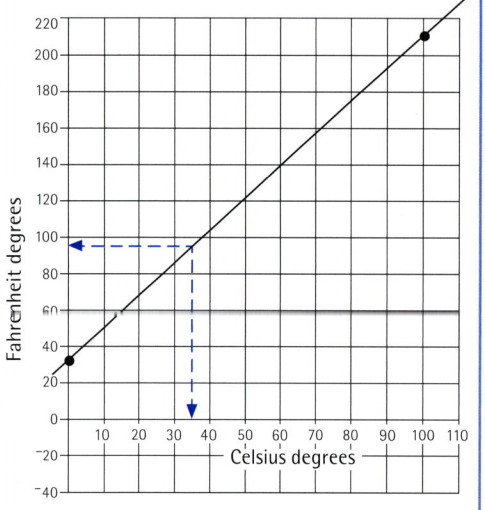

linear graph

A linear graph is a graph in which all the points representing the relationship between the quantities lie on a straight line.

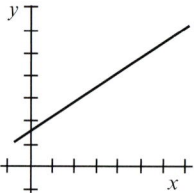

quadratic graph

A quadratic graph is a graph in which the relationship between the variables is given by a quadratic equation. Its shape is that of a parabola.

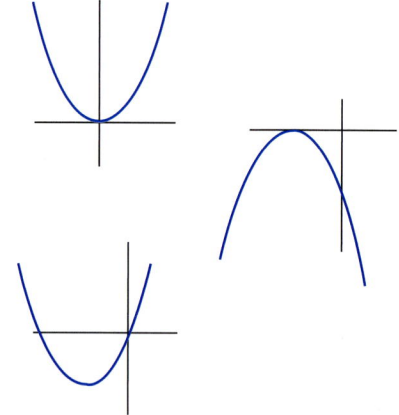

scatter graph

A scatter graph shows how two sets of numerical data are related, by treating matching pairs of numbers as coordinates and plotting them as a single point, repeating this as necessary for each data-pair.

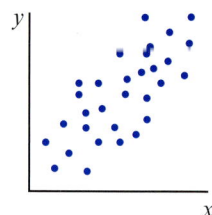

topological graph (*also* network)

A topological graph is made up of a set of points and lines joining them. It is also known as a network.

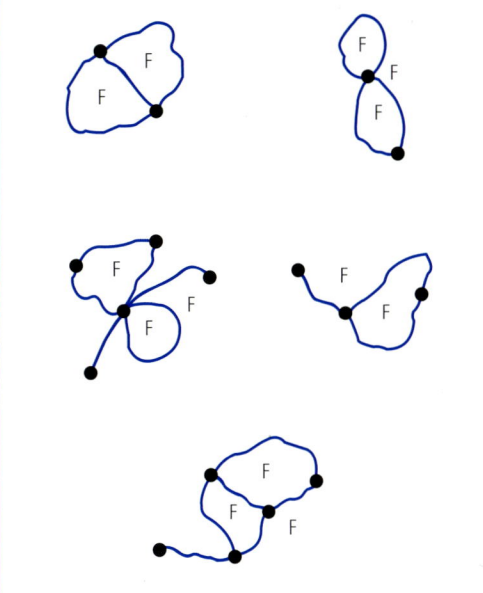

graphics calculator *see* **calculator**

. . . .

gravitational acceleration

The rate of acceleration on the Earth's surface due to gravity is 9.80665 metres per second squared.

. . . .

great circle

A great circle is any circle drawn on the surface of a sphere (e.g. the Earth) whose centre is at the centre of the sphere. All great circles on a sphere are of the same size, and any one divides the sphere into two hemispheres.

SEE ALSO Greenwich Meridian

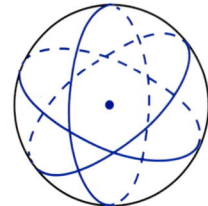

great circles on a sphere and their common centre

WORD BUILD

equator

The equator is the great circle around the Earth that is perpendicular to the axis of rotation. It is equidistant from either pole, and divides the Earth into northern and southern hemispheres.

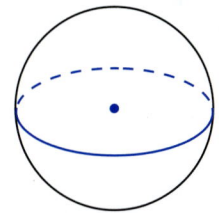

latitude

A line of latitude is a small circle on the Earth's surface, parallel to the equator, whose position is given north or south of the equator.

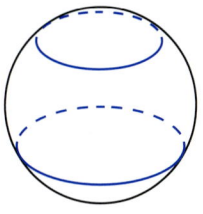

circles of latitude

longitude

A line of longitude is a meridian whose position is given, East or West, relative to the Greenwich Meridian as measured by the angle at the centre of the Earth between the great circles forming those two meridians.

meridian

A meridian is half of a great circle on the Earth's surface going from one pole to the other. It appears as a line running north and south, crossing the equator at right angles.

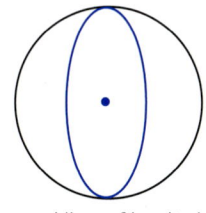

meridians of longitude　　　　　　》

small circle

A small circle is any circle drawn on the surface of a sphere (e.g. the Earth) that is not a great circle.

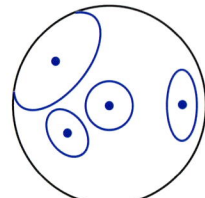

small circles on a sphere and their different centres

Greek number system *see* **number system**

Greenwich Meridian

The Greenwich Meridian is the meridian which passes through a fixed point in the old Greenwich Observatory (in London).

SEE ALSO **great circle**

grid

A grid is usually two or more sets of parallel lines crossing each other. Most grids are squares but they can be rectangles or triangles.

grid reference

Grid references give the position of a point on a map by stating its shortest distances from two fixed reference lines set at right angles to each other. They are a Cartesian coordinate system.

SEE ALSO **coordinate**

gross

❶ A gross amount of weight or money is that total which exists at the beginning before any deductions are made for any reason.

SEE ALSO **net**

EXAMPLE:

A person's wages are £270 **gross** but taxes totalling £75 are taken off, so £195 is left.

£195 is the net wage.

❷ A gross is a dozen dozens or 144.

group

A group is a set under a binary operation for which all the following statements are true:
  – The operation is closed.
  – The operation is associative.
  – The set has an identity.
  – Every object in the set has an inverse.
• *Integers under addition are a* **group***, but not integers under multiplication since inverses (i.e. fractions) do not exist within the set.*

grouped data *see* **data**

Hh

half-angle formula

Half-angle formulas are useful in solving triangles when the lengths of all three edges are known.

FORMULA:

$$\sin \frac{A}{2} = \sqrt{\frac{(s-b)(s-c)}{bc}}$$

$$\cos \frac{A}{2} = \sqrt{\frac{s(s-a)}{bc}}$$

$$\tan \frac{A}{2} = \sqrt{\frac{(s-b)(s-c)}{s(s-a)}}$$

where a, b, c are the lengths of the edges of the triangle.

$$s = \frac{(a+b+c)}{2}$$

Hamiltonian walk

A Hamiltonian walk is a path traced out on a topological graph which visits every vertex once and once only—except possibly for the start and finish which might be on the same vertex.

happy number see number

harmonic progression

a series of quantities whose reciprocals are in arithmetical progression, such as $\frac{1}{3}, \frac{1}{5}, \frac{1}{7}, \frac{1}{9}$
SEE ALSO series

harmonic series see series

Harshad number see number

haversine see versine

HCF

stands for highest common factor.
SEE ALSO factor

height see dimension, slant height

helix plural helices

A helix is the shape drawn on the curved surface of a cylinder or cone by a point which moves along the surface at a constant angle.
• *Two common examples of a **helix** are a circular staircase and a corkscrew.*

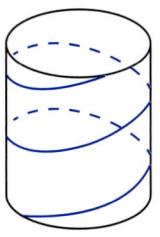

helix on a cylinder

helix on a cone

hemisphere

A hemisphere is one half of a sphere.

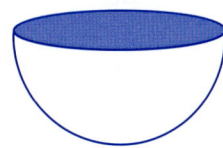

Heronian triangle see triangle

hexadecimal see number base

hexiamond *see* **polyiamond**

....

highest common factor *see* **factor**

....

Hindu–Arabic number system
see **number system**

....

histogram

A histogram is a frequency diagram using rectangles whose widths are proportional to the class interval and whose areas are proportional to the frequency.

• *In this* **histogram**, *the blocks represent 1,000 people divided by age groups.*

SEE ALSO **frequency diagram**

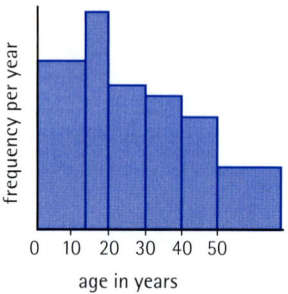

⚠ WATCH OUT

A **histogram** and a **bar chart** are two types of frequency diagram which look very similar.

They are differentiated by the way the frequency is represented: by the length of the bars in a **bar chart** and by the area of the bars in a **histogram**.

Bar charts tend to be used for **discrete data** while histograms are nearly always used for **continuous data**.

....

horizontal

A horizontal line at any point on the Earth is a straight line that lies at right angles to the vertical at that point. It is often described as 'level'.

• *Usually, in drawings, a* **horizontal** *line means one which goes across the page.*

SEE ALSO **vertical**

....

hyperbola *plural* **hyperbolas, hyperbolae**
A hyperbola is the locus of a point that moves in such a way as to make its distance from a focus always greater than its distance from a directrix in some ratio.

SEE ALSO **directrix, focus, locus**

FORMULA:

Once the focus, directrix and ratio are fixed, two hyperbolas are possible.

They may be drawn as graphs using the equation

$$\frac{x^2}{a^2} - \frac{y^2}{b^2} = 1$$

where

a, b are constant values affecting the size of the hyperbola.

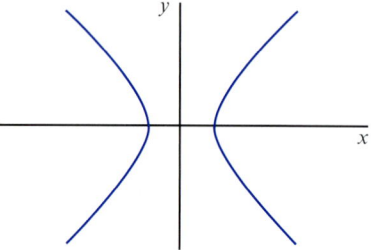

➤ **hyperbolic** related to or in the form of a hyperbola

rectangular hyperbola

A rectangular hyperbola is the hyperbola produced by a graph having the equation $xy = k$ where k is a constant.

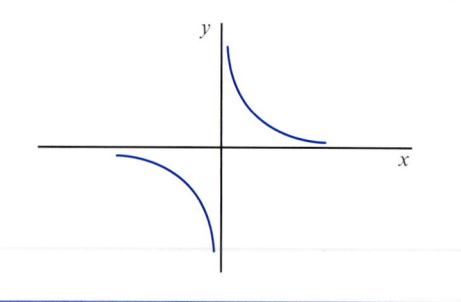

....

hyperbolic function

The hyperbolic functions sinh x, cosh x, and tanh x are to the hyperbola as the ordinary trigonometry functions sinx, cosx, and tanx are to the circle. They are spoken as 'sinsh, cosh, and tansh'. Their inverse functions are written as sinh^{-1} x, cosh^{-1} x, and tanh^{-1} x.

hyperbolic paraboloid *see* **paraboloid**

hyperbolic spiral *see* **spiral**

hypocycloid *see* **cycloid**

hypotenuse

The hypotenuse is the edge of a right-angled triangle which is opposite to the right angle. It is also the longest edge of that triangle.

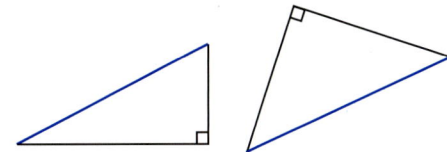

hypothesis *plural* **hypotheses**

A hypothesis is a statement which is usually thought to be true, and serves as a starting point in looking for arguments (or evidence) to support it. This word is mostly used in statistics.

SEE ALSO **conjecture**

hypothesis test

A hypothesis test is a statistical test which compares data gained from experiment or observation with that calculated from a mathematical model. The comparison is said to be 'statistically significant' if the difference between the two sets of data has a sufficiently high probability of not happening.

i *see* **unit vector**

identical *see* **congruent**

identification number *see* **number**

identity

❶ An identity in algebra is an equation that is true for all values of the variable(s).

• *The ≡ sign should he used instead of the = sign to show that it is an **identity**.*

SEE ALSO **condition, P, Q**

EXAMPLE:

$$x^2 - y^2 \equiv (x + y)(x - y)$$

$$3(x + 5) \equiv 3x + 15$$

❷ The identity for a binary operation on a set is an object in that set which, when combined (by the operation) with any second object from the set, produces a result which is equal to the second object.

EXAMPLE:

Addition of numbers has the **identity** 0 since $0 + 5 = 5 + 0 = 5$.

Multiplication of numbers has the **identity** 1 since $1 \times 7 = 7 \times 1 = 7$.

This is generally expressed as $0 + x = x + 0 = x$ and $1 \times x = x \times 1 = x$.

left identity

A left identity is an identity which works only on the left side of the other object.

right identity

A right identity is an identity which works only on the right side of the other object.

EXAMPLE:

Subtraction has a **right identity** of 0 since $x - 0 = x$ but no **left identity** since $0 - x \neq x$.

Division has a **right identity** of 1.

a b c d e f g h i j k l m n o p q r s t u v w x y z

identity matrix *see* **matrix**

. . . .

iff
is a short way of writing 'if and only if' and is equivalent to ⇔.

SEE ALSO condition, P, Q

EXAMPLE:

If P is 'x is divisible by 6',
and Q is 'x is divisible by 2 and 3',
then P ⇐ Q and Q ⇐ P, so P **iff** Q

. . . .

illusion
An illusion is a visual trick showing something that cannot exist.

EXAMPLE:

The trick illustrated shows an area of sixty-four squares cut up and rearranged to make a 5 by 13 oblong with an area of sixty-five squares.

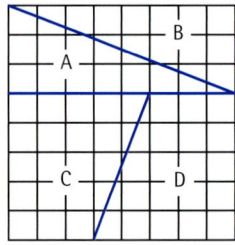

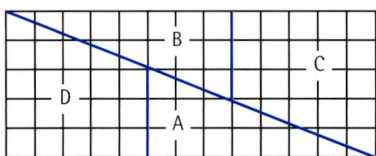

➤ **illusory** means imagined and not real. An illusory diagram or illustration is one which shows a visual trick or something that cannot exist.

. . . .

image
An image is the shape which appears after a transformation has been applied to an object.

. . . .

imaginary number *see* **number**

. . . .

implicit function *see* **function**

. . . .

improper fraction *see* **fraction**

. . . .

incentre *see* **incircle**

. . . .

incircle
An incircle to any polygon is the circle drawn on the inside of that polygon which touches all its edges. Each edge is a tangent to the incircle.
• *Not every polygon has an associated incircle, but every regular polygon has one, and so do all triangles.*

SEE ALSO escribed circle, circumcircle

FORMULA:

$$\text{Radius of incircle} = \frac{2 \times \Delta}{a + b + c}$$

where

a, b, c are lengths of edges

Δ is the area of the triangle

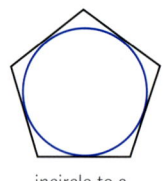

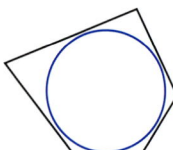

| incircle to a regular pentagon | incircle to an irregular pentagon |

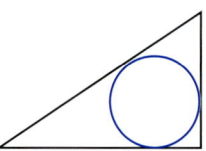

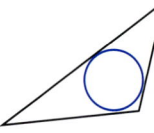

incircles to triangles

WORD BUILD

incentre
the position of the centre of an incircle

. . . .

income tax
is a tax which is taken from a person's earnings by the government of the country to help them pay for all the things needed to run the country.

....

indefinite integral *see* integral calculus

....

independent equation *see* equation

....

independent event *see* event

....

independent variable *see* variable

....

indeterminate equation *see* equation

....

index *plural* indexes, indices (*also* power)
An index or a power indicates the number of times a number is multiplied by itself. It is written in superscript.

SEE ALSO laws of indices

EXAMPLE:

In the term 4^3 the **index** is 3.

We can also say that 4^3 is a **power** of 4.

$4^3 = 4 \times 4 \times 4 = 64$

negative index
An index having a negative value indicates a reciprocal has to be taken after the index has been applied to the base.

EXAMPLE:

$x^{-1} = \dfrac{1}{x}$

$x^{-2} = \dfrac{1}{x^2}$

$2^{-3} = \dfrac{1}{2^3} = \dfrac{1}{8}$

positive index
A positive index is an index which is greater than zero.

zero index
A zero index is an index which is equal to zero. Any non-zero number raised to a zero index is equal to 1.

EXAMPLE:

$1^0 = 1$

$2^0 = 1$

$99^0 = 1$

$x^0 = 1$

....

index notation (*also* exponential form)
is a way of indicating how a number (or symbol) must be operated on by using another number written as a superscript to the first. This second number is called an index or power.

EXAMPLE:

When the index is a positive whole number, that number indicates how many of the first number or symbol must be multiplied together.

$A^2 = A \times A$

$5^3 = 5 \times 5 \times 5 = 125$

When the index is a fraction, then it indicates a root has to be found.

$9^{\frac{1}{2}} = \sqrt{9} = 3$

....

index number
Index numbers are used to compare the growth of some measurable quantity by studying the multiplier needed to make the new value from the old one. The old value is referred to as the base value and all subsequent values are measured by comparison with that.

• *Index numbers are frequently used in economics, for example the Consumer Prices Index or Retail Prices Index.*

⚠ **WATCH OUT**

An **index number** (which is a multiplier) should not be confused with **index notation** (where the index is an exponent).

....

indices *see* **index, laws of indices**

....

indirect proof *see* **proof**

....

indirect proportion *see* **proportion**

....

indirect variation *see* **proportion**

....

induction *see* **proof**

....

inequality
An inequality is shown by an expression such as $y < 3 - x$, meaning that y can take any value which is less than that of $3 - x$.
• *An **inequality** is shown on a graph by drawing the line of $y = 3 - x$ and shading the region where y is always less than that.*

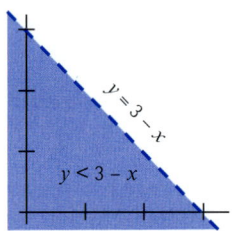

....

infinite
A quantity is said to be infinite if it clearly has some size but it cannot be counted or measured in any way.

SEE ALSO **finite**

....

infinite series *see* **series**

....

infinite set *see* **set**

....

infinitesimal
An infinitesimal quantity is one which is so small that it is almost indistinguishable from zero.

....

infinity
The concept of infinity is of a space, time, or quantity that knows no bounds; it goes on forever and cannot be measured on any practical scale that we know of. In terms of number, no matter what number may be thought of, it is clear that there must be another number which is bigger, and so on, and so on—to infinity.
• *The symbol used to represent **infinity** is ∞.*
➤ **tends to infinity** While infinity as a value cannot ever be reached, we can consider the case of a number (usually n) which is growing without restraint and always moving towards infinity. This is expressed as 'n tends to infinity' and written $n \rightarrow \infty$.

....

infix notation *see* **notation**

....

inflation
is a measure of the rate at which the cost of goods is changing over some period of time (usually a year) and is usually expressed as a percentage.
• *The rate of **inflation** can be negative but it is usually positive.*

FORMULA:

$$\text{Rate of inflation (\%)} = \frac{E - B}{B} \times 100$$

where

B is the cost at the beginning of the period

E is the cost at the end of the period

EXAMPLE:

In November 2018, the Consumer Prices Index was 106.9 and in November 2019 it was 108.5.

So the rate of consumer price **inflation** for that year is:
$$\frac{108.5 - 106.9}{106.9} \times 100 = 1.5\%$$

....

inner product *see* **scalar product**

....

inscribe

A second shape is said to be inscribed in a first shape if the second is completely inside the first, generally touching it at several points, but not cutting it. It is usual to require the inscribed shape to be the largest possible under the conditions given. The most common examples are the incircle to a polygon and the insphere to a polyhedron.

SEE ALSO **circumscribe, incircle**

in-sphere

An in-sphere is the sphere which can be drawn inside a polyhedron so as to touch all its faces. The tables show data for circumspheres and in-spheres within regular convex polyhedrons. *C*-radius and *I*-radius refer to the radii of the circumsphere and in-sphere respectively. *e* is the length of one edge. Inexact values are given to 6 significant figures.

• *It is always possible to draw an **in-sphere** for a regular convex polyhedron, but it may not be possible for others.*

SEE ALSO **circumsphere**

Name	No. of faces	Area = $e^2 \times$ ...	Volume = $e^2 \times$ ...
tetrahedron	4	1.73205	0.117851
cube	6	6	1
octahedron	8	3.46410	0.471405
dodecahedron	12	20.6458	7.663312
icosahedron	20	8.66025	2.18170

Name	C-radius = $e^2 \times$ ...	I-radius = $e^2 \times$ ...
tetrahedron	0.612372	0.204124
cube	0.866025	0.5
octahedron	0.707107	0.408248
dodecahedron	1.40126	1.113516
icosahedron	0.951057	0.755761

instalment

An instalment is an amount of money paid at regular intervals over some agreed period of time, for example when repaying a loan (plus interest) or keeping up a hire purchase agreement.

• *It is usual to arrange **instalments** of equal size (payable weekly or monthly) so that the loan and the interest are paid off together. The size of instalment needed to do this can be calculated from the formula below.*

FORMULA:

$$\text{Instalment} = \frac{A\, r\, F^n}{F^n - 1}$$

where

A is the amount of loan

r is the rate of interest (%) per period ÷ 100

F is $r + 1$

n is the number of periods

EXAMPLE:

£300 is loaned for 12 months at 2% per month compound interest.

$A = 300$ $r = 0.02$ $F = 1.02$ $n = 12$

Monthly instalments to the nearest penny $= \dfrac{300 \times 0.02 \times 1.02^{12}}{1.02^{12} - 1} = £28.37$

integer *see* **number**

integral

An integral of a curve on a graph is a measurement of its area between two points on the *x*-axis, and the curve and the *x*-axis. In effect this means that the area under the graph of f(*x*) between the stated end-points ($x = a$, $x = b$) is being found.

SEE ALSO **calculus**   »

EXAMPLE:

The shaded area on the graph shown is given by
$\int_{a}^{b} f(x)\,dx$

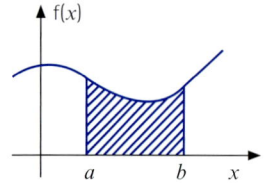

➤ **indefinite integral** An indefinite integral is one in which the range over which the integral is to be calculated is not given.

• *An **indefinite integral** could be written as $\int f(x)\,dx$, meaning that the integral is to be done with regard to x but without a range being given.*

➤ **integral of a function** An integral of a function is the integral of its curve when the function is drawn on a set of axes.

. . . .

integral calculus *see* **calculus**

. . . .

integrate
to find the integral of a quantity

. . . .

integration *see* **calculus**

. . . .

intercept
The intercept of a graph is the point at which it cuts across an axis. For linear graphs this word is usually reserved for the point at which the line cuts the y-axis.

EXAMPLE:

$y = mx + c$ is the equation of a straight line which has a gradient of value m and an **intercept** at c.

$y = 3x - 4$ has a gradient of 3 and an **intercept** of -4.

In the linear graph shown the **intercept** is -2.

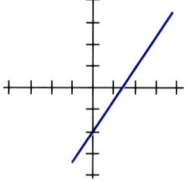

interest
Interest is the amount of extra money paid in return for having the use of someone else's money.

SEE ALSO **principal**

compound interest
Compound interest is worked out at the end of each period on the principal plus any previous interest already earned.

• *Compound interest is usually calculated as a total amount owing, rather than separate interest.*

FORMULA:

Total amount owing $= p \times (r + 1)^{n}$

where

p is the principal amount

r is the rate of interest (%) per period $\div$ 100

n is the number of periods

simple interest
Simple interest is worked out at the end of each period only on the principal of the original amount.

• *Simple interest is not very often used as a method today.*

FORMULA:

Total simple interest $= (p \times r \times n) \div 100$

where

p is the principal amount

r is the rate of interest (%) per period

n is the number of periods

EXAMPLE:

For a loan of £300 at 2% per month, **simple interest** would mean that at the end of each month interest of £6 would be owing. At the end of a year, the total interest owing would be £72 (plus the loan which still has to be repaid).

rate of interest (*also* interest rate)

The rate of interest states how the interest is to be worked out. It is usually stated as a percentage of the principal for each given period.
• *The **rate of interest** on the loan is set at 2% per month.*

interior angle *see* polygon

interpolation

An interpolation is an estimation of the likely value of an unknown piece of data, falling within the range of some known data and based on the evidence provided by that known data.
• *Interpolation usually involves using the trend line.*
SEE ALSO extrapolation, trend line
➤ **interpolate** to estimate the likely value of an unknown piece of data using interpolation

EXAMPLE:

In the graph, the values of the known data are shown by black dots, and the **interpolated** value by a blue dot.

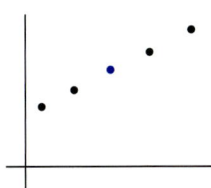

interquartile range *see* quartile

intersecting chord *see* chord

intersection

❶ The intersection of lines is the point at which they cross.
❷ The intersection of two or more sets is the single set made containing only members which are common to all the original sets.
• *∩ is the symbol for the **intersection** of sets.*

EXAMPLE:

$\{4, 7, 13, 20\} \cap \{2, 7, 10\}$ is $\{7\}$

➤ **intersect** If lines intersect, they cross each other. Intersecting lines may be straight or curved.

interval

An interval is the amount of time or space between two things.

EXAMPLE:

The **interval** between 6, 9, 12, and 15 is 3.

intuitive

Understanding (of a statement or a piece of knowledge) is described as intuitive when it is, or can be, reached without support of any argument.

invalid *see* valid

invariable

Any property of an object which never changes is said to be invariable.
• *With a shear transformation, the area of a shape is **invariable**.*

invariant point

An invariant point on a line or shape is a point which does not change its position under a given transformation.
SEE ALSO transformation

inverse

The inverse of an object in a set under a binary operation is another object in the same set which, when combined with the original object, produces the identity as the result.
• *For numbers under addition any number x has the **inverse** −x since x + −x = 0 (the identity for addition).*

inverse cosine *see* **trigonometric ratio**

inverse function *see* **function**

inverse matrix *see* **matrix**

inverse proportion *see* **proportion**

inverse sine *see* **trigonometric ratio**

inverse square

An inverse square relationship is $y = \dfrac{k}{x^2}$, where k can be any number.

EXAMPLE:

A graph showing an **inverse square** relationship has a general shape like the one shown.

If k is negative, then it will be reflected into the third and fourth quadrants.

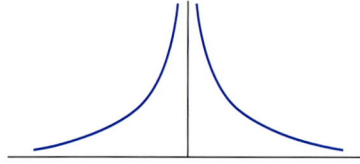

inverse tangent *see* **trigonometric ratio**

irrational number *see* **number**

irreducible

An irreducible expression is one that cannot be reduced.

irregular quadrilateral *see* **quadrilateral**

isogon *see* **polygon**

isometric drawing

An isometric drawing tries to show a three-dimensional view of an object in a two-dimensional drawing. The faces to be seen are plotted within a framework of three-dimensional coordinates, and all lengths are measured (to scale) along, or parallel to, one of these three axes. On the paper the vertical axis is drawn vertically, and the two horizontal axes are drawn on either side of this vertical line and at an angle of 60° to it.

SEE ALSO **elevation, plan**

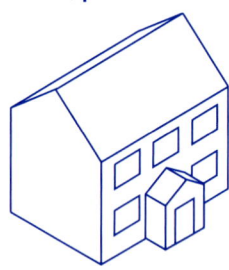

isometry

An isometry is a transformation or combination of transformations, such that every distance measured between a pair of points in the object is the same as the distance between the corresponding pair of points in the image. The object and image are the same shape and size.

• *Translations, rotations, reflections, and glide reflections are all* **isometries**.

SEE ALSO **translation, rotation, reflection**

direct isometry

an isometry in which either no reflection, or else an even number of them, has been used

opposite isomety

an isometry in which an odd number of reflections has been used

isosceles trapezium *see* **trapezium**

isosceles triangle *see* **triangle**

iteration

An iteration is a procedure which is repeated many times so that, from an estimated solution to a particular problem, each repeat produces a better approximation to the solution.

EXAMPLE:

Solutions in an **iteration** are usually numbered by means of a subscript, as in $x_1, x_2, x_3, x_4, ...,$ x_n, x_{n+1}, etc.

➤ **iterative** An iterative procedure is one that uses an iteration.

EXAMPLE:

An **iterative** formula to find the cube root of a number N is $x_{n+1} = \sqrt{\sqrt{N \times x_n}}$

Given $N = 4$ and starting with $x_1 = 1$,
then $x_2 = 1.4142$, $x_3 = 1.5422$, $x_4 = 1.5759$,
and so on to $x_{13} = 1.587401 ...$
which is accurate to 6 decimal places.

j *see* **unit vector**

Jordan curve *see* **curve**

k *see* **unit vector**

Kaprekar's constant

Kaprekar's constant is 6174.

FORMULA:

This is the result eventually produced by carrying out the following operations:

Make a four-digit number by using at least two different, non-zero, digits.

Place the digits in order: largest to smallest and smallest to largest, to make two other numbers.

Subtract the smaller from the larger to make a new number.

Continue repeating this process until 6174 is obtained.

Starting with 1998: $1998 \rightarrow 9981 - 1899 = 8082$

$8082 \rightarrow 8820 - 0288 = 8532$

$8532 \rightarrow 8532 - 2358 = 6174$

Kelvin scale *see* **temperature**

a
b
c
d
e
f
g
h
i
j
k
l
m
n
o
p
q
r
s
t
u
v
w
x
y
z

kinematic equation (*also* suvat equation)

Kinematic equations, sometimes called the suvat equations, are five equations which give the relationships between the five variables controlling movement under conditions of uniform motion.

FORMULA:

$$v = u + at$$

$$s = \frac{1}{2}(u + v)t$$

$$s = ut + \frac{1}{2}at^2$$

$$s = vt - \frac{1}{2}at^2$$

$$v^2 = u^2 + 2as$$

where

s is the distance moved

u is the initial velocity

v is the final velocity

a is the acceleration

t is the time taken

kinematics

is the branch of mathematics dealing with the motion of objects and considering only their movement in relation to space and time, disregarding the effects of their mass or any forces acting upon them.

kite

A kite is a quadrilateral which has two pairs of adjacent edges of the same length, and no interior angle is bigger than 180 degrees. It has one line of symmetry and its diagonals cross each other at right angles.

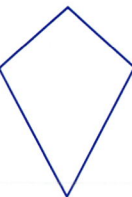

knot

A knot is a speed of 1 nautical mile per hour.

Ll

Latin square

A Latin square of size *n* by *n* is one in which *n* different objects are each repeated *n* times and arranged in a square array so that none of them is repeated in any row or column.

Graeco-Latin square (*also* Euler square)

A Graeco-Latin square is made by combining two different Latin squares (each of which is made of a different set of objects) so that no pair of objects is repeated.
• *Graeco-Latin squares are useful in the design of experiments.* • *A problem based on this is to take sixteen playing cards, A, K, Q, J of each suit, and put them in a 4 by 4 array, so that no two cards of the same value or suit are in line.*

A	B	C	D		1	2	3	4		A1	B2	C3	D4
C	D	A	B	+	4	3	2	1	=	C4	D3	A2	B1
D	C	B	A		2	1	4	3		D2	C1	B4	A3
B	A	D	C		3	4	1	2		B3	A4	D1	C2

Graeco-Latin square

latitude *see* great circle

laws of indices

are those rules which control the operations of combining numbers written in index (exponential) form.

FORMULA:

Where $x, y > 0$ and m, n are integers, then

$$x^m \times x^n = x^{m+n}$$

$$x^m \div x^n = x^{m-n}$$

$$(x^m)^n = x^{mn}$$

$$x^m \times y^m \neq (xy)^m$$

$$x^{-n} = \frac{1}{x^n}, x \neq 0$$

$$x^0 = 1, x \neq 0$$

EXAMPLE:

$$2^3 \times 2^5 = 2^8$$

$$2^3 \div 2^7 = 2^{-4}$$

$$(2^3)^5 = 2^{15}$$

$$2^{-3} = \frac{1}{2^3} = \frac{1}{8}$$

LCD *see* **lowest common denominator**

leading diagonal *see* **diagonal**

least squares
The method of least squares is used to determine the position of a line of best fit for two sets of data plotted on a scatter graph.
• *In the method of **least squares** (devised by Gauss) the line is the one which ensures that the total sum of all the squares of the distances between the various pieces of data and that line is as small as possible*

left-handed system *see* **right–handed system**

left identity *see* **identity**

lemma
A lemma is a theorem which is used in the proof of another theorem.
• *A **lemma** is useful as a way of simplifying the proof of the final theorem by reducing its length.*

length *see* **dimension**

level
A level is an instrument used to make sure that a line, or the surface of an object, is parallel to the horizontal plane of the Earth's surface at that place.
• *A common example of a **level** is the spirit-level, in which the movement of an air-bubble inside a curved glass tube will show when the instrument is horizontal.*

light year
A light year is approximately a distance of 9.4605×10^{15} metres.

likely
In mathematics, likely is most often used as having the same meaning as probable.
An outcome that is likely has a better chance of happening than not.
• *How **likely** is it that I will throw a 4 with this die?*
➤ **equally likely** A set of outcomes associated with a particular activity are described as being equally likely when each occurs as readily as any other.

like term *see* **term**

limit
❶ the point, line, or level beyond which something does not continue, or the greatest quantity or value allowed
❷ a quantity which a function or the sum of a series can be made to approach as closely as desired

EXAMPLE:

Consider the sequence of fractions:

$$\frac{1}{1} \quad \frac{1}{2} \quad \frac{1}{3} \quad \frac{1}{4} \cdots \quad \frac{1}{100} \cdots \frac{1}{1,000} \cdots \quad \frac{1}{n}$$

Clearly it can go on forever with no **limit** on the value of n.

Since we cannot have $n = \infty$ we must consider what happens as n gets indefinitely large, or as n tends to infinity.

Noting that as n gets bigger the fraction gets smaller, and as the **limit** on smallness is zero, we reach the conclusion that, in the **limit** as n tends to infinity the fraction becomes zero.

This is written as

$$\lim_{n \to \infty} \frac{1}{n} = 0$$

line

A line is the path followed by a point when it moves from one position to another so that it has a measurable size (its length) only along that path. A line has only one dimension—its width is ignored.

SEE ALSO **line segment**

➤ **linear** means relating to or arranged in a straight line

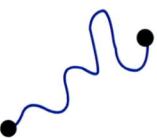

linear equation see **equation**

linear graph see **graph**

linear programming

is a method used to find the 'best' solution to problems which can be expressed in terms of linear equations or inequalities. Solutions are usually found by drawing graphs of inequalities and looking for optimum values that satisfy the required conditions.

• *Linear programming is widely used in business and industrial contexts and the problems often relate to obtaining maximum profits for given costs and production levels.*

line of best fit see **trend line**

line of symmetry

A line of symmetry is a line along which a plane shape can be folded so that one half of the shape fits exactly on the other half.

• *A shape can have several **lines of symmetry**.*
• *In the illustration, the **lines of symmetry** are shown in blue.*

line segment

A line segment is a piece of a straight line. The single word 'line' is usually taken to mean 'line segment'.

• *Strictly speaking, a straight line is fixed by two separate points and goes on indefinitely in both directions so that it cannot be measured. It is only the **line segment** which is measurable.*

line symmetry see **symmetry**

literal expression see **expression**

local maximum see **maximum**

local minimum see **minimum**

locus plural **loci**

A locus is the line of a path along which a point moves so as to satisfy some given conditions. A locus is usually a curve but does not have to be. In the illustration, the locus trails the end of a string unwinding from a rectangular block.

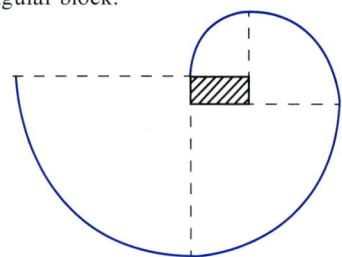

• *A point that moves so that it is always the same distance from another (fixed) point will follow a **locus** in the shape of a circle.*

SEE ALSO **ellipse**

logarithm

The logarithm of a number N to a particular base b is the index to which that base must be raised to equal that number.

• *Logarithms were important before the existence of electronic calculators because they could be used to simplify multiplication and division by using the laws of indices.*

FORMULA:

Number = base$^{logarithm\ of\ the\ Number}$ or $N = b^{\log N}$

If $M = b^{\log M}$ and $N = b^{\log N}$

then

$M \times N = b^{\log M} \times b^{\log N} = b^{\log M + \log N}$

common logarithm

Common logarithms are calculated to a base value of 10 and were the logarithms used in the past for doing arithmetical calculations.

natural logarithm

Natural logarithms are calculated to a base value of e (≈ 2.71828), and arise in work involving the ideas of the calculus. This is now the principal use for logarithms rather than the simplification of arithmetic.

logic

The logic of a system is the whole structure of rules that must be used for any reasoning within that system.
• *It is always necessary to state, or otherwise have it understood, what rules are being used before any logic can be applied.*
➤ **logical** A logical system follows a structure of rules for any reasoning within it.
• *Most of mathematics is based upon a well-understood structure of rules and is considered to be highly logical.*

long division *see* **division**

longitude *see* **great circle**

look-see proof *see* **proof**

loss
a profit that is a negative amount
SEE ALSO **profit**

lower quartile *see* **quartile**

lowest common denominator (*also* LCD, least common denominator)

The lowest common denominator of two fractions is the smallest number into which all of their denominators will divide. It is the LCM of the denominators.
• *The LCD of the following fractions is 24:*

$$\frac{2}{3} \quad \frac{1}{8} \quad \frac{5}{6}$$

lowest common multiple (*also* LCM, least common multiple)

The lowest common multiple of two or more numbers is the smallest possible number into which all of them will divide exactly.
• *The LCM of 3, 4, and 8 is 24.*

lowest terms

If a fraction is in its lowest terms it is in its simplest form, so that the only common factor of both the numerator and the denominator is 1.
SEE ALSO **lowest common denominator, fraction, simplify**

EXAMPLE:

$\frac{12}{15}$ in its **lowest terms** is $\frac{4}{5}$.

Both the numerator and denominator have been divided by 3 and cannot be divided any further by one common factor or number. So the fraction is in its **lowest terms**.

lozenge *see* **diamond**

Lucas sequence *see* **sequence**

lucky number sequence *see* **sequence**

a
b
c
d
e
f
g
h
i
j
k
l
m
n
o
p
q
r
s
t
u
v
w
x
y
z

lune (*also* **crescent**)

When two circles (lying in the same plane) overlap, then a lune is the shape which is formed between the outside of one circle and the inside of the other. The two circles may be the same, or different, in size.

• *Two overlapping circles form two* **lunes** *whose difference in areas is equal to the difference in the areas of the two circles making them.*

EXAMPLE:

In the diagram, the shaded area is a **lune**.

The area of **lune** ADBC can be found by subtracting the area of segment ABC of circle 1 from the area of segment ABD of circle 2.

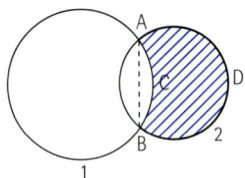

Mm

magic square

A magic square is a set of numbers arranged in the form of a square so that the total of every row, column, and diagonal is the same. It is usual to require that every number is different. In most cases the numbers also form some kind of sequence.

using 1 to 9		
8	3	4
1	5	9
6	7	2

using 1 to 16			
16	2	3	13
5	11	10	8
9	7	6	12
4	14	15	1

using primes only		
17	89	71
113	59	5
47	29	101

magnitude

❶ (*also* **modulus**) The magnitude of a vector is a measure of its length when it is represented by a single straight line and is the positive square root of the scalar product of the vector with itself. It is also known as the modulus.

• |*v*| *is the symbol for the magnitude of a vector* v.

EXAMPLE:

Given $v \equiv (3, 1, 8)$ then

$$|v| = \sqrt{v.v} = \sqrt{3^2 + 1^2 + 8^2} = \sqrt{74}$$

❷ The magnitude of something is a measure of its size. Magnitude is generally used in relation to some scale so that comparisons can be made. Earthquakes and the brightness of stars use such scales. In mathematics, using a number's standard form allows us to compare its magnitude with others.

SEE ALSO **order, standard form**

EXAMPLE:

It is easy to see 2.45×10^{15} is bigger than 9.67×10^{14} but not when they are written out in full.

main diagonal *see* **diagonal**

major arc *see* **arc**

major axis *see* **ellipse**

major sector *see* **sector**

major segment *see* **segment**

many-to-one correspondence
see **correspondence**

map
❶ To map the elements of a set is to match them to elements of another set by use of a rule.
• *The elements to be **mapped** are usually numbers of some type (integer, real, complex, etc.) or they could be algebraic.*
❷ A spatial pattern is said to be mapped onto itself if a translation, reflection, rotation, glide reflection, or any combination of them, acting on the whole pattern, serves to place each motif of the pattern exactly onto another copy of that motif—so the pattern matches with itself.
➤ **mapping** A mapping is the matching of the elements from one set to the elements of another set by use of a rule.
• *For the purpose of **mapping** a pattern, it is important to assume that the pattern goes on indefinitely.*

mapping diagram
A mapping diagram is a drawing used to show the effect of a mapping by listing the two sets and drawing arrows indicating how the elements are to be matched.

• *The **mapping diagram** illustrated shows what happens for the rule 'multiply by 3 and add 1' for some values.*

$$1 \rightarrow 4$$
$$2 \rightarrow 7$$
$$3 \rightarrow 10$$
$$4 \rightarrow 13$$

mark-up
is a term used, mainly in the retail trade, to indicate what has to be added on to the cost price of an article to find the selling price.
• ***Mark-up** is usually expressed as a percentage of the cost price.*

EXAMPLE:

A shopkeeper buys boxes of chocolates at £2.50 each.

Their **mark-up** is 150% of the original price = £3.75

Their selling price then is £2.50 + £3.75 = £6.25

mass
The mass of a body is the quantity of matter that it contains.

⚠ WATCH OUT

The words **mass** and **weight** are commonly used as though they were identical. This does not matter for ordinary use, but there is a difference.

The **mass** of a body is a measure of how much matter it contains and is the property of that body that governs the way it will behave under the action of a force.

The **weight** of a body is a measure of the force the body itself produces when in a gravitational field.

The **mass** of a body is unchanged wherever it is in the universe, whereas the **weight** depends on the gravitational force at the place it is being weighed. Objects do not change their mass, but weigh less when on the Moon than when they are on the Earth.

matrix *plural* matrices

A matrix is a rectangular array of elements.
Usually the elements in a matrix are all of
the same type (numbers, symbols, algebraic
expressions, etc.) and the array is enclosed in
either square or round brackets.

• *The individual elements in a **matrix** are separated
only by spaces; commas or other dividing marks are
not used.*

SEE ALSO **determinant, diagonal**

EXAMPLE:

$$\begin{pmatrix} 1 & 4 & -3 \\ 6 & 1.5 & 7 \end{pmatrix} \begin{pmatrix} A & X \\ Y & B \end{pmatrix} \begin{pmatrix} 3x+8 & y+1 \\ 3y-4 & 2x-7 \end{pmatrix}$$

➤ **addition of matrices** Two matrices may be
added to make a new matrix, provided they are of
the same order, by adding corresponding elements
in each to form elements for the new matrix. The
new matrix will be of the same order.

EXAMPLE:

$$\begin{pmatrix} 1 & 2 \\ 3 & 4 \end{pmatrix} + \begin{pmatrix} 5 & 9 \\ 7 & 8 \end{pmatrix} \rightarrow \begin{pmatrix} 1+5 & 2+9 \\ 3+7 & 4+8 \end{pmatrix} = \begin{pmatrix} 6 & 11 \\ 10 & 12 \end{pmatrix}$$

➤ **multiplication of matrices** Two matrices
may be multiplied, provided that the number
of columns in the first matrix is the same as
the number of rows in the second matrix.
It is done by laying each row of the first matrix
against each column of the second matrix,
multiplying the pairs of elements, and adding the
results together to make a single element for the
answer matrix.

⚠ **WATCH OUT**

Matrix multiplication depends on the order in
which the two are written. Changing the order
may give a different answer, or multiplication
may not be possible.

EXAMPLE:

$$\begin{pmatrix} 4 & 2 \\ 3 & 1 \end{pmatrix} \begin{pmatrix} 5 & 7 & 8 \\ 6 & 0 & 9 \end{pmatrix} \rightarrow$$

$$\begin{pmatrix} 4\times5+2\times6 & 4\times7+2\times0 & 4\times8+2\times9 \\ 3\times5+1\times6 & 3\times7+1\times0 & 3\times8+1\times9 \end{pmatrix} =$$

$$\begin{pmatrix} 32 & 28 & 50 \\ 21 & 21 & 33 \end{pmatrix}$$

but $\begin{pmatrix} 5 & 7 & 8 \\ 6 & 0 & 9 \end{pmatrix} \begin{pmatrix} 4 & 2 \\ 3 & 1 \end{pmatrix}$ cannot be done.

column matrix

A column matrix has only a single column.

diagonal matrix

A diagonal matrix is a square matrix which has
all its elements equal to zero, except for those
on the main diagonal.

identity matrix

The identity matrix (for multiplication) is a
square matrix whose elements in the main
diagonal are all 1s, and the others are all zero.

• $\begin{pmatrix} 1 & 0 \\ 0 & 1 \end{pmatrix}$ is the 2 by 2 **identity matrix** for multiplication.

inverse matrix

The inverse, for multiplication, of a square
matrix (which must not be singular) is another
matrix such that when the two are multiplied
together, in any order, then the result is the
identity matrix.

EXAMPLE:

The inverse of $\begin{pmatrix} 2 & 1 \\ 5 & 3 \end{pmatrix}$ is $\begin{pmatrix} 3 & -1 \\ -5 & 2 \end{pmatrix}$ since

$$\begin{pmatrix} 2 & 1 \\ 5 & 3 \end{pmatrix} \begin{pmatrix} 3 & -1 \\ -5 & 2 \end{pmatrix} = \begin{pmatrix} 1 & 0 \\ 0 & 1 \end{pmatrix}$$

row matrix

A row matrix has only a single row.

EXAMPLE:

(3 4 10) is a **row matrix**.

It is also a 1 by 3 matrix.

singular matrix

A singular matrix is a square matrix with
determinant = zero.

square matrix

A square matrix has the same number of rows
and columns.

EXAMPLE:

$\begin{pmatrix} 4 & -1 \\ 0 & 6 \end{pmatrix}$ is a **square matrix**.

It is also a 2 by 2 matrix.

maximum *plural* maximums, maxima

A maximum is a stationary point passed through by the curve made by the graph of $f(x)$, when the value of $f(x)$ is increasing before the stationary point and decreasing after it.

global maximum

A maximum when no greater value of $f(x)$ exists is a global maximum.

local maximum

A maximum when a greater value of $f(x)$ exists is a local maximum.

mean

The mean value of a data set is usually taken to be the arithmetic mean.

SEE ALSO median, mode

arithmetic mean

The arithmetic mean of a set of data is the numerical value found by adding together all the separate values of the data and dividing by the number of pieces of data there are.

• x *is the symbol for the **arithmetic mean** of a set of values of x.*

EXAMPLE:

For the data 9, 3, 3, 15, 11, the **arithmetic mean** is $41 \div 5 = 8.2$

geometric mean

The geometric mean of a set of n positive numbers is found by multiplying them all together and taking the positive nth root of the result.

EXAMPLE:

The **geometric mean** of $\{2,3\}$ is $\sqrt{6}$; and of $\{4, 5, 6\}$ is $\sqrt[3]{120}$.

weighted mean

The weighted mean of a set of data is the mean value found after each piece of data has been multiplied by some factor which gives a measure of its importance or its frequency of occurrence.

EXAMPLE:

The table shows the distribution of shoe sizes among 100 people.

The mean shoe size could be given as $(2 + 3 + 4 + 5 + 6 + 7) \div 6 = 4.5$

But this does not allow for the fact that some sizes are a lot more common than others.

The **weighted mean** shoe size is $[(2 \times 15) + (3 \times 19) + (4 \times 35) + (5 \times 18) + (6 \times 8) + (7 \times 5)] \div 100 = 4$.

Shoe size	2	3	4	5	6	7
No. of people	15	19	35	18	8	5

working mean

A working mean is an assumed value for the mean of a set of data. The use of a working mean allows other calculations to be done as the data is being entered and a correction made once the true mean is known.

mean deviation

The mean deviation of a set of data is the mean distance between the value of each piece of data and some fixed value. The fixed value is usually the mean of all the data, but it can be the median. All the distances are considered to be positive.

measure of central tendency

A measure of central tendency of a set of data is any values about which the distribution of the data may be considered to be roughly balanced.

measuring problem

Measuring problems have always been popular because they are easy to understand and relate to something familiar in ordinary life.

• *Some **measuring problems** are based on the use of weights, while others require lengths to be measured with imperfectly marked rulers.*

EXAMPLE:

One of the earliest types of **measuring problem** was introduced by Tartaglia:

There are three uncalibrated containers of 3, 5, and 8 litres capacity called A, B, and C respectively. C is full. How can the 8 litres be divided into two lots of 4 litres?   **»**

Pour 5 litres from *C* into *B*. Pour 3 litres from *B* into *A*.

Empty *A* back into *C*. Empty *B* into *A*.

Pour 5 litres from *C* into *B*. Pour 1 litre from *B* into *A*.

Finally empty *A* into *C*.

median

❶ The median value of a set of data is the numerical value of the piece of data in the middle of the set, after arranging the set in size order. If there is an even number of pieces of data, the mean of the middle two is taken as the median.

SEE ALSO **mean, mode**

EXAMPLE:

{9, 3, 3, 15, 11} has a **median** of 9 (middle of 3, 3, 9, 11, 15).

{6, 2, 12, 4, 7, 18} has a **median** of 6.5 (mean of middle pair 6 and 7).

❷ The median of a triangle is a straight line joining one vertex of a triangle to the middle of the opposite edge. Any triangle has three medians and they all cross each other at the same point.

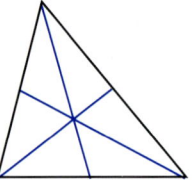

median triangle *see* **triangle**

mediator

A mediator can be used to mean any axis of symmetry, but is usually a perpendicular bisector of a line.

SEE ALSO **bisector, symmetry**

member (*also* **element**)

A member or an element of a set is one of the objects contained in that set.

• ∈ *is the symbol meaning 'is a* **member** *of'.*

SEE ALSO **set**

meridian *see* **great circle**

Mersenne prime

Mersenne primes are those prime numbers which can be made from the expression $2^n - 1$.

• *The formula for* **Mersenne primes** *only works when n itself is prime but even then there are times when it does not work.* • *For instance, it works when n = 2, 3, 5, or 7 but not when n = 11 or 23, as well as many other prime values.*

mid-ordinate rule

The mid-ordinate rule is a method for finding the approximate area under a curve by dividing the space into strips; finding the areas of the separate strips by multiplying the length of the middle ordinate of each strip by the width of that strip; and finally adding the areas of the strips together.

• *The* **mid-ordinate rule** *is a practical method that can be used when the equation of the curve is not known.*

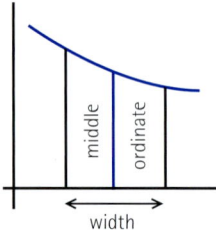

WORD BUILD

trapezium rule (*also* **trapezoidal rule**)

The trapezium rule or trapezoidal rule is a method for finding the approximate area under a curve which is similar to the mid-ordinate rule but treats each strip as a trapezium.

• *The* **trapezium rule** *can be very accurate if the strips are made as narrow as is practicable.*

• *By using strips of equal widths, the whole procedure can be reduced to a formula.*

FORMULA:

If the width of each strip is w and the lengths of the ordinates are $y_1, y_2, y_3, ..., y_n$ then the area is given by:

$$w \frac{1}{2}(y_1 + y_n) + y_2 + y_3 + y_4 + ... + y_{n-1}$$

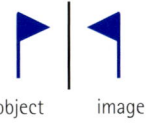

minimum *plural* **minimums, minima**
A minimum is a stationary point passed through by the curve made by the graph of $f(x)$, when the value of $f(x)$ is decreasing before the stationary point and increasing after it.

global minimum
A minimum when no smaller value of $f(x)$ exists is a global minimum.

local minimum
A minimum when a smaller value of $f(x)$ exists is a local minimum.

minor arc *see* **arc**

minor axis *see* **ellipse**

minor sector *see* **sector**

minor segment *see* **segment**

minuend
In a subtraction sum, the minuend is the number from which the other number must be subtracted.
SEE ALSO **subtrahend**

FORMULA:

minuend − subtrahend = difference

minute
❶ A minute is a unit of time equal to 60 seconds.
SEE ALSO **second**
❷ A minute is the angle made by $\frac{1}{60}$ part of a degree.
SEE ALSO **degree**

⚠ **WATCH OUT**

Degrees and **decimal fractions** increasingly tend to be used for angles rather than **minutes** and **seconds**, except in navigation.

mirror line
A mirror line is the fixed line used in making a reflection.

EXAMPLE:

Each of these pictures shows the effect of reflecting an object in the **mirror line**, which is shown as a single black line.

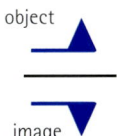

object   image

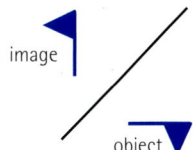

object

image

image

object

mirror symmetry *see* **symmetry**

mixed number *see* **number**

Möbius band (also Möbius strip)

A Möbius band or strip is made by taking a rectangular strip of paper like that shown as *ABCD* and fastening the two shorter edges together (*AB* and *CD*) but, before fastening, giving the strip a half twist so that *A* fastens to *D* and *B* to *C*. The strange property of this band is that it now has only one edge and one side.

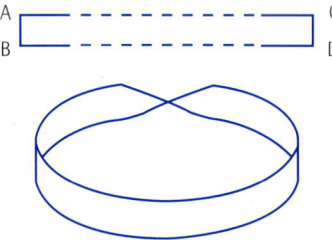

---

mod *see* modulus

---

modal class

The modal class of a set of grouped data is the class which has the greatest frequency.

• *In the table below, the **modal class** for the set is the group of those with size 4 feet as it has the most members.*

SEE ALSO **mode**

Shoe size	2	3	4	5	6	7
No. of people	15	19	35	18	8	5

---

mode

The mode of a set of data is the piece of data found most often.

• *Data 9, 3, 3, 15, 11 has a **mode** of 3 (as there are most 3s).*

SEE ALSO **mean, median**

---

modulo arithmetic *see* modulus

---

modulus

❶ The modulus of a particular system of arithmetic is an integer value which is used as a divisor throughout that system.

❷ The modulus of a vector is its magnitude.

WORD BUILD

modulo (also mod)

Modulo or its abbreviation mod is used to identify the number being used as the modulus.

• *When the modulus is 4, the system is working modulo 4 or mod 4.*

modulo arithmetic

is a system of arithmetic based on relating numbers to each other only by their residues for some given modulus.

EXAMPLE:

A multiplication table (mod 4) is shown.

It is not a group, as there are no inverses for 0 and 2: both $0 \times x = 1$ and $2 \times x = 1$ have no solution.

x	0	1	2	3
0	0	0	0	0
1	0	1	2	3
2	0	2	0	2
3	0	3	2	1

---

mosaic *see* tiling

---

motif

In a spatial pattern the motif is the basic object or element which is repeated to make the pattern.

• *A **motif** can be a single object or made up of a collection of objects. It can be any drawing so long as it is the basic element which is repeated throughout the pattern.*

---

moving average *see* average

---

multigrade

A multigrade is an equality between two expressions, each requiring some numbers to be raised to a power and added, which is true for more than one value of that power.

EXAMPLE:

For $n = 1$ or 2, the following are **multigrade** expressions:

$1^n + 2^n + 6^n = 4^n + 5^n$

$1^n + 6^n + 8^n = 2^n + 4^n + 9^n$

multinomial

A multinomial expression is one having two or more terms.

SEE ALSO **polynomial**

WORD BUILD

binomial

A binomial expression is a multinomial having two terms.
• *3x + 4, x − y, and 5 − 7y are all **binomial** expressions.*

trinomial

A trinomial expression is a multinomial having three terms.
• *3x² − 5x + 4 and x − y + 7 are **trinomial** expressions.*

multiple

A multiple is a number made by multiplying together two other numbers. A number is a multiple of any of its factors.
• *12 is a **multiple** of 2 since 12 = 2 × 6*
SEE ALSO **lowest common multiple**

multiplicand

In a multiplication sum the multiplicand is the first of the two numbers given.
SEE ALSO **multiplier, product**

FORMULA:

multiplicand × multiplier = product

multiplication

is the operation which combines several equal measures of size giving the result as a single number. × and * are both symbols for multiplication.

SEE ALSO **matrix, scalar multiplication**

EXAMPLE:

With whole numbers, **multiplication** can be seen as equivalent to the addition of several numbers of the same size; the more general case for all numbers is an extension of that.

There are four rooms with six people in each, so in total there are 6 + 6 + 6 + 6 or 6 × 4 people.

This extends to cases like 3.28 × 5.74.

➤ **multiply** To multiply several numbers or measures of the same size is to combine them giving the result as a single number.

multiplier

In a multiplication sum the multiplier is the second of the two numbers given.
• *Since multiplication is commutative and order does not matter, the multiplicand and **multiplier** can be changed around, so the names are only for identifying them in a particular case.*
SEE ALSO **multiplicand, product**

FORMULA:

multiplicand × multiplier = product

multiply *see* multiplication

mutually exclusive event *see* event

a
b
c
d
e
f
g
h
i
j
k
l
m
n
o
p
q
r
s
t
u
v
w
x
y
z

Nn

Naperian logarithm

is an alternative name for natural logarithms.

SEE ALSO logarithm

Napier's rods (*also* Napier's bones)

Napier's rods or bones were invented to help with multiplication, based on the gelosia multiplication method. Each rod was a flat strip with a single digit at the top and nine cells underneath containing the result of multiplying this top digit by 1 to 9 in order from top to bottom.

SEE ALSO gelosia multiplication

EXAMPLE:

Rods for 3, 5, 6, and 7 are shown in the picture. The index rod indicates the multiplier used on each level.

Three of the rods are shown put together to form the number 635 (at the top).

The shaded areas show the cells used when multiplying 635 by 2, 4, and 7 respectively.

Remembering that the figures have to be added diagonally, the three answers are 1,270, 2,540, and 4,445.

natural logarithm *see* **logarithm**

natural number *see* **number**

natural number sequence *see* **sequence**

nautical mile

is the unit for measuring distance at sea and is slightly longer than the mile. The international nautical mile is 1852 metres.

nearest *see* **rounding**

necessary and sufficient condition *see* **condition**

necessary condition *see* **condition**

negative angle *see* **angle**

negative correlation *see* **correlation**

negative gradient *see* **gradient**

negative index *see* **index**

negatively skewed *see* **skewed distribution**

negative number *see* **number**

negative vector *see* **vector**

nephroid *see* **cycloid**

nested multiplication

is a way of rewriting an expression so that it is easier to work with when calculating values

• *Nested multiplication* is especially useful with a

calculator where the value of the variable can be kept in, and recalled from, the memory.

EXAMPLE:

$4x^3 - 5x^2 + 7x - 8$ is easier to use as

$[(4x - 5)x + 7]x - 8$

net

❶ A net is an arrangement of polygons connected at their edges, all lying in one plane, which can be folded up to make a polyhedron.

• *There is always more than one way of folding up a net. It is also known as a development.*

SEE ALSO **polyhedron**

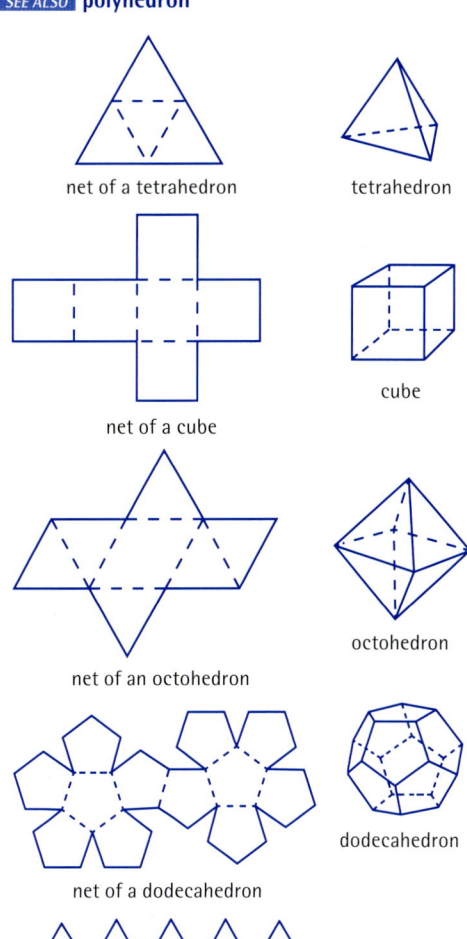

net of a tetrahedron   tetrahedron

cube

net of a cube

octohedron

net of an octohedron

dodecahedron

net of a dodecahedron

net of an icosahedron   icosahedron

❷ A net amount of weight or money is the amount remaining after any necessary deductions have been made.

SEE ALSO **gross**

EXAMPLE:

A packet containing rice weighs 760 grams (gross) but the packet weighs 40 grams.

The **net** weight (= weight of the contents) is 720 grams.

network *see* **graph**

n–gram *see* **star polygon**

node *see* **vertex**

nominal value *see* **value**

nomogram

A nomogram is a set of three or more marked scales (which may be straight or curved) made so that when sufficient values are known, a line joining them will also pass through the unknown value.

EXAMPLE:

The **nomogram** in the picture connects the radius, height and volume of a cylinder, so that when the values of any two are known, the third value is in line with them.

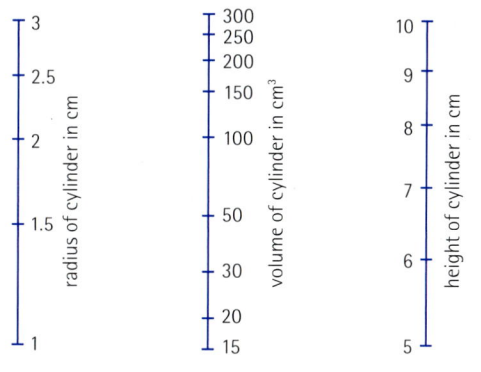

non-convex polyhedron *see* **polyhedron**

....

non-periodic tiling *see* **tiling**

....

normal distribution *see* **distribution**

....

notation

In general, notation is a system of signs or symbols representing numbers or quantities. For example, triangle notation often identifies each vertex with 3 capital letters (such as A, B, and C) and each edge with 3 small letters (such as *a*, *b*, and *c*) as shown in the image.

SEE ALSO **standard form, tiling, triangle, vector**

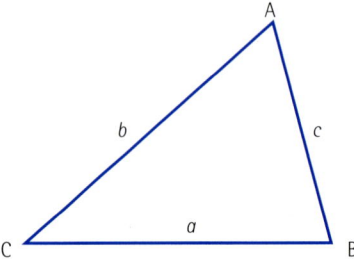

index notation

is a way of indicating how a number (or symbol) must be operated on by using another number written as a superscript to the first; this second number is called an index or power.
- *When the **index** is a positive whole number, that number indicates how many of the first number or symbol must be multiplied together.*
- *When the **index** is a fraction, then it indicates a root has to be found.*

EXAMPLE:

$A^2 = A \times A$

$5^3 = 5 \times 5 \times 5 = 125$

$9^{\frac{1}{2}} = \sqrt{9} = 3$

infix notation

is the method used in writing mathematical expressions where the operators are written between the two numbers (or expressions) on which they have to operate.
- *You should use BIDMAS to evaluate the operators used in a particular order, or else expressions using infix notation may be evaluated wrongly.*

SEE ALSO **BIDMAS**

EXAMPLE:

Examples of **infix notation** are $1 + 2$, 3×4, $(5 + 6) \times (7 - 8)$, and so on.

Using BIDMAS, $\times$ has to be done before $+$ so $2 + 3 \times 4$ equals 14 not 20.

reverse Polish notation (*also* postfix notation)

was designed to remove all possible ambiguities of the infix notation by putting each operator immediately after the pair of numbers on which it must operate. Brackets are not needed.

EXAMPLE:

$2 + 3 \times 4$ becomes $2\ 3\ 4 \times +$ meaning first 3×4 then $+ 2$.

$(2 + 3) \times 4$ becomes $4\ 2\ 3 + \times$ meaning first $2 + 3$ then $\times 4$.

$2\ 3\ 4 + \times 5\ 6 \times 7 + \times$ should produce the answer 518.

The 'trick' is to take each operator in turn working from left to right, use it on the two preceding numbers and replace them and the operator with the result at each stage.

....

null set *see* **set**

....

null vector *see* **vector**

....

number

Numbers are the basic elements of arithmetic which are used for expressing and recording quantities or measures of various kinds.

SEE ALSO polygon number

abundant number

An abundant number is a number whose proper factors add up to more than the number itself.
• *20 is an **abundant number** since 1 + 2 + 4 + 5 + 10 = 22.*

algebraic number

An algebraic number is a real number which can arise as the root of a polynomial equation whose coefficients are all whole numbers.
• *All rational numbers are **algebraic**, but only some irrational numbers are **algebraic**. $\sqrt{3}$ is an **algebraic number** since $\sqrt{3}$ is a root of $x^2 = 3$.*

automorphic number

An automorphic number is a number whose last digits are unchanged after the number has been squared.
• *76 and 625 are **automorphic** since $76^2 = 5,776$ and $625^2 = 390,625$.*

cardinal number

A cardinal number is a natural number used to describe 'how many' objects there are in a set.

EXAMPLE:

In the following statement 8 and 6 are used as **cardinal numbers:**

The set R B Z N F B R X has 8 letters altogether but only 6 are different.

complex number

A complex number is a combination of real and imaginary numbers. It is written in the form $a + bi$, where a and b are real numbers.
• *$\mathbb{C}$ is the symbol for the set of all **complex numbers**.*

composite number

A composite number is a number that has three or more factors. It cannot be 1 or a prime number.
• *4, 6, 8, 9, 10, 12, 15 are all **composite numbers**.*

consecutive number

Consecutive numbers are whole numbers that follow each other in order when arranged in a sequence from smallest to largest.
• *3, 4, 5 and 19, 20, 21, 22 are both groups of **consecutive numbers**.*

cutting number

Cutting numbers are that sequence of numbers produced when a given shape is cut up into the maximum number of pieces by a succession of 1, 2, 3, 4 ... cuts and without re-arranging the pieces between cuts.
• *A line makes 2, 3, 4, 5 ... pieces after 1, 2, 3, 4 ... cuts.* • *A circle produces 2, 4, 7, 11 ... pieces after 1, 2, 3, 4 ... cuts.*

deficient number

A deficient number is a number whose proper factors add up to less than the number itself
• *16 is a **deficient number** since 1 + 2 + 4 + 8 = 15.*

even number

An even number is a whole number which, when divided by 2, has no remainder.
• *20, 348, 1,356 are all **even numbers**.*
• *Any number which ends in 0, 2, 4, 6, or 8 must be even.*

happy number

A number has all its digits squared and added together to make a new number. This process is repeated until a 1 is obtained, when the original number is described as 'happy'. If a 1 is never obtained, then the original number is said to be 'sad'.
• *$19 \to 1^2 + 9^2 = 82 \to 8^2 + 2^2 = 68 \to 6^2 + 8^2 = 100 \to 1^2 = 1$ so 19 is a **happy number**.* **»**

Harshad number

A Harshad number is a number which can be divided exactly by its digit sum
• *1,729 is a **Harshad number** since its digit sum (1 + 7 + 2 + 9) is 19, and 19 divides exactly into 1,729.*

identification number

An identification number is a number which is neither cardinal nor ordinal but which is given to objects or persons to help distinguish it in some way.
• *Your national insurance number and your PIN are both **identification numbers**.*

imaginary number

An imaginary number is the square root of a negative number. It is called imaginary since the square root of a negative number cannot be real.

EXAMPLE:

The way in which **imaginary numbers** are expressed is based on this argument:

$\sqrt{-k}$ can always be re-written as $\sqrt{k} \times \sqrt{-1}$ and k is positive so $\sqrt{k}$ is real.

Suppose $\sqrt{k} = b$ then $\sqrt{-k} = \sqrt{k} \times \sqrt{-1} = b\mathrm{i}$.

So any **imaginary number** can be written in the form $b\mathrm{i}$, where b is real.

index number

An index number is used to compare the growth of some measurable quantity by studying the multiplier needed to make the new value from the old one. The old value is referred to as the base value and all subsequent values are measured by comparison with that.
• *Index numbers are frequently used in economics, for example the Consumer Prices Index or Retail Prices Index.*

⚠ **WATCH OUT**

Take care: an **index number** (which is a multiplier) should not be confused with **index notation** (where the index is an exponent).

irrational number

An irrational number can only be written in number form (using no symbols) as a never-ending, non-repeating decimal fraction. An irrational number cannot be written in the form of a rational number.

EXAMPLE:

1.23456789101112 ... is an **irrational number**. To generate this number it is only necessary to write out the natural numbers and it could go on forever without repeating.

The square root of any prime number is an **irrational number**.

π and e are both **irrational numbers**.

mixed number

A mixed number is a number made up of two parts: a whole number followed by a proper fraction.
• *$1\frac{1}{2}$, $5\frac{7}{8}$, and $-2\frac{5}{6}$ are all **mixed numbers**.*

natural number (*also* counting number)

A natural number is a member of the set of numbers 1, 2, 3, 4, 5, 6, ... as used in counting. It is a matter of choice whether 0 is included or not.
• *$\mathbb{N}$ is the symbol for the set of all **natural numbers**.*

negative number

A negative number is a real number less than 0.

odd number

An odd number is a whole number which, when divided by 2, has a remainder of 1.
• *17, 243, and 8,645 are all **odd numbers**.* • *Any number which ends in 1, 3, 5, 7, or 9 must be **odd**.*

ordinal number

An ordinal number is a natural number used to describe the 'position' of an object in a set which is arranged in order.
• *The most common **ordinal numbers** are first, second, third, etc.*

In this statement eighth and six are used as **ordinal numbers**:

The set C N B I Z K F R G has R as the eighth letter and in position six there is a K.

perfect number

A perfect number is a number whose proper factors add up to the number itself.

6 is a perfect number since $1 + 2 + 3 = 6$.

28 is a perfect number since $1 + 2 + 4 + 7 + 14 = 28$.

The next three perfect numbers are 496, 8,128, and 33,550 336.

No odd perfect numbers are known.

polite number

A polite number is a number made by adding together two or more consecutive whole numbers.
• $15 = 1 + 2 + 3 + 4 + 5$ and $4 + 5 + 6$ and $7 + 8$, so 15 is a **polite** number.

positive number

A positive number is a real number greater than 0.

prime number prime

A prime number is a number with two, and only two, factors.
• 1 is not a **prime number** since it only has one factor.

coprime, Mersenne prime

rational number

A rational number is a number written in the form $\frac{a}{b}$ where a and b are both integers and b is not zero.
• $\mathbb{Q}$ is the symbol for the set of all **rational numbers**.

$-4.5 \qquad 1\frac{1}{3} \qquad 0.0909090909 \ldots \qquad 3.14285\dot{7} \qquad 8$

are all **rational numbers** since they can be re-written as

$\dfrac{-9}{2} \qquad \dfrac{4}{3} \qquad \dfrac{1}{11} \qquad \dfrac{22}{7} \qquad \dfrac{8}{1} \qquad$ respectively.

real number

A real number is a number that is either rational or irrational.
• $\mathbb{R}$ is the symbol for the set of all **real numbers**.

transcendental number

A transcendental number is any irrational number which is not algebraic.
• The best known **transcendental numbers** are π and e.

whole number

A whole number is a number which has no fraction attached. Whole number is sometimes used to mean a natural number and sometimes to mean an integer, depending on the context.
• 8, 13, 207 are **whole numbers**. • 2.5 is not a **whole number**.

WORD BUILD

integer (also directed number, signed number)

An integer is any natural number or zero with or without a negative sign in front of it.
• The **integers** are: ..., $-5, -4, -3, -2, -1, 0, 1, 2, 3, 4, 5, \ldots$ • $\mathbb{Z}$ is the symbol for the set of all **integers**. • The set of positive integers is the set of all integers not including negative numbers or zero.

Gaussian integer

A Gaussian integer is a complex number in which both the real and imaginary parts are whole numbers.

$3 + 8i$ and $10 + 2i$ are **Gaussian integers**.

$7.6 + 5i$ is not.

number base (*also* **base**)

The base of a place-value number system controls the relationship between the places. Usually it is also the number of different symbols used in that system.

WORD BUILD

binary

A binary number system uses a base of 2.

EXAMPLE:

In **binary**, the two symbols used to make numbers are 0 and 1.

Numbers in **binary** look like 1001101 ($\equiv$ 77 in decimal).

decimal (*also* denary)

A decimal number system uses a base of 10. This is the system used in ordinary arithmetic.
* *In **decimal**, the 10 symbols used to make numbers are 0, 1, 2, 3, 4, 5, 6, 7, 8, and 9*

duodecimal

A duodecimal number system uses a base of 12.

hexadecimal

A hexadecimal number system uses a base of 16. This system is used widely in computer work.

EXAMPLE:

In **hexadecimal**, the sixteen symbols used are 0, 1, 2, 3, 4, 5, 6, 7, 8, 9, A, B, C, D, E, and F.

To signal that a **hexadecimal** number is intended, it is usually prefaced with the symbol &.

The largest two-symbol number in the **hexadecimal** system is &FF, which is 255 in decimal.

octal

An octal number system uses a base of 8. This system is used in some computer work.
* *In **octal**, the eight symbols used are 0, 1, 2, 3, 4, 5, 6, and 7.*

ternary

A ternary number system uses a base of 3.
* *In **ternary**, the three symbols used are 0, 1, and 2.*
* *Numbers in **ternary** look like 1020211 ($\equiv$ 913 in decimal).*

number line

A number line is a graduated straight line along which it is possible (in theory) to mark all the real numbers.

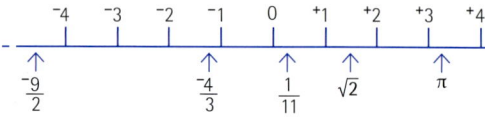

number pattern *see* pattern

number system

A number system is made up of a set of defined symbols and the numbers they represent, together with rules for forming larger numbers from those symbols.

SEE ALSO number base

additive number system

a number system in which the bigger numbers are formed by using enough of the basic symbols to add up to the number required
* *With **additive number systems** the symbols can be placed in any order; it is only necessary to make clear to which group, or number, each symbol belongs.*

place-value number system

a number system in which the positions of the symbols affect the overall value of the number. Place-value number systems have a base.
* *In a **place-value system**, the symbol 3 in the number 7,361 has a value of 3–hundreds, but in the number 4,138 it has a value of 3–tens.*

Babylonian number system

The Babylonians used a mixture of an additive number system, with some subtraction, and a place-value system with a base of 60.
• *The Babylonian number system needed only three symbols: for 1, 10, and subtraction.*

Egyptian number system

In ancient Egypt they used an additive number system, using the following symbols

$| \equiv 1$ $\cap \equiv 10$ $9 \equiv 100$ $\equiv 1,000$ $\equiv 10,000$

EXAMPLE:

$\equiv 5 + 30 + 200 + 1,000 = 1,235$

Greek number system

Ancient Greeks used an additive number system, using their alphabet as number symbols.
• *σ π θ is 200 + 80 + 9 ≡ 289*

Hindu–Arabic number system

The Hindu-Arabic number system is the number system which is now used for ordinary arithmetic. The symbols are the digits 0 to 9.

Roman number systems

Romans mainly used an additive number system, with a little subtraction.
• *The Roman number system used the symbols I, V, X, L, C, D, and M to represent the numbers 1, 5, 10, 50, 100, 500, and 1,000. • Symbols in the Roman number system had to be written in size order from left to right, but if a smaller one preceded a larger one then the smaller had to be subtracted from the larger; this could only be applied to an adjacent pair of symbols.*

EXAMPLE:

III ≡ 3

IV (1,5 so 5 − 1) ≡ 4

XCV (10, 100, 5, so 100 − 10 + 5) ≡ 95

CCCXX ≡ 320

MCMXLIV ≡ 1,944

MMXX ≡ 2,020

number theory

is a branch of mathematics which is concerned only with the study of numbers. It includes matters such as types of numbers (primes, squares, etc.) and their occurrence and relationship to each other, how number systems work, the effect of using different bases, and the development and improvement of arithmetic processes.
• *A much used tool in **number theory** is modulo arithmetic. • **Number theory** mainly deals with positive whole numbers, but work is often extended to other sorts of number (negatives, irrationals, etc.) and algebraic ideas are used to find and prove many of the results.*
SEE ALSO **modulus, number base, number system**

numeral *see* digit

numerator

The numerator is the top number in a common fraction.
• *In the fraction $\frac{8}{9}$, 8 is the **numerator**, 9 is the denominator.*
SEE ALSO **denominator**

numerical data *see* data

Oo

object

❶ An object of an operation is something that is being processed. In the operations of addition, subtraction, multiplication, and division the objects being processed are numbers.

❷ The object of a transformation is the original shape before the transformation is applied.

SEE ALSO image

....

oblique

Oblique lines are sloping or slanting. They are not horizontal or vertical.

....

oblique circular cone *see* cone

....

oblique pyramid *see* pyramid

....

oblong

An oblong is a rectangle in which one pair of edges is longer than the other pair. It has two lines of symmetry and rotational symmetry of order 2. Both diagonals are the same length and bisect each other.

....

obtuse angle *see* angle

....

obtuse triangle *see* triangle

....

octal *see* number base

....

odd number *see* number

....

odds

are a type of probability.

• The **odds** against a successful outcome happening are written as 'number (of other outcomes in the activity)' to 'number (of ways outcome can happen)'.

EXAMPLE:

The **odds** against getting a 3 with a single die are 5 to 1 since there are five other numbers and only one 3, so there are five ways of losing against only one way of winning.

The probability of getting a 3 is $\frac{1}{6}$ or $\frac{1}{5+1}$

FORMULA:

Odds of a to b equal a probability of $\frac{b}{(a+b)}$

A probability of $\frac{a}{b}$ converts to odds of $(b-a)$ to a.

....

odd vertex *see* vertex

....

offset

An offset is a line, and its measurement, which is taken off at right-angles to a base line.

• *The table shows the economical way in which all the measurements can be recorded.*

84	30
60	50
48	20
34	20
26	28
14	15

EXAMPLE:

The diagram shows a thick blue base line with thin blue **offsets** and their lengths, used to fix the position of the black line which represents the boundary of the space being surveyed.

The figures along the base line give the distance from one end.

The trapeziums formed in this method help in calculating the area.

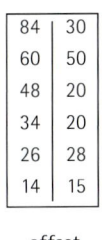

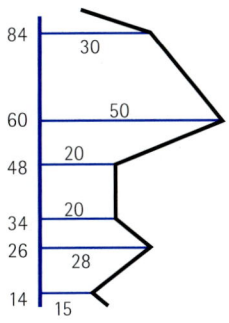

offset

binary operation

A binary operation is an operation which combines two objects to produce a third.
• *Addition, subtraction, multiplication, and division are all **binary operations**, since they all require two numbers from which a third number is made.*

unary operation

A unary operation is an operation requiring only one object to work on from which it produces another.
• *Finding the square root of a number is a **unary operation**.*

ogee (*also* **sigmoid**)
An ogee is a shallow S-shaped curve often used in the ornamentation of arches and ceilings, especially in buildings dating from classical times.

ogive
An ogive is the name sometimes given to a cumulative frequency diagram where the curve is usually in the shape of an ogee.

one-dimensional pattern *see* **pattern**

one-to-many correspondence
see **correspondence**

one-to-one correspondence
see **correspondence**

operation
An operation is a rule or body of rules for processing one or more objects. The most basic operations of arithmetic are those of addition, subtraction, multiplication, and division. The objects being processed are numbers.
• *In mathematics generally the **operations** can be much more complex and the objects are usually algebraic in form.*
SEE ALSO **order**

operator
An operator is the symbol used to show the operation that is to be done.
• *The symbols* $+ - \times \div$ *are all **operators**.*

opposite isometry *see* **isometry**

order
❶ The order of a matrix is a measure of its size. It is stated as 'the number of rows by the number of columns'.
• *This is a 2 by 4 matrix:* $\begin{pmatrix} 7 & -6 & 0 & 7 \\ 9 & 1 & 8 & 3 \end{pmatrix}$
❷ The order of a vertex is a number which states how many edges are joined to that vertex.

ordered pair
An ordered pair is the two numbers, written in a particular order, needed to give the position of a point in the Cartesian coordinate system. The convention is to give the x-number first, and the y-number second.
• *The point where the two axes cross is identified by the **ordered pair** (0, 0).*
SEE ALSO **coordinate, ordinate, origin**

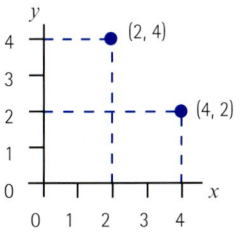

»

A B C D E F G H I J K L M N O P Q R S T U V W X Y Z

ordered triple

An ordered triple is the three numbers, written in a particular order, needed to give the position of a point in three-dimensional space.

order of magnitude

Two values are said to be of the same order of magnitude if their difference is small in relation to the size of the numbers being compared.

• *The phrase* **order of magnitude** *is generally used with large numbers.*

SEE ALSO **magnitude**

EXAMPLE:

32 million and 35 million have a difference of 3 million but, as this is less than 10% of either of them, it could be said that they are of the same **order of magnitude**.

order of operations

In arithmetic, the order of operations is the established order in which operations must be done. Anything in brackets has to be done first, then division and multiplication, and then addition and subtraction. This order is commonly known as BIDMAS.

• *The* **order of operations** *is necessary because it is possible to get different answers from the same expression according to the order in which the operations are done.*

SEE ALSO **BIDMAS**

EXAMPLE:

From the expression $2 + 4 \times 3 - 1$:

working from left to right $(+ \times -)$ gives 17

using $(+ - \times)$ gives 12

using $(\times + -)$ gives 13

using $(- \times +)$ gives 10

order of rotational symmetry
see **rotational symmetry**

ordinal number *see* **number**

ordinate

The ordinate of a point in Cartesian coordinates is its distance from the x-axis, as measured on the y-axis. It is the value of the second number in the ordered pair for that point.

• *The* **ordinate** *of the point shown in the image is 3.*

SEE ALSO **coordinate, ordered pair**

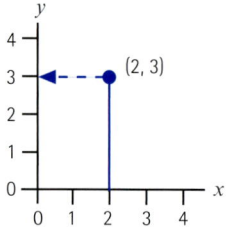

origin

The origin in the Cartesian coordinate system is the point where the two axes cross. It is the point identified by the ordered pair (0, 0).

SEE ALSO **coordinate**

orthocentre

The orthocentre of a triangle is the point at which its three perpendiculars (extended if necessary) cross.

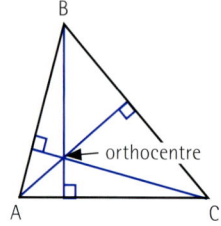

orthocentre of acute triangle ABC

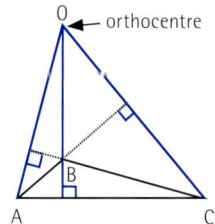

orthocentre of obtuse triangle ABC

orthogonal

❶ another word for perpendicular

❷ Two intersecting circles are said to be orthogonal if, at their two points of intersection, their circumferences cross at right angles to each other. At the point of intersection, the radius of one circle will be perpendicular to that of the other.

EXAMPLE:

The circle centred at A with a radius of r will be **orthogonal** to the circle centred at B with a radius of R if the distance $AB = \sqrt{R^2 + r^2}$

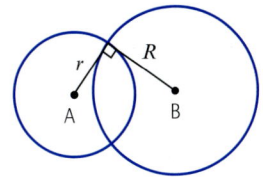

. . . .

orthogonal vector *see* **vector**

. . . .

outcome

An outcome is the actual result of an activity. It is sometimes called an event.

SEE ALSO **event**

. . . .

overhead

An overhead is a cost involved in running a business which is not directly connected with the products being handled by that business.

• *Items such as rent, council tax, heating, lighting, administration, and research would be classed as **overheads** for a shop selling books.*

. . . .

Pp

P, Q

In logic, P and Q are symbols used to represent statements.

SEE ALSO **condition**

➤ $P \Leftarrow Q$ is a symbolic way of saying 'P is implied by Q'; or 'when Q is true, then so also is P'; or 'P is a necessary condition for Q'. It also means that Q is a sufficient condition for P.

• *If P is 'x is divisible by 5', and Q is 'x is divisible by 10', then $\mathbf{P \Leftarrow Q}$.*

➤ $P \Rightarrow Q$ is a symbolic way of saying 'P implies Q'; or 'when P is true then so is Q'; or 'P is a sufficient condition for Q'. It also means that Q is a necessary condition for P.

• *If P represents 'x is a prime number greater than 2', and Q represents 'x is an odd number', then $\mathbf{P \Rightarrow Q}$.*

➤ $P \Leftrightarrow Q$ is a symbolic way of saying that P and Q must both be true (or false) together; or 'P implies and is implied by Q' or 'P is a necessary and sufficient condition for Q'.

• *If P is 'x is divisible by 6', and Q is 'x is divisible by 2 and 3', then $P \Rightarrow Q$ and $Q \Rightarrow P$ so $\mathbf{P \Leftrightarrow Q}$.*

. . . .

pair of dividers *see* **dividers**

. . . .

palindrome

A palindrome is a number or word which is unchanged whether it is read from left to right or from right to left.

• *77, 565, 34843, and 1962691 are all **palindromes**.*

➤ **palindromic** A palindromic number or word reads the same from left to right as from right to left.

. . . .

pandigital

A pandigital number or expression is one which contains each of the digits 1 to 9 (or 0 to 9) once and once only.

• *26 + 48 + 79 = 153 is a **pandigital** expression.*

• *139,854,276 and 9,814,072,356 are **pandigital** squares.*

. . . .

pantograph

A pantograph is an instrument used to copy drawings while making them either smaller or

a
b
c
d
e
f
g
h
i
j
k
l
m
n
o
p
q
r
s
t
u
v
w
x
y
z

bigger but always keeping them similar to the original.

EXAMPLE:

In the outline drawing of a **pantograph**, the 4 links AQ, AF, CF, BC are joined together at A, B, C, and F, but are free to swivel at those points. Point F is held still.

$AF = BC$ and $AB = FC$

If the lines of the diagram to be copied are followed by point P, then point Q will trace out an enlargement of the original diagram.

A reduction can be made by changing over the roles of P and Q.

The scale of the enlargement or reduction can be changed by altering the relative positions of P and Q along their respective links.

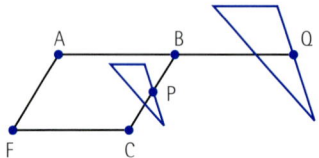

----

parabola *plural* **parabolas, parabolae**
A parabola is the locus of a point that moves in such a way as to be always the same distance from a focus as it is from a directrix. Once the focus and the directrix are fixed, only one parabola is possible.
• *A parabola may be drawn as a graph using the equation $y = ax^2$ where a is a constant.*

SEE ALSO directrix, locus

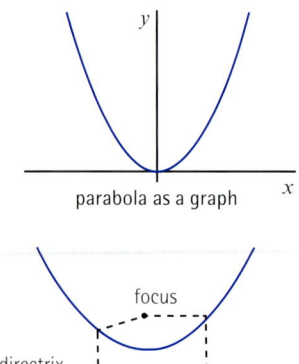

parabola as a graph

parabola as a locus

paraboloid
A paraboloid is a three-dimensional shape which is produced by rotating a parabola about its axis of symmetry.

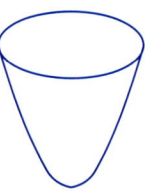

circular paraboloid
a paraboloid in which all cross-sections perpendicular to the axis of symmetry are circles
• *Circular paraboloids are the simplest type of paraboloid. Wine glasses are circular paraboloids.*

FORMULA:

Volume of circular paraboloid $= \dfrac{\pi d^2 h}{8}$

where

d is the diameter of the circular end

h is the height of paraboloid

elliptic paraboloid
a paraboloid in which all cross-sections perpendicular to the axis of symmetry are ellipses

hyperbolic paraboloid
a paraboloid in which all cross-sections perpendicular to the axis of symmetry are hyperbolas

----

paradox
A paradox is a valid statement which is self-contradictory or appears to be wrong. Paradoxes are important to the development of logic systems.

EXAMPLE:

The Potato **paradox** presents a problem with a counter-intuitive answer as follows:

Fred brings home 100 kg of potatoes, which (being purely mathematical potatoes) consist of 99% water. He then leaves them outside overnight so that they consist of 98% water. What is their new weight?

The surprising answer is 50 kg.

parallel

Two or more lines, which must lie in the same plane, are said to be parallel if, no matter how far they are extended in either direction, they are always the same distance apart.
• *Usually only straight lines are said to be **parallel**, but it can be applied to curves that remain a constant distance apart.*

parallelepiped

A parallelepiped is a solid having six faces, each of which is a parallelogram. Opposite faces are parallel.
• *A cuboid is a special case of a **parallelepiped** where each of the faces is a rectangle.*

SEE ALSO rhombohedron

FORMULA:

Volume of parallelepiped = area of one face × the perpendicular distance between that face and the opposite face

parallelogram

A parallelogram is a quadrilateral which has two pairs of parallel edges. It has a rotational symmetry of order 2, and its diagonals bisect each other. Usually one pair of edges is longer than the other pair, no interior angle is a right angle, and it has no lines of symmetry.

FORMULA:

Area of a parallelogram = base × perpendicular height

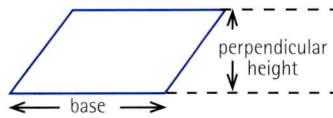

perpendicular height

base

parallel ruler *see* ruler

parallel vector *see* vector

parametric equation

Parametric equations are those that link two or more variables, not directly, but by expressing them in terms of equations using another variable that is common to all the equations.

EXAMPLE:

A parabola can be described as $y = x^2$.

This can be turned into the **parametric equations** $x = t$, $y = t^2$.

An ellipse can be described using the following **parametric equations**:

$x = a \cos t$, $y = b \sin t$

where

a and b are the radii of major and minor axes.

parity

The parity of a number refers to the fact of it being either even or odd.
• *The numbers 4 and 10 have the same **parity** (both even).* • *3, 7, and 15 have the same **parity** (all odd).* • *5 and 8 are of opposite **parity** (5 is odd and 8 is even).*

partial fraction

If an algebraic fraction can be simplified to become a sum of fractions with simple denominators, those simpler fractions are called partial fractions.

EXAMPLE:

$\dfrac{5x - 1}{x^2 - x - 2} \equiv \dfrac{3}{x - 2} + \dfrac{2}{x + 1}$ has two partial fractions on the right-hand side.

partial sum

A partial sum of an infinite series is found by using only a finite number of terms. The starting and finishing terms to be used are indicated by the n values written respectively below and above the summation sign.
• $\displaystyle\sum_{n=1}^{n=7} n$ *means* $1 + 2 + 3 + 4 + 5 + 6 + 7 = 28$

partition

❶ To partition a number is to break it up into a separate set of numbers which add up to make the original number. Whole numbers are used. The number itself is included but zero is not.

EXAMPLE:

4 can be **partitioned** in five different ways:

1 + 1 + 1 + 1

1 + 1 + 2

1 + 3

2 + 2

4

❷ A set of numbers made when partitioning a number is called a partition.
• *Reordering the set does not constitute a different partition.*
❸ A partition is an act of division when something is physically divided or shared out.

SEE ALSO quotition

Pascal's triangle

is an array of numbers in the shape of a triangle, having a 1 at the top and also at the ends of each line. All the other numbers are made by adding the pair of numbers closest to them in the line above.

EXAMPLE:

The picture shows a **Pascal's triangle**. You can see, for example, in the lines 5 and 6 from the top:

1 + 4 = 5

4 + 6 = 10

6 + 4 = 10

4 + 1 = 5

```
              1
            1   1
          1   2   1
        1   3   3   1
      1   4   6   4   1
    1   5  10  10   5   1
  1   6  15  20  15   6   1
```

pattern

a set of objects or elements arranged in order according to a rule. Repetition underlies all patterns.

frieze pattern (*also* border pattern, strip pattern)

A frieze pattern is a spatial pattern which 'grows' in one dimension only, and which can be mapped onto itself. There are just seven different frieze patterns and the picture shows all of them. Each pattern starts with the same motif. All patterns can be mapped onto themselves by means of a translation.
• *The only possible rotation for a frieze pattern is a half-turn.*

SEE ALSO motif

translation only

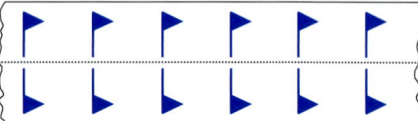

reflection in horizontal mirror line

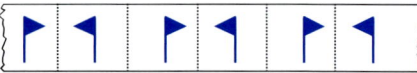

reflection in vertical mirror line

half-turn rotation (about any one of the dots)

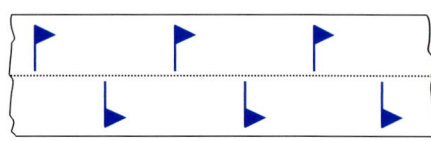

glide reflection (using mirror line)

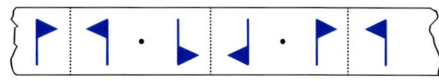

reflection in vertical mirror lines OR half turn rotation

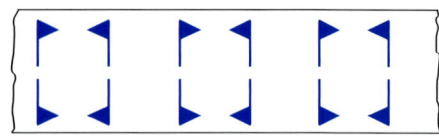

all transformations can be used to
map this pattern on to itself

number pattern

A number pattern is a set of numbers arranged according to a rule or rules involving repetition.
• *Number patterns are usually different from spatial patterns in that they do not have a motif.* • *Number patterns can be found in many sequences and arrangements such as Pascal's triangle.*

one-dimensional pattern

A one-dimensional pattern is a pattern which grows in only one dimension, such as a frieze pattern.

spatial pattern

A spatial pattern is an arrangement of objects or elements in space according to a rule or rules involving repetition.

three-dimensional pattern

A three-dimensional pattern is a pattern having three dimensions which can be mapped onto itself.
• *There are 230 different **three-dimensional** patterns. They play an important part in the scientific study of crystals.*

two-dimensional pattern

A two-dimensional pattern is a pattern which grows in two dimensions, such as a wallpaper pattern.

wallpaper pattern

A wallpaper pattern is a spatial pattern which 'grows' in two dimensions and the pattern can be mapped onto itself. The only possible rotations for a wallpaper pattern are through 180°, 120°, 90°, and 60°.
• *There are only 17 different **wallpaper patterns**. Care needs to be taken in analysing these patterns so that the full extent of the motif is properly identified.*
SEE ALSO   **tiling**

Pearson's product-moment correlation coefficient (*also* PMCC)

is a measure of the linear correlation between two sets of data. The two sets must be matched by means of a mapping showing a one-to-one correspondence, meaning it can be displayed graphically as a scatter plot.
• *r is the symbol for this coefficient.*

EXAMPLE:

To calculate r first identify each piece of data in one set as x-values and the others as y-values, so that for each x-value there is a corresponding y-value, and there are n pieces of data in each set. Then:

A. Multiply matching x-values and y-values together; add them up; multiply by n.

B. Add up all x-values; add up all y-values; multiply the two results together.

C. Subtract result of B from A. This might be negative.

D. Square all x-values, add them up, multiply the total by n. Repeat for y-values.

E. Add together all x-values and square the total. Repeat for y-values.

F. Subtract the x-result in E from that in D. Repeat for y-results.

G. Multiply the two answers from F together and take the square root.

r = result from C ÷ result from G

Peaucellier's straight line mechanism

is a system of links devised in 1864 to enable a rotary motion to be changed into movement along a straight line.   »

EXAMPLE:

Peaucellier's mechanism uses a total of seven links: LR and LS which are equal in length; PR, PS, QR, and QS which are all equal in length; and OP which is equal in length to distance OL.

O and L are fixed in position.

As P turns in a circle about O, Q moves up and down in a straight line.

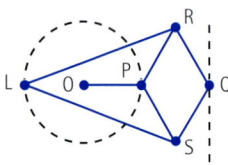

pedal triangle *see* **triangle**

pentomino *see* **polyomino**

per cent

A value given per cent means that the number stated is a measure of the number of parts in every 100 parts.
• *The symbol for* **per cent** *is* %. • *45* **per cent** *or 45% means 45 in every 100 or the fraction* $\frac{45}{100}$

percentage

A percentage is an amount or rate expressed as a value per cent.

SEE ALSO **reverse percentage**
➤ **percentage point** A percentage point is the value of the difference between two percentages.

⚠ **WATCH OUT**

A **percentage point** is not the same as the percentage change.

A report that 'The government reduced the interest rate of 5% by 1 **percentage point** means that the new rate is $(5 - 1)\% = 4\%$ and not 5% reduced by 1% (of 5%) to make it 4.95%.

percentage error *see* **error**

percentile

When a set of data is arranged in size order, the nth percentile is the value such that n% of the data must be less than or equal to that value; and n must be a whole number from 1 to 99.

EXAMPLE:

When the data (arranged in size order) is the set of numbers: 3.7, 4.5, 7.3, 8.3, 8.4, 9.6, 10.1, 10.8, 11.6, and 12.4, then the 30th **percentile** is 7.3.

Percentiles should only be used with large sets of data so that dividing it up into 100 equal parts (as the word 'percentiles' implies) seems realistic.

perfect number *see* **number**

perfect square *see* **square**

Perigal's dissection

is a visual way of illustrating Pythagoras' theorem.
• *In the diagram, cutting out and moving the necessary pieces shows how the square drawn on the hypotenuse AB is made up of the (blue) square drawn on the shorter edge AC plus the square drawn on the other edge BC which is divided into the four numbered quadrilaterals.*

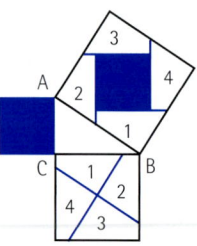

perigon *see* **angle**

perimeter

The perimeter of a shape is the total distance around the edges defining the outline of that shape.
• *The **perimeter** of a quadrilateral is found by adding together the lengths of its four edges.*

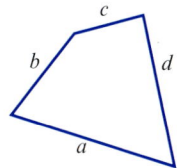

period

The period of a periodic decimal (a recurring decimal) is the number of digits which are repeated each time.
• *$0.\dot{1}4285\dot{7}$ has a **period** of 6.*

periodicity

The periodicity of a curve is a measure of the distance a curve goes before it repeats itself.
• *The sine and cosine curves both have a **periodicity** of 360°.* • *The tangent curve has a **periodicity** of 180°.*

periodic tiling *see* tiling

periodic variation *see* variation

per mil

A value given per mil means that the number stated is a measure of the number of parts in every 1000 parts.
• *‰ is the symbol for **per mil**.* • *68 **per mil** or 68‰ is the fraction $\frac{68}{1,000}$*

SEE ALSO per cent

permutation

A permutation of a set of objects is an ordered arrangement of those objects. The set of letters *ABC* has six **permutations**: *ABC, ACB, BAC, BCA, CAB,* and *CBA*. $^{n}P_{r}$ is the symbol for the total number of **permutations** possible when, from a set of *n* objects, *r* are chosen at a time.

FORMULA:

With *n* different objects:

There are *n*! permutations possible in total.

$$^{n}P_{r} = \frac{n!}{(n-r)!}$$

⚠ **WATCH OUT**

A **combination** and a **permutation** of a set of objects both mean an arrangement of those objects.

A **combination** is unordered which means that *ABC* is considered to be *the same as BCA* or *CAB* or *CBA*, etc.

A **permutation** is ordered which means that *ABC* is considered to be *different from BCA* or *CAB* or *CBA*, etc.

perpendicular (*also* orthogonal)

❶ Two straight lines (or planes) are said to be perpendicular to each other if, at their crossing or meeting, a right angle is formed.

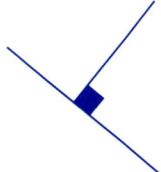

❷ A perpendicular line is a line which meets or crosses another line so as to form a right angle.
• *In ordinary (Euclidean) geometry, from any one given point to any one line only one* ***perpendicular*** *exists.*
❸ A perpendicular of a triangle is a line from a vertex to the opposite edge which is at right angles to that edge.
• *Any triangle has three* ***perpendiculars***, *and these three (extended if necessary) all cross at the same point, called the orthocentre.*

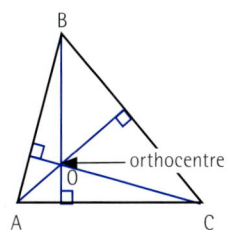

➤ **drop a perpendicular** To drop a perpendicular from a given point on to a given straight line is to draw a line from, or through, that point so that it forms a right angle with the line. It is assumed that the given point is not on the given line.
• *In the diagram we have* **dropped a perpendicular** *from point P onto the line XY.*

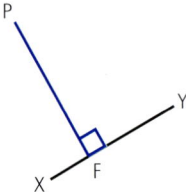

➤ **foot of a perpendicular** The foot of a perpendicular is that point at which it meets the line with which it forms a right angle.
• *In the diagram the* **foot of the perpendicular** *from P to XY is the point F.*

. . . .

perpendicular bisector *see* **bisector**

. . . .

perpendicular height (*also* **altitude**)
❶ The perpendicular height of a triangle is the length of a line from a vertex to the opposite edge and at right angles to that edge.
❷ The perpendicular height of a cone is the distance of its vertex above the plane of its base.
❸ The perpendicular height of a pyramid is the distance of its apex from the plane of its base.

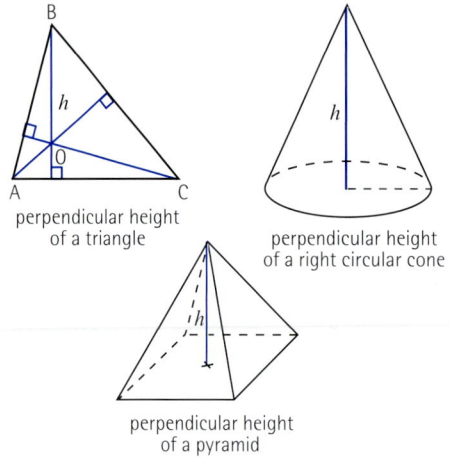

perpendicular height
of a triangle

perpendicular height
of a right circular cone

perpendicular height
of a pyramid

. . . .

perpendicular vector *see* **vector**

. . . .

persistence
The persistence of a number is measured in the following way: its digits are multiplied together to make another number. This process is continued on each new number until only a single digit is obtained. The number of times the process has to be repeated to achieve this is a measure of the persistence of the original number.
• *79 → 63 → 18 → 8 so 79 has a* **persistence** *of 3.*

. . . .

pi
Pi is a spelling out of the Greek letter π, the symbol used to represent a particular number that relates the radius or diameter of a circle to its area and circumference.
• *Pi is 3.142159 to 6 decinal places. It is an irrational number.*

FORMULA:

$$\frac{\text{circumference}}{\text{diameter}} = \pi$$

Circumference of a circle $= 2\pi r$

Area of a circle $= \pi r^2$

pi(n)
π(*n*) means the number of primes equal to, or less than, *n*.
• *π(13) is 6. The six primes are 2, 3, 5, 7, 11, and 13.*

. . . .

Pick's theorem
A grid of dots is marked out in a square array, then a polygon is drawn on this grid by joining up dots with straight lines to make the edges of the polygon, with none of these edges crossing.

FORMULA:

$$\text{Area} = \left(\frac{b}{2} + i - 1\right) \times u$$

where

b is the number of dots on the boundary of the polygon

i is the number of dots inside the polygon

u is the area of a unit square

EXAMPLE:

In the polygon shown, $b = 10$, $i = 4$

The area of the unit square (coloured black) $u = 1$

So the area of the polygon = $(5 + 4 - 1) \times 1 = 8$

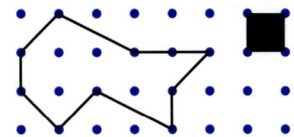

pictogram

A pictogram is a frequency diagram using a symbol to represent so many units of data. The symbol usually relates to the data being shown.

• *This **pictogram** shows the total number of computers owned in each class.*

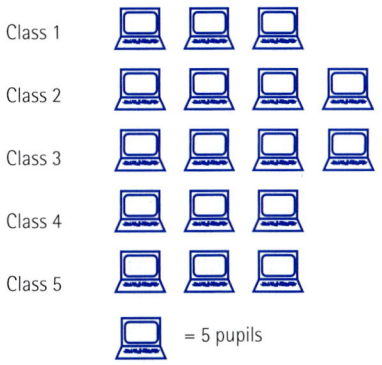

| Class 1 |
| Class 2 |
| Class 3 |
| Class 4 |
| Class 5 |

= 5 pupils

pie chart *see* **chart**

place-holder (*also* **zero**)

In a place-value sytem, a place-holder is necessary in order to know in which each of the other symbols should be placed, and so know its true value. The place-holder in the Hindu-Arabic number system is the symbol for zero (0).

• *In 3,024 the 3-symbol is valued at 3-thousands. If the **place-holder** 0 was left out as there were no hundreds, then 342 would value the 3-symbol at 3-hundreds.*

SEE ALSO **number system**

place value

The place value of a digit or symbol is the numerical value that it has by virtue of its position in a number.

• *In a system that uses **place value**, the symbol 3 in the number 7,361 has a value of 3-hundreds, but in the number 4,138 it has a value of 3-tens.*

SEE ALSO **number base, number system**

➤ **place-value headings** The column headings needed for any place-value system are fixed by the base used in that system.

• *In decimal (base 10), the **place-value headings** are units, tens, hundreds, thousands, and so on. Also tenths, hundredths, thousandths, and so on on the other side of the decimal point.* • *The table shows the **place-value headings** for other number systems where b is the value of the base.*

		b^3	b^2	b	units
binary	$b = 2$	8	4	2	1
ternary	$b = 3$	27	9	3	1
octal system	$b = 8$	512	64	8	1
decimal	$b = 10$	1,000	100	10	1
duodecimal	$b = 12$	1,728	144	12	1
hexadecimal	$b = 16$	4,096	256	16	1

place-value number system
see **number system**

plan

A plan drawing of an object is the two-dimensional horizontal view that is seen when the object is looked at from a position above the object and looking straight down.

• ***Plans** are usually drawn to scale so that measurements can be taken from them.*
• *The drawing shows a **plan** for a house. Compare these to the elevation drawings and isometric drawing elsewhere in the dictionary.*

SEE ALSO **elevation, isometric drawing**

a
b
c
d
e
f
g
h
i
j
k
l
m
n
o
p
q
r
s
t
u
v
w
x
y
z

plane

A plane surface is one where, if any two points on it are joined by a straight line, the line lies entirely on that surface. It is more commonly known as a flat surface.

➤ **planar** of or in the form of a plane

plane curve see curve

plane geometry see geometry

plane of symmetry

A plane of symmetry is a plane (flat surface) along which a mirror could be placed so that the reflection of a three-dimensional shape looks exactly the same as the part of the shape being covered up by the mirror.

• *A shape can have several **planes of symmetry**.*
• *The illustration shows the **plane of symmetry** for the shape in blue.*

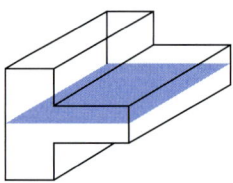

plane shape see shape

plane surveying see surveying

plane symmetry see symmetry

plane table survey see radial survey

plane vector see vector

planimeter

A planimeter is an instrument used for measuring the area of any shape on a plane drawing.

EXAMPLE:

The diagram shows the simplest type of **planimeter**.

PI and *IT* are two arms which are free to move. *P* is a fixed point. *T* is used to trace around the perimeter of the drawing.

The relative movements of the two arms as *T* moves is recorded by a unit fixed on the joint at *I*, known as the integrator, which then displays the size of the shaded area enclosed by *T*'s movements.

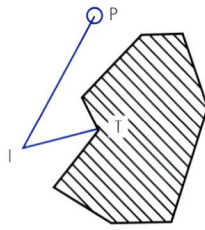

Platonic solid see solid

plumb line

A plumb line is a length of cord with a weight (usually made of lead) fastened at one end so that when the weight is allowed to hang freely, and is still, the cord will give a line which is vertical to the Earth's surface at that place.

PMCC see Pearson's product–moment correlation coefficient

point

A point indicates a position. In any work involving a point its size is ignored. It has no dimensions.

point of inflection

If, at a stationary point, the curve of $f(x)$ is neither a maximum nor a minimum then it is a point of inflection.

• *A **point of inflection** occurs at any point where the tangent to the curve crosses the curve.* • *In the diagram the blue dots are all stationary points, although **points of inflection** do not have to be stationary points.*

SEE ALSO **stationary point**

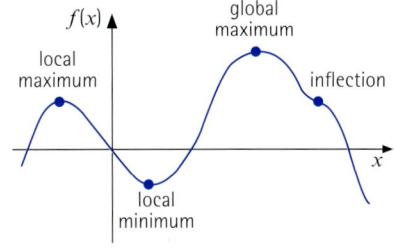

polite number *see* **number**

....

polycube

A polycube is a three-dimensional shape made from identical cubes joined together by their faces.

• ***Polycubes** are often used in puzzles.* • *The table shows the number of different shapes that can formed with a given number of **polycubes**. Note that there is no formula to govern this relationship.*

No. of cubes	1	2	3	4	5	6
No. of shapes	1	1	2	8	29	166

No. of cubes	7	8	9	10
No. of shapes	1,023	6,922	48,311	346,543

WORD BUILD

Soma cube

Soma cubes are the seven different polycubes that can be made from three or four cubes, with each shape having at least one concave edge.

• *It needs twenty-seven cubes to make all seven **Soma cubes**. They can be assembled to make models of a wide variety of objects, and can be used to make a cube in 240 different ways.*

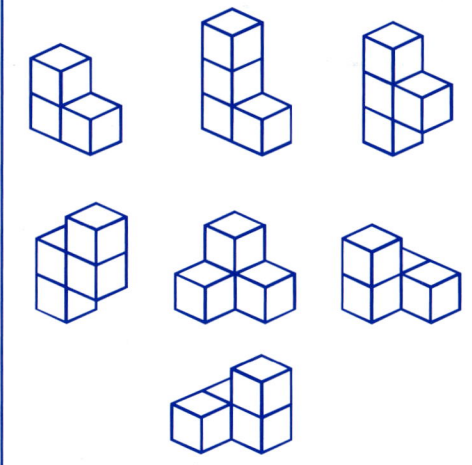

....

points of the compass *see* **compass**

....

point symmetry *see* **rotational symmetry**

....

Poisson distribution

The Poisson distribution has an asymmetrical frequency diagram. It relates to events which are unlikely to occur in a given time interval.

SEE ALSO **distribution**

....

polar axis *see* **axis**

....

polar coordinates *see* **coordinate**

....

pole

❶ A pole is a fixed point used in polar coordinates.

SEE ALSO **coordinate**

❷ A pole is one of two positions (one North, one South) on the Earth's surface through which the axis of rotation of the Earth passes.

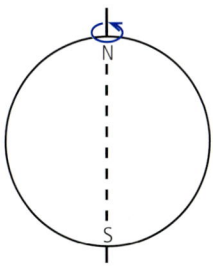

....

polygon *plural* polygons, polygona

A polygon is a flat shape completely enclosed by three or more straight edges. Usually edges are not allowed to cross one another.

• *Polygons are named by the number of edges or angles they have.* • *The word polygon is not often used for shapes having fewer than five edges.*

SEE ALSO **Reuleaux polygon, star polygon**

No. of edges	Name of polygon
3	triangle
4	quadrilateral
5	pentagon
6	hexagon
7	heptagon
8	octagon
9	nonagon
10	decagon
12	dodecagon

➤ **exterior angle of a polygon** The exterior angle of a polygon is the angle formed outside the polygon between any one edge and the edge adjacent to it, extended.

• *Size of exterior angle = 180° minus interior angle (it may be negative).* • *For any polygon, the sum of all the exterior angles is 360°.*

➤ **interior angle of a polygon** An interior angle is the angle formed inside a polygon between two adjacent edges.

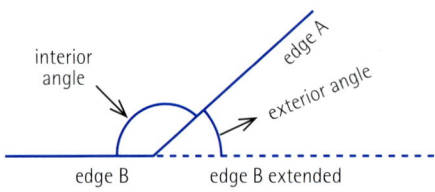

interior angle

edge A

exterior angle

edge B   edge B extended

concave polygon (*also* re-entrant polygon)

a polygon having at least one interior angle which is greater than 180°

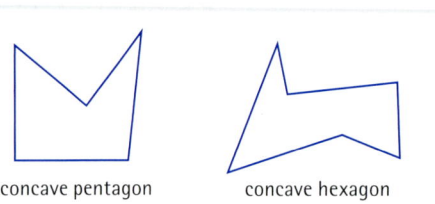

concave pentagon   concave hexagon

convex polygon

a polygon whose interior angles are all less than 180°. All regular polygons are convex.

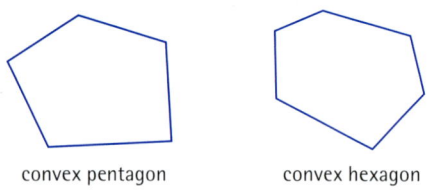

convex pentagon   convex hexagon

equiangular polygon (*also* isogon)

a polygon whose interior angles are all the same size

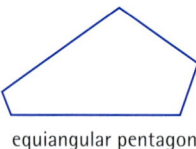

equiangular pentagon

equilateral polygon

a polygon whose edges are all the same length

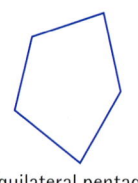

equilateral pentagon

regular polygon

a polygon which is both equilateral and equiangular

....

polygon number (*also* figurate number)

A polygon number is a number which states the quantity of objects needed for the objects to be arranged in the shape of a regular polygon with all the possible smaller similar polygons included in it.

• *A polygon number is named after the shape— triangle number, square number, etc—and a sequence can be formed of all the numbers which make that shape.* • $P_e (n)$ *is used to indicate a polygon number where e is the number of edges in the polygon and n is the number of objects along the length of one edge. n is also the position of the number in the sequence. The table shows some values of $P_e (n)$ for* *various values on n and e. • The images show **polygon numbers** and their growth. The blue dots show what is being added each time.*

FORMULA:

The general formula is:

$$P_e(n) = n\,[2 + (e - 2)(n - 1)] \div 2$$

name	e	$P_e(1)$	$P_e(2)$	$P_e(3)$	$P_e(4)$
triangle	3	1	3	6	10
square	4	1	4	9	16
pentagon	5	1	5	12	22
hexagon	6	1	6	15	28

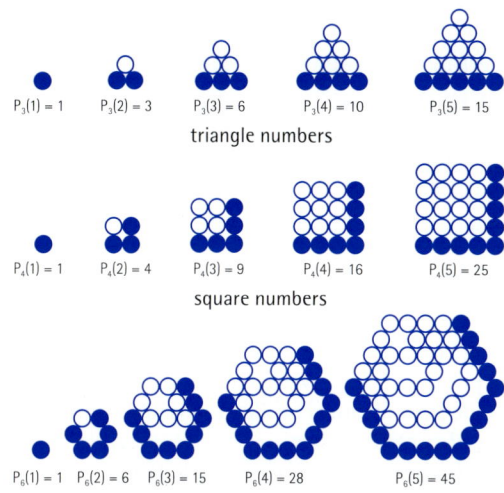

$P_3(1) = 1$ $P_3(2) = 3$ $P_3(3) = 6$ $P_3(4) = 10$ $P_3(5) = 15$

triangle numbers

$P_4(1) = 1$ $P_4(2) = 4$ $P_4(3) = 9$ $P_4(4) = 16$ $P_4(5) = 25$

square numbers

$P_6(1) = 1$ $P_6(2) = 6$ $P_6(3) = 15$ $P_6(4) = 28$ $P_6(5) = 45$

hexagon numbers

centred polygon number

One of the numbers made by taking e triangle numbers of the same size and adding 1.
• *The names of **centred polygon numbers** are determined by the value of e: centred triangle number, centred square number and so on.*
• $C_e(n)$ *is used to indicate a **centred polygon number**, where e is the number of edges in the polygon and n is the number of objects along the length of one edge.* • *The images show **centred polygon numbers** and their growth. The blue dots show what is being added each time.*

FORMULA:

The general formula is:

$$C_e(n) = [en(n - 1) \div 2] + 1$$

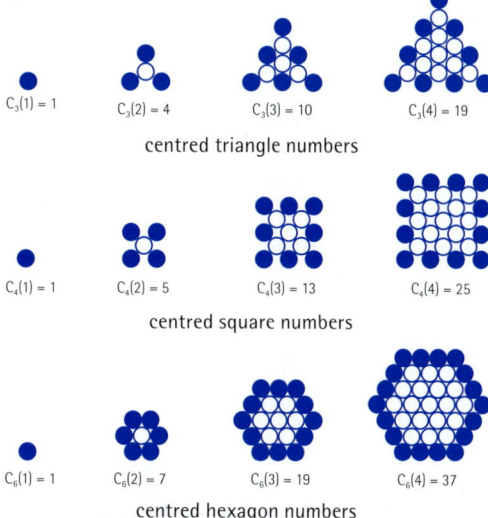

$C_3(1) = 1$ $C_3(2) = 4$ $C_3(3) = 10$ $C_3(4) = 19$

centred triangle numbers

$C_4(1) = 1$ $C_4(2) = 5$ $C_4(3) = 13$ $C_4(4) = 25$

centred square numbers

$C_6(1) = 1$ $C_6(2) = 7$ $C_6(3) = 19$ $C_6(4) = 37$

centred hexagon numbers

WORD BUILD

pyramid number

A pyramid number is made by adding together a consecutive set of polygon numbers, starting at 1 (all of them being the same shape).
• *The names of the **pyramid numbers** are inherited from the name of the polygon numbers making them: triangle pyramid numbers, square pyramid numbers and so on.* • *Using the triangle number series (1, 3, 6, 10, 15, 21, etc.), the **triangle pyramid numbers** 1, 4, 10, 20, 35, 56, and so on can be made.* • *An orderly stacking of **pyramid numbers** into the shape of a pyramid is only possible for the triangular and square types.*

FORMULA:

In any sequence of pyramid numbers based on a polygon having e edges, the nth number of the sequence is given by $n(n - 1)\,[e(n - 1) - 2n + 5] \div 6$

n	1	2	3	4	5	6	7	8
triangular pyramid	1	4	10	20	35	56	84	120
square pyramid	1	5	14	30	55	91	140	204
pentagonal pyramid	1	6	18	40	75	126	196	288
hexagonal pyramid	1	7	22	50	95	161	252	372

polygram

is the general name for puzzles which are similar to tangrams (puzzles requiring arrangements of 7 pieces of a square to make up a given shape) but which use a different dissection of the square or even a different hape altogether

• *The pictures show some varieties of **polygram** that have been commercially produced, with their names.*

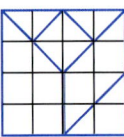

Pythagoras

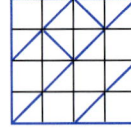

Chie No Ita

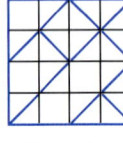

Tormentor

Cross breaker

. . . .

polyhedral formula (*also* Descartes–Euler polyhedral formula)

is a formula that connects the number of faces, edges and vertices of any simply connected polyhedron or polygon. It states that

FORMULA:

$$V + F - E = 2$$

where

V is the number of vertices

F is the number of faces

E is the number of edges

. . . .

polyhedron *plural* polyhedrons, polyhedra

A polyhedron is a three-dimensional shape whose faces are all polygons. It must have at least four faces.

• *The name of a **polyhedron** is based on the number of faces it has. For example, a tetrahedron has four faces. A pentahedron has five faces.*

convex polyhedron

A convex polyhedron is one in which any straight line joining one vertex to another lies entirely on or inside the polyhedron.

non–convex polyhedron

A non-convex polyhedron is one which is not convex.

regular polyhedron (*also* platonic solid)

A regular polyhedron has all of its faces identical, and the same number of edges meeting at each vertex. There are only nine possibilities, of which five are convex. These five are known as the platonic solids.

polyiamond

A polyiamond is a two-dimensional shape made from identical equilateral triangles joined together by their edges.

• ***Polyiamonds** are often used in puzzles.*

• *Each type of **polyiamond** is named from the number of triangles it uses: four triangles makes a tetriamond, five triangles makes a pentiamond and so on.*

WORD BUILD

hexiamond

Hexiamonds are the twelve different polyiamonds that can be made from six equilateral triangles.

• *The image shows the twelve **hexiamonds** with their names. All twelve can be combined to make a rhombus.*

regular polyhedrons

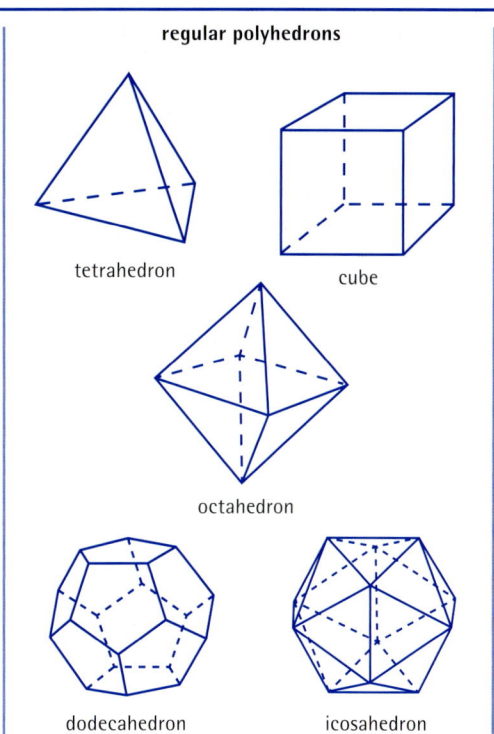

tetrahedron   cube

octahedron

dodecahedron   icosahedron

semi–regular polyhedron

A semi-regular polyhedron is a polyhedron of which every face is a regular polygon and every vertex is identical. Excluding prisms and antiprisms, there are only thirteen possibilities and these are known as the Archimedean solids.

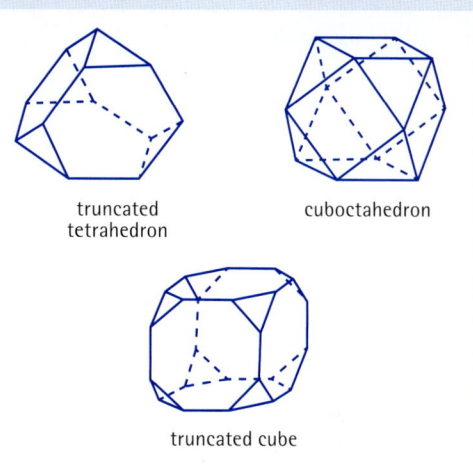

truncated tetrahedron   cuboctahedron

truncated cube

hexiamonds

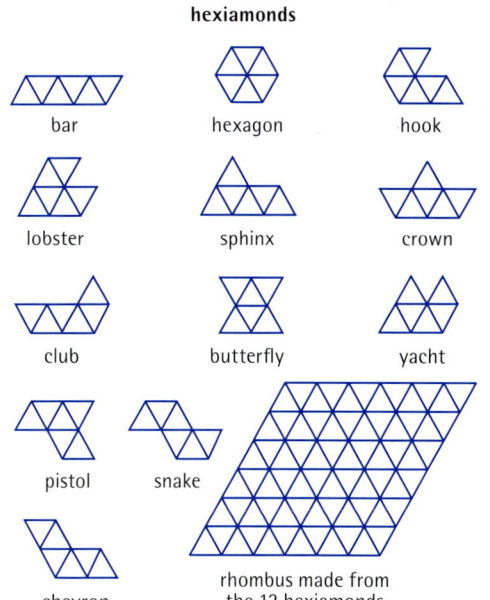

bar   hexagon   hook

lobster   sphinx   crown

club   butterfly   yacht

pistol   snake

chevron   rhombus made from the 12 hexiamonds

polynomial

A polynomial expression or polynomial is an expression made of two or more terms where each term consists of a coefficient and a variable or variables raised to some non-negative power which must be a whole number. The non-negative power could be zero.

• *$4x^3 - 5xy^2 + y^3 + 2$ is a **polynomial** but $x^2 + x^{-1}$ is not.*

SEE ALSO **multinomial**

. . . .

polyomino

A polyomino is a two-dimensional shape made from identical squares joined together by their edges.

• *Each type of **polyomino** is named from the number of squares it uses: four squares makes a tetromino, six squares makes a hexomino, and so on.* • *There is no formula to determine the number of different **polyominoes** that can be made with any given number of squares as shown in the table.* »

No. of squares	1	2	3	4	5	6
No. of shapes	1	1	2	5	12	35

No. of squares	7	8	9	10
No. of shapes	108	369	1,285	4,655

WORD BUILD

pentomino

Pentominoes are the twelve different polyominoes that can be made from five squares.
• *Each pentomino is named for a letter as shown in the illustration.*

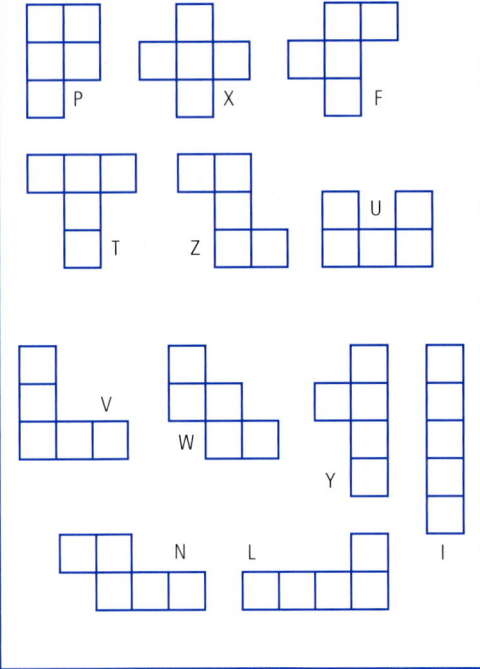

population pyramid

A population pyramid consists of two bar charts used 'back-to-back' to display two sets of data against a common base-line for purposes of comparison.
• *This population pyramid shows how many people there are in some of the given age-groups in the UK. The left-hand bar chart gives the figures for males, the right-hand one gives the figures for females.*

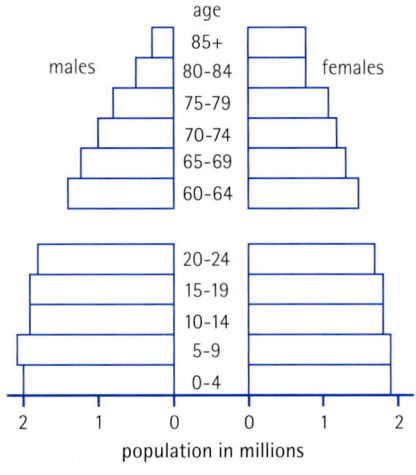

position

❶ The position of an object is where it can be found—its place or location.
• *A coordinates grid is used to find the position of objects drawn on a grid.*
SEE ALSO coordinate
❷ Position also describes the order in which objects or people are placed.
SEE ALSO order

position vector *see* vector

positive angle *see* angle

population

A population is the complete set of objects (values or people) which is being studied by some statistical method.

positive correlation *see* **correlation**

positive index *see* **index**

positive integer *see* **integer**

positively skewed *see* **skewed distribution**

positive number *see* **number**

possible
A possible outcome can happen.
SEE ALSO **probable**
➤ **possibility** A possibility is an outcome that
can happen.

postfix notation *see* **notation**

power *see* **index**

premise *see* **assumption**

primary data *see* **data**

prime factor *see* **factor**

prime number *see* **number**

principal
The principal is the amount of money involved
(usually at the start) in some transactions such as
lending, borrowing, or saving.
• *On opening an account with £250 there is a*
***principal** of £250.*

principal diagonal *see* **diagonal**

prism
A prism is a 3D shape with a regular cross section,
so that any plane cut made parallel
to the ends produces a cross-section the
same shape and size as the ends. All faces,
other than the ends, are rectangles or
parallelograms.
• ***Prisms** are named after the shape of the cross-
section (if it has a name) as in 'triangular prism'
or 'hexagonal prism'. • The volume of a **prism**
can be found by multiplying the area of one of
the end faces by the perpendicular distance between
the two ends.*

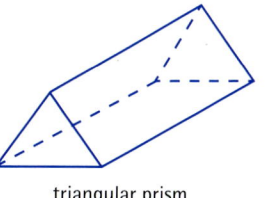

triangular prism

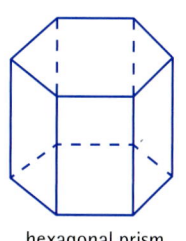

hexagonal prism

right prism

a prism whose faces, other than the ends,
are rectangles

prismoid
A prismoid resembles a prism in having
two polygonal end faces parallel to each
other, but they do not have to be identical,
though both must have the same number
of vertices.
• *All the other faces of a **prismoid** (which must be
plane or flat) will be rectangles, parallelograms
or trapeziums. • Corresponding vertex angles of the
two end faces will be equal, but the edge lengths
can be different. The cross-section will vary
in size.*   **»**

FORMULA:

$$\text{Volume of a prismoid} = \frac{h}{6}(A_1 + 4A_m + A_2)$$

where

h is the height (or length) between two ends

A_1 and A_2 are the areas of two end faces

A_m is the area of the cross-section midway between two ends

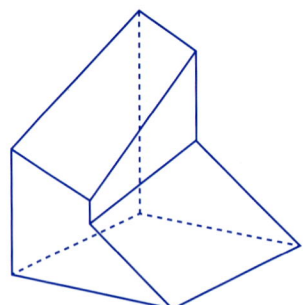

WORD BUILD

prismatoid

Like a prism and a prismoid, a prismatoid has two parallel end faces which are polygons but these two polygons do not have to have the same number of vertices. The faces connecting the two ends must be either triangles or quadrilaterals, with all vertices being coincident with one or other of the vertices of the two end faces.

....

probability

The probability of an outcome (or event) is a measure of how likely that outcome is. Probability may be given as a common fraction, a decimal fraction, or a percentage.
• *A **probability** value of 0 means an outcome is impossible, while 1 means it is certain. In all other cases the value must lie between 0 and 1.* • *P( ) or Pr( ) is the symbol for the **probability** of the outcome named in brackets.*

SEE ALSO odds, frequency

EXAMPLE:

The probability of getting heads when tossing a coin is P(heads) = $\frac{1}{2}$ or 0.5 or 50%.

conditional probability

is the probability of an outcome happening when it is dependent upon, or following, some other outcome.

EXAMPLE:

A bag contains eight red and two black counters.

The probability of drawing two red counters, if the first drawn is not replaced, is given by the probability of the first counter being red times the probability of the second being red.

$$P(\text{red, red}) = \frac{8}{10} \times \frac{7}{9} = \frac{28}{45}$$

theoretical probability

The theoretical probability of an outcome is the value predicted from the fraction given by

$$\frac{\text{Number of ways that named outcome(s) can happen}}{\text{Number of all possible outcomes which can be obtained from that activity}}$$

• *The **theoretical probablity** can only be calculated when the item(s) on which the activity is based (dice, cards, coins, etc.) have outcomes which are all equally likely.*

EXAMPLE:

The probability of rolling a 4 on a six-sided dice is P(4) = $\frac{1}{6}$ or 0.1̇6̇ or 16.6̇%

The probability of getting more than 4 is P(>4) = $\frac{2}{6}$ or 0.3̇ or 33.3̇%

The probability of getting 1, 2 or 5 is P(1,2,5) = $\frac{3}{6}$ or 0.5 or 50%

The probability of getting a 7 is P(7) = 0

....

probability scale

A probability scale is a line numbered 0 to 1 or 0 to 100% on which outcomes (or events) can be placed according to their probability.

....

probable

An outcome is described as probable if it is more likely to happen than not.

> ⚠ **WATCH OUT**
>
> Use **possible** to describe an event that is within the bounds of reason.
>
> Use **probable** to describe an event if the chance of it happening is a good one, or if it is more likely to happen than not.
>
> For example, you could say 'It is **possible** for me to roll a 6 six times in a row, but it is not **probable**.'

problem

In mathematics, a problem is something that can be represented, analysed, or solved using mathematical methods.

SEE ALSO Delian problem, Diophantine problem, ferry problem, four-colour problem, counting-out problem, Fermat's problem

produce

To produce a line means to extend it, or make it longer, in order to match certain conditions.
• *Produce the line AB so as to meet the line XY.*

product

The product is the result given by the operation of multiplication.
• *The product of 1.6 and 7 is 1.6 × 7 which is 11.2*
SEE ALSO scalar product, vector

continued product

A continued product is made by placing multiplication signs between the terms of a sequence.
• *Π is the symbol used to show that a continued product is being given.*

EXAMPLE:

$\prod_{n=1}^{n=7} n$ means $1 \times 2 \times 3 \times 4 \times 5 \times 6 \times 7 = 5{,}040$ and is another way of writing factorial n or $n!$, or in this case, 7!

profit

is a measure of the gain, usually financial gain, made in a transaction or enterprise. The profit could be a negative amount, in which case it is more generally known as a loss.

FORMULA:

Profit (%) $= \dfrac{(s - c)}{c \times 100}$

where

s is the selling price

c is the cost price

programmable calculator *see* **calculator**

projection

A projection is a representation in 2-dimensions of a 3-dimensional object. Three common projections are a plan (what a 3D object looks like from above), a front elevation (what it looks like from the font) and a side elevation (what it looks like from a side).
• *If a circle is held in a beam of light and the shadow is allowed to fall on a plane surface which is not parallel to the circle, the shadow (its **projection**) will be in the shape of an ellipse*

proof

A proof is a sequence of statements (made up of axioms, assumptions, and arguments) leading to the establishment of the truth of one final statement.

direct proof

A direct proof is a proof in which all the assumptions used are true and all the arguments are valid.

EXAMPLE:

To prove the proposition that adding two odd numbers makes an even number:

Any odd number is of the form $2n + 1$; (n is a whole number).

Adding two of this form produces $(2n + 1) + (2m + 1) = 2(n + m) + 2 = 2(n + m + 1)$, which is clearly even. **»**

indirect proof (also proof by contradiction, reductio ad absurdum)

An indirect proof is a proof in which one assumption is made. Then, using valid arguments, a statement is arrived at which is clearly false; so the original assumption must have been false.

• *Indirect proof can only be used in a system in which statements must be either true or false, so that proving the first assumption is false allows only one possibility for its alternative form, which must be true.*

EXAMPLE:

To prove $\sqrt{2}$ is irrational, first assume that it is rational.

Then $\sqrt{2} = \dfrac{a}{b}$, where a, b are whole numbers with no common factors.

This leads to $a^2 = 2b^2$, and a^2 must be even and so must be a.

Put $a = 2c$ then $\sqrt{2} = \dfrac{2c}{b}$ and $2c^2 = b^2$ and b must be even.

But a, b had no common factors so both cannot be even.

The assumption must be false and $\sqrt{2}$ is not rational.

Therefore $\sqrt{2}$ must be irrational.

proof by exhaustion

A proof by exhaustion is a proof which is established by working through every possible case and finding no contradictions.

• *Usually a proof by exhaustion is only possible if the proposition to be proved has some restrictions placed upon it.*

EXAMPLE:

The statement that 'Between every pair of square numbers there is at least one prime number' would be impossible to prove by looking at every possibility.

However, by writing it as 'Between every pair of square numbers less than 1,000 there is at least one prime number' it can be proved by exhaustion—looking at every case.

This might then be considered as enough evidence to make it a conjecture about all numbers.

proof by induction

A proof by induction is a proof which shows that if one particular case is true then so is the next one; it also shows that one particular case is true. From those two actions it must follow that all cases are true.

visual proof (also look–see proof)

A visual proof is a proof in which the statements are presented in the form of diagrams.

EXAMPLE:

The diagrams shown are used to prove the proposition that adding two odd numbers makes an even number.

Any odd number can be shown as the top part of the image.

Adding two odd numbers is shown below and clearly makes an even number.

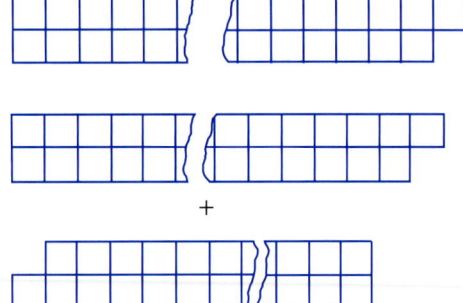

+

proper divisor *see* **factor**

. . . .

proper factor *see* **factor**

. . . .

proper fraction *see* **fraction**

. . . .

proper subset *see* **subset**

. . . .

property
A property of an object or, more usually
a group of objects, is some particular fact
which is true for that object or, all the objects
in the group.
• *It is a* **property** *of squares that their diagonals
cross at right angles.*

. . . .

proportion
One set of quantities is said to be in proportion
to another set if a mapping between the two
sets can be made either by using a constant
multiplier, or by matching the pairs from each
set so that their product is always the same
constant value.
• *∝ is the symbol for 'is in* **proportion** *to' and k is
used for the constant.*

> **direct proportion** (*also* **direct variation**)
>
> When two sets are in proportion using a
> constant multiplier so that an increase in one
> matches an increase in the other, they are said
> to be in direct proportion.
> • *The set {12, 20, 32} is in* **direct proportion** *to
> {3, 5, 8} and the constant multiplier is 4.*
> • *Even when interchanged, the two sets are still
> in* **direct proportion** *but the constant is now $\frac{1}{4}$.*
> • *$y \propto x$ – y is in proportion to x means y is in*
> **direct proportion** *to x; or y = kx where k is a
> numerical constant.*

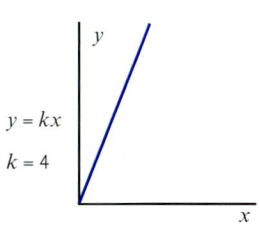

direct proportion

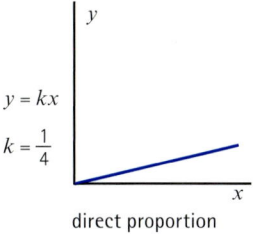

direct proportion

> **inverse proportion** (*also* **indirect variation**)
>
> When two sets are in proportion and an
> increase in one matches a decrease in the other,
> they are said to be in inverse proportion.
> • *The sets {40, 24, 15} and {3, 5, 8} are in*
> **inverse proportion** *to each other since 40 × 3 = 120,
> 24 × 5 = 120 and 15 × 8 = 120.*
> • *$y \propto \frac{1}{x}$ – y is in proportion to 1 over x means y
> is in* **inverse proportion** *to x; or $y = \frac{k}{x}$ where k is
> a numerical constant.*

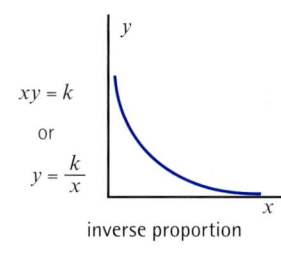

inverse proportion

. . . .

proposition
A proposition is a statement whose correctness
(or otherwise) is to be shown by the use of an
argument.
• *A* **proposition** *most often serves as an introduction
by saying, in effect, what the argument is going
to show.*

. . . .

a
b
c
d
e
f
g
h
i
j
k
l
m
n
o
p
q
r
s
t
u
v
w
x
y
z

pro rata

is a Latin term used to mean that something has to be changed or shared 'in proportion'.

EXAMPLE:

Two people buy something for £10, one paying £7 and the other £3.

They sell it for £20 and share the money pro rata according to what each paid, which gives them £14 and £6 respectively.

....

protractor

A protractor is an instrument made as a flat shape (usually a circle or semicircle of clear plastic) with a set of graduated marks, and is used for measuring angles.

• *The picture shows a common type of* ***protractor*** *with dual scales for measuring in either direction.*

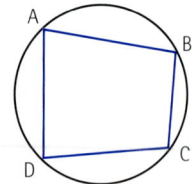

....

Ptolemy's theorem

states that, if ABCD is a cyclic quadrilateral (the vertices being lettered in order), then

$(AB \times CD) + (BC \times AD) = AC \times BD$.

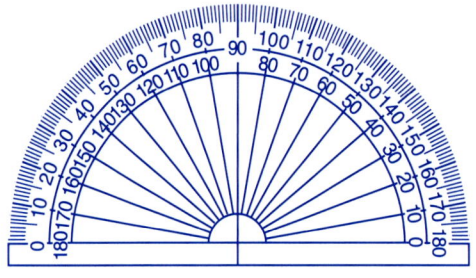

....

pyramid

A pyramid is a polyhedron having any polygon as one face, with all the other faces being triangles meeting at a common vertex. The pyramid is named after the polygon forming the face from which the triangles start.

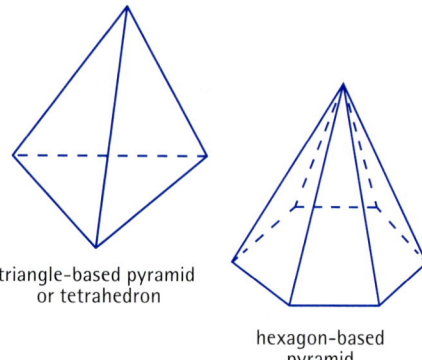

triangle-based pyramid
or tetrahedron

hexagon-based
pyramid

oblique pyramid

An oblique pyramid is a non-right pyramid.

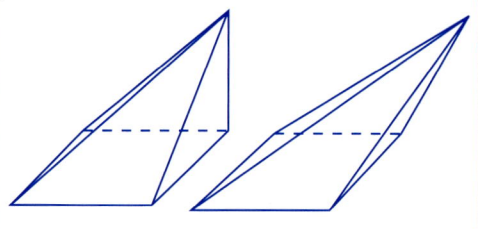

oblique pyramids

right pyramid

A right pyramid is one having all its triangular faces equal in size. The base is a regular polygon, the apex is perpendicularly above the centre of the base, and all the triangular faces make the same angle with the base.

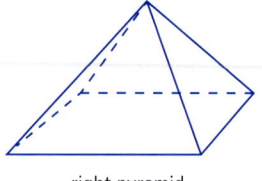

right pyramid

right square-based pyramid

A right square-based pyramid is a right pyramid having a square base. It is what is usually meant when only the word 'pyramid' is used and is the type seen in Egypt as a tomb of the Pharaohs.

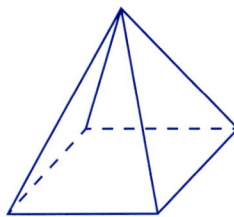

right square-based pyramid

· ·

pyramid number *see* **polygon number**

· ·

Pythagoras' theorem

states that, in any right-angled triangle, the area of the square drawn on the hypotenuse is equal to the total area of the squares drawn on the other two edges.

• *In the diagram, the area of square Z is equal to the areas of square X and square Y added together.*

FORMULA:

In terms of the edge lengths a, b, and c as shown in the right-angled triangle under trigonometric ratios:

$c^2 = a^2 + b^2$ or $a^2 = c^2 - b^2$ or $b^2 = c^2 - a^2$

where c must be the hypotenuse.

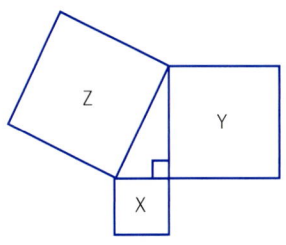

· ·

Pythagorean triplet

Pythagorean triplets are groups of three rational numbers (a, b, c) which satisfy the equation $a^2 + b^2 = c^2$.

FORMULA:

Choose two numbers m, n ($m > n$) with no common factors (except 1). Then:

$a = m^2 - n^2$

$b = 2mn$

$c = m^2 + n^2$

From any basic triplet, others can be made by multiplying each of its three numbers by some constant.

So (3, 4, 5) gives (6, 8, 10) or (21, 28, 35) and so on.

· ·

a
b
c
d
e
f
g
h
i
j
k
l
m
n
o
p
q
r
s
t
u
v
w
x
y
z

Qq

Q *see* **P, Q**

. . . .

quadrant

The two axes of a coordinate system divide the plane into four separate sections known as quadrants. These are identified as the first, second, third, and fourth quadrants as shown in the picture.

second 2nd	first 1st
third 3rd	fourth 4th

. . . .

quadratic equation (*also* **quadratic**)

A quadratic equation is an equation involving an expression, or expressions, containing a single variable, of degree 2.

EXAMPLE:

$$x^2 + 3x - 5 = 0$$

$$3(x + 1)^2 = 0$$

$$4x^2 - 3x + 4 = 0$$

➤ **roots of a quadratic** The two roots of a quadratic equation, when it is drawn as a graph, are indicated by the points at which the line of the graph crosses the x-axis.
• *If the line crosses the x-axis, the two x-values at those crossings are the* **roots** *of that quadratic.*
• *If the line touches, but does not cross, the x-axis, the two* **roots** *are equal and are referred to as a 'repeated* **root***'.* • *If the line does not cross or touch the x-axis, the* **roots** *are complex numbers.*

FORMULA:

If a quadratic equation can be put in the form $ax^2 + bx + c = 0$, then its roots can be found by using the formula:

$$x = \frac{-b \pm (b^2 - 4ac)}{2a}$$

EXAMPLE:

The graph shows that the roots of the quadratic equation $x^2 - x - 2$ are −1 and 2.

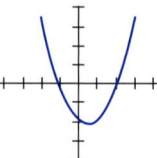

. . . .

quadratic graph *see* **graph**

. . . .

quadrature

The quadrature of a shape, usually one made of curves, is the process of making a square that is equal to it in area.
➤ **quadrature of the circle** (*also* **squaring the circle**) An unsolved problem for 2,000 years, squaring the circle challenged mathematicians to create a square the same area as a given circle using a geometrical construction. In 1882, it was proved that this was impossible.
SEE ALSO **geometrical construction**

. . . .

quadrilateral

A quadrilateral is a polygon which has four edges. Its four interior angles add up to 360 degrees.

cyclic quadrilateral

A cyclic quadrilateral is a quadrilateral around which a circle (known as the circumcircle for that quadrilateral) can be drawn to pass through all of its vertices. The opposite angles of a **cyclic quadrilateral** add up to 180 degrees.
• *Rectangles and isosceles trapeziums are always* **cyclic quadrilaterals**. • *Kites and irregular quadrilaterals are sometimes* **cyclic quadrilaterals**. • *The rhombus, parallelogram and arrowhead are never* **cyclic quadrilaterals**.

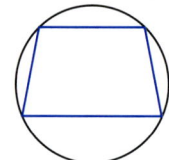 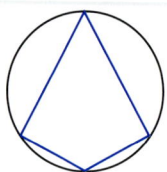

irregular quadrilateral

Strictly speaking, an irregular quadrilateral is any quadrilateral that is not a square, but it is usually taken to be one not having a special name.

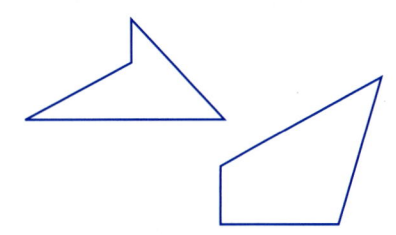

regular quadrilateral

another name for a square

quadrivium

In the Middle Ages the quadrivium was the four subjects arithmetic, geometry, astronomy, and music. Combined with the trivium (the three subjects grammar, rhetoric and logic) they formed the seven liberal arts, the basis of most university educations at that time.

qualitative data *see* **data**

quantitative data (*also* **quantitive data**)
see **data**

quartic (*also* **biquadratic**)

A quartic or biquadratic equation, expression, or function is one of degree 4.
• *$3x^4 - 5x^2 + 7$ is a* **quartic** *or* **biquadratic** *expression.*
SEE ALSO **cubic**, **quintic**

quartile

one quarter (25%) of a set of data arranged in size order
SEE ALSO **percentile**

lower quartile

The lower quartile of a set of data is the 25th percentile. One quarter (25%) of all the data must have a value of less than, or equal to, the value of the lower quartile.

EXAMPLE:

One method to find the lower quartile of a set of n terms is to find the value of $\frac{n+1}{4}$.

For the data set 7 11 15 17 20 21 22 23 28 30 31, $n = 11$.

$\frac{11+1}{4} = 3$, so the **lower quartile** is the 3rd value which is 15.

upper quartile

The upper quartile of a set of data is the 75th percentile. Three quarters (75%) of all the data must have a value that is less than, or equal to, the value of the upper quartile.

EXAMPLE:

One method is to find the upper quartile of a set of n terms is to find the value of $\frac{3(n+1)}{4}$.

For the data set 7 11 15 17 20 21 22 23 28 30 31, $n = 11$.

$\frac{3 \times (11+1)}{4} = 9$, so the **upper quartile** is the 9th value which is 28.

WORD BUILD

interquartile range

The interquartile range of a set of data is the difference in value between the lower and upper quartiles for that data. It is one way of measuring the dispersion of the data.
• *The* **interquartile range** *for the data set shown above is 28 − 15 = 13.*

semi–interquartile range

one-half of the interquartile range
• *The* **semi-interquartile range** *for the data set shown above is 13 ÷ 2 = 6.5.*

a b c d e f g h i j k l m n o p q r s t u v w x y z

quincunx

A quincunx is an arrangement of five objects in a square, so that there is one in each corner and one in the middle.
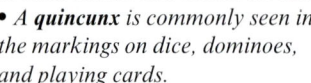
• *A **quincunx** is commonly seen in the markings on dice, dominoes, and playing cards.*

quinquangle

A quinquangle is an old name for a pentagon, which is now rarely used.

quintic

A quintic equation, expression or function is one of degree 5.
• *$f(x) = 3x^5 - 7x^2 + 4x$ is a **quintic** function.*
• *Unlike those of degree 4 or less, the general equation of a **quintic** or higher degree cannot be solved by use of straightforward formulas.*

SEE ALSO cubic, quartic

quota sampling see sample

quotient

The quotient is the result given by the operation of division.
• *In $32 \div 8 = 4$, the **quotient** is 4.*

quotition

A quotition is an act of division when something is physically divided into parts.

⚠ **WATCH OUT**

The words **partition** and **quotition** both describe a type of division applied to a physical situation, where whatever is being divided is named, or has units attached.

If the dividend and divisor have different types of names it is a **partition**.

If the dividend and divisor have the same type of name it is a **quotition**.

Dividing (sharing) 100 apples among 10 people is a **partition** (apples ÷ people).

Finding how many 10 cm lengths can be cut from a 1 metre strip is a **quotition** (length ÷ length).

radial survey

A radial survey is done by establishing a fixed point inside the shape to be surveyed, running traverses from that fixed point to selected points on the edges of the shape, and then measuring the length of each traverse and the angles between them.
• *A **radial survey** is an easy method to use and very suitable for fields and similar shapes which are reasonably flat.*

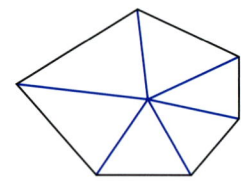

WORD BUILD

plane table survey

A plane table survey is a type of radial survey which does not require the angles to be measured.

SEE ALSO alidade

EXAMPLE:

Paper is fixed to a horizontal flat surface (like a drawing-board) placed above a fixed point on the ground and then, using an alidade, the direction of identifiable points on the boundary are drawn directly onto the paper.

The table is then moved a measured distance to a second fixed point and set up facing the same compass direction as before.

The position of the second fixed point is plotted on the paper (to scale) and another set of direction lines are sighted and drawn through that.

The intersections of the two sets of directions fixes the relative positions of all the identifiable points.

radian

A radian is the angle made at the centre of a circle between two radii when the length of the arc on the circumference between them is equal to the length of one radius.

• *The* **radian** *as a unit of angle measurement is used a lot in further mathematical work.* • *There are 2π* **radians** *in a full turn.* • *There are π* **radians** *in 180°.*

FORMULA:

To change radians into degrees, multiply by 180 and divide by π.

To change degrees into radians, multiply by π and divide by 180.

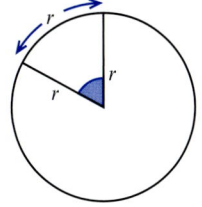

radical

a quantity forming, or expressed as, the root of another

radius *plural* radii, radiuses

❶ A radius of a circle is any straight line from the centre to the curve.
❷ The radius of a circle is the length of any straight line from the centre to the curve.

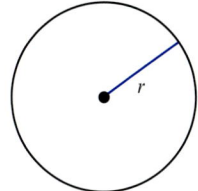

A circle with a radius of length r

radius vector

When using polar coordinates, the radius vector is the line joining the pole and the point whose position is being given.

random

❶ A result of an experiment is said to be random if, from all the results that could happen as a consequence of that experiment, each result has the same chance of happening and, no matter how many results have already been found, the next cannot be predicted.
❷ A random selection is any process by which objects (or numbers) are chosen in such a way that the appearance of each object is random.

• *Rolling a fair die and reading numbers from a printed random number table are both* **random** *selection processes.*

SEE ALSO **sample**

random sample *see* sample

random sequence *see* sequence

random variation *see* variation

range

❶ The range of a set of numerical data is the numerical difference between the smallest and the greatest values to be found in that data.

• *For the data 9, 3, 3, 15, 11, the* **range** *is $15 - 3 = 12$.*
❷ The range of a mapping is made up of those elements in the codomain which are actually used in the mapping.

EXAMPLE:

The mapping shown uses the same set for both the domain and codomain and the rule 'multiply by 2'.

The **range** is only the even numbers.

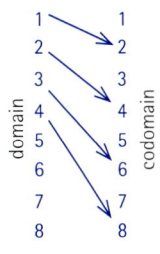

a b c d e f g h i j k l m n o p q r s t u v w x y z

rangefinder

A rangefinder is an instrument which measures the distance from the observer to some distant object. The simplest rangefinders use two lenses mounted one at each end of a base-line of known length. The distance of the object is determined by the amount these lenses have to be turned to view the object.

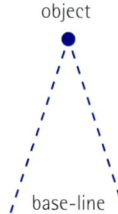

object

base-line

• *More sophisticated and accurate rangefinders work by calculating the distance from the time needed for some form of electromagnetic beam to travel to the object and back again.*

rate

Rate is a measure of how quickly an amount changes compared to another. It is also a measure of how quickly an event happens.
• *Water flows from a hose at a faster rate than from a tap.* • *If it takes 1 hour to drive 60 km, the rate at which the journey was completed is 60 kilometres per hour.*

rate of change

When one quantity x causes a change in another quantity y, the instantaneous rate of change of y is a measure of how quickly y is changing when x has a particular value. However, the average rate of change of y as x changes over a range of values is found by dividing the change in y by the change in x. Graphically, the instantaneous rate of change is the gradient of a tangent, and the average rate of change is the gradient of a chord.
SEE ALSO **gradient, derivative**

rate of exchange (*also* exchange rate)

The rate of exchange between two systems is a statement of how a value in one system may be given as an equivalent value in the other system.
• *A rate of exchange is most often used in changing money between countries.*

EXAMPLE:

If the **rate of exchange** between euros (€) and pounds (£) is €1.20 to £1 then:

£47 would be worth 47 × 1.20 = €56.40

€150 would be worth 150 ÷ 1.20 = £125

rate of interest *see* interest

ratio

is used to compare the sizes of two (or more) quantities.
• *When making pastry for pies, the **ratio** of flour to fat to water is 3 : 2 : 1.* • *When making mortar for building walls, the **ratio** of cement to sand is 2 : 7.*
SEE ALSO **golden ratio, trigonometric ratio**

rationalizing

A fraction with a denominator containing a surd can be simplified by making the denominator a rational number. This process is called rationalizing the denominator.
SEE ALSO **surd**

EXAMPLE:

$\dfrac{1}{\sqrt{2}}$ is rationalized to become $\dfrac{\sqrt{2}}{2}$

A similar process can be used to divide one complex number by another.

rational number *see* number

raw data *see* data

real number *see* number

real variable *see* variable

rearrange

To rearrange an equation or formula is to change it (under definite rules) to produce an equivalent version. This is usually done in order to simplify it or make it easier to work with.
• *The equation $4x + y = 5$ can be **rearranged** to $y = 5 - 4x$.*

reciprocal

The reciprocal of a number is the value given by dividing 1 by that number, or dividing that number into 1.
• *The **reciprocal** of 2 is $\frac{1}{2}$ or $1 \div 2 = 0.5$*
• *The **reciprocal** of 7 is $\frac{1}{7} = 0.142857...$*

reciprocal bearing *see* **bearing**

recreational mathematics
covers games, puzzles, and similar activities in
which mathematical principles are used in
some way: to create them, to play them, or to
solve them.

rectangle
A rectangle is a quadrilateral in which every
interior angle is a right angle.

FORMULA:

Area of a rectangle = length × width

Perimeter of a rectangle = 2 × (length + width)

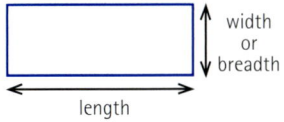

rectangular coordinates *see* **coordinate**

rectangular hyperbola *see* **hyperbola**

rectilinear shape *see* **shape**

recurrence relation
A recurrence relation defines a sequence based on
a rule which gives the next term of the sequence
as a function of the previous term or terms. Initial
values are needed to begin the process.
SEE ALSO **sequence**

recurring decimal *see* **decimal fraction**

recursive sequence *see* **sequence**

reduce
To reduce a fraction or expression is to change it
into its simplest possible form.
• *To* **reduce** *a fraction, you keep dividing its
numerator and denominator by the same value*

until it becomes impossible to do so. • *To* **reduce** *an
expression, you rewrite it as a product of its factors.*

EXAMPLE:

To **reduce** $\frac{150}{240}$ divide both by 10 to get $\frac{15}{24}$
then divide both by 3 to get $\frac{5}{8}$

$x^3 - 4x^2 + 3x - 12$ has two factors and is
reduced to $(x^2 + 3)(x - 4)$

reducible
A reducible expression is one which has at least
two factors.

reductio ad absurdum *see* **proof**

re-entrant polygon *see* **polygon**

reflection
A reflection is a transformation such that any two
corresponding points in the object and the image
are both the same distance from a fixed straight
line, and a line drawn between those points would
be perpendicular to that fixed line. It is described
by giving the position of the fixed line.

glide reflection
A glide reflection is a transformation made
by combining a translation with a reflection
whose mirror line is parallel to the direction of
the translation.
• *A repeated* **glide reflection** *can be used to make
a pattern.*

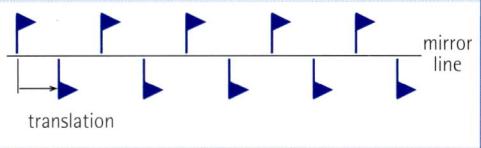

reflective symmetry *see* **symmetry**

reflex angle *see* **angle**

region *see* **face**

regular polygon see polygon

----

regular polyhedron see polyhedron

----

regular quadrilateral see quadrilateral

----

regular tiling see tiling

----

relative error see error

----

relative frequency see frequency

----

relatively prime see coprime

----

remainder

The remainder is the amount left over in a division operation when one quantity cannot be divided exactly by another.

> **EXAMPLE:**
>
> $23 \div 4 = 5$ with a **remainder** of 3.
>
> This is usually written as $5\ r\ 3$ or 5 rem 3.
>
> Dividend ÷ divisor = quotient plus remainder that cannot be shared out.

----

rep–tile (also replicating tile)

A rep-tile or replicating tile is a two-dimensional shape of which multiple copies can be put together to make another shape which is similar to the original.
• *The simplest **rep-tiles** are the right-angled isosceles triangle and an oblong (or parallelogram) whose edges are in the ratio $1 : \sqrt{2}$ which are the proportions used by A-sized papers.* • *The image shows a more complex set of **rep-tiles**. Many others can be found.*

----

repunit

A repunit is a number made up only of 1s (repeated units). A short way of writing such numbers is 1_n where n is the number of 1s to be used.

> **EXAMPLE:**
>
> $1_3 = 111$
>
> $1_6 = 111111$
>
> The **repunits** 1_2, 1_{19}, and 1_{23} are all primes.

----

residue

The residue of any number is the remainder after that number has been divided by a specified modulus.
• *Using a modulus of 4, the **residue** of 7 is 3. This is the same as 7 = 3 (mod 4).*

----

resultant

A resultant is the vector produced by the addition and/or subtraction of two or more vectors. It is the single vector which can replace all the other vectors and still produce the same result.

Retail Prices Index (also RPI, Consumer Price Index, Cost of Living Index)

The Retail Prices Index or RPI is a measure of how the cost of things that people need for everyday life is changing. The figure is produced by noting the overall change in the cost of a large, carefully balanced sample of items including nearly everything that people spend their money on, including food, lighting, heating, travel, entertainment, etc. The base value is set at 100 in one particular year (most recently 1987) and the changes are measured against that.

Every country in the world carries out a similar survey of retail prices at least once a year. In the UK the survey (started in 1914) is done every month by the Office for National Statistics based on a total of over 100,000 items.

The table gives the RPI (in January) for the UK between 2015 – 2019. We can see that in a few years time, the cost of things will be about three times as much as they were when the base value of 100 was set in 1987.

2015	258.5
2016	263.1
2017	272.5
2018	281.6
2019	288.8

----

retardation *see* **deceleration**

Reuleaux polygon (*also* **curve of constant width**)

A Reuleaux polygon is similar in appearance to a polygon except that all its edges are curved in such a way that the distance between any pair of parallel lines touching the edges at opposite points is always the same.

• *The polygon used as the basis of a **Reuleaux polygon** must have an odd number of vertices but does not have to be regular.*

• *The vertices of a **Reuleaux polygon** can also be rounded by drawing further suitable curves. The diagram shows a Reuleaux triangle.*

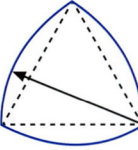

----

reverse percentage

is the name of the technique used when finding the original value of something, knowing only its current value and the percentage of the original value by which its original value was increased.

• *Reverse percentage is commonly used when a price including a tax is known and the price without the tax is needed.*

FORMULA:

original value = [100 × current value] ÷ [100 + R]

where

R is the percentage charge made to the original value

If a decrease has been made, original value = [100 × current value] ÷ [100 − R].

EXAMPLE:

A lawnmower costs £372 which includes VAT at 20%.

Its cost without VAT must be [100 × 372] ÷ [100 + 20] = £310.

----

reverse Polish notation *see* **notation**

----

revolve

If something revolves, it turns around or moves in a circle about a certain point.

➤ **revolution** A revolution is a complete turn about a point or axis.

SEE ALSO **rotate**

----

rhomb *see* **rhombus**

----

rhombohedron

A rhombohedron is a parallelepiped whose faces are rhombuses. In scientific work (on crystals) it is often called a rhomboid.

----

rhomboid

A rhomboid is a parallelogram having adjacent edges of different lengths. The word is little used because of possible confusion.

SEE ALSO **rhombohedron**

----

rhombus *plural* **rhombuses, rhombi**

A rhombus is a quadrilateral whose edges are all the same length. Its diagonals bisect each other at right angles and both are also lines of symmetry. Usually no interior angle is a right angle and then it can be referred to as a diamond, lozenge, or rhomb.

FORMULA:

Area of a rhombus = $b \times h$

where

b is the base

h is the perpendicular height

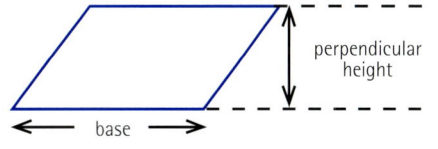

----

right angle *see* angle

right-angled triangle *see* triangle

right circular cone *see* cone

right circular cylinder *see* cylinder

right-handed system

Three vectors *a*, *b*, *c* (in that order, not all in the same plane, and all starting at O) form a right-handed system if, when looking in the direction of *c*, vector *a* can be rotated clockwise about O through an angle of less than 180° to lie on *b*. If the required rotation (which must be <180°) is anticlockwise then it is a left-handed system.
• *If the vectors a, b, c form a **right-handed system** then so also do b, c, a and c, a, b.* • *A **right-handed system** becomes left-handed if one vector is reversed.* • *The unit vector system i, j, k is always a **right-handed system**.*

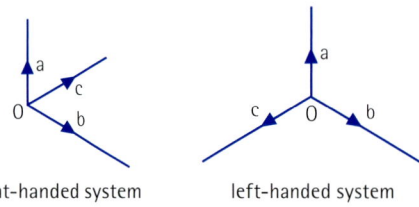

right-handed system   left-handed system

right identity *see* identity

right prism *see* prism

right pyramid *see* pyramid

right square-based pyramid *see* pyramid

Roman number system *see* number system

root

A root of an equation is a value that will satisfy the equation. Roots may be real or complex numbers.
• *The maximum number of **roots** for any given equation equals the degree of the expression.*
SEE ALSO **quadratic equation**

EXAMPLE:

$x^2 - 8x + 15 = 0$ has the two **roots**: $x = 3$ or 5

$x^3 - 4x^2 - x + 4 = 0$ has the three **roots**:
$x = -1$, 1 or 4

root mean square

the square root of the arithmetic mean of the squares of a set of numbers

rotation

A rotation is a transformation about a fixed point, called the centre of rotation, such that every point in the object turns through the same angle relative to that fixed point.
• *A **rotation** is described by giving the angle and direction of the turn, and the position of the fixed point about which the turn is made.*

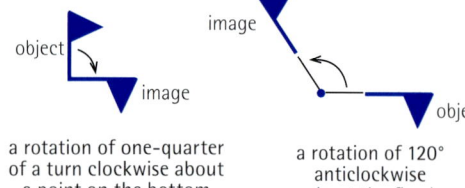

a rotation of one-quarter of a turn clockwise about a point on the bottom of the object   a rotation of 120° anticlockwise about the fixed point marked

➤ **rotate** To rotate a shape or line is to turn it relative to a fixed point.

axis of rotation

An axis of rotation is a line about which a shape or another line is turned.

centre of rotation

The centre of rotation is the fixed point about which a rotation takes place.

rotational symmetry (*also* point symmetry)

Rotational symmetry is the symmetry of a shape which may be turned and fitted onto itself somewhere other than in its original position.

• *These examples of* **rotational symmetry** *show the centres, about which the shape is turned, in blue.*

WORD BUILD

centre of symmetry

The centre of symmetry is the point about which a shape having rotational symmetry is turned.

order of rotational symmetry

The order of rotational symmetry of a shape counts the number of times that a shape can be turned to fit on to itself until it comes back to its original position. Every shape has an order of rotational symmetry of at least 1, but this is usually ignored.

• *Note how marking a shape in some way can change its* **order of rotational symmetry**. *In the illustration, the cross would normally have an* **order of rotational symmetry** *of 4, but with a dot on one of its outer squares, its order is 1 instead.*

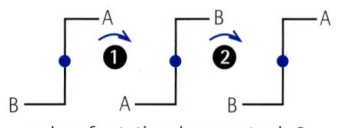

order of rotational symmetry is 2

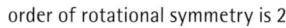

order of rotational symmetry is 3

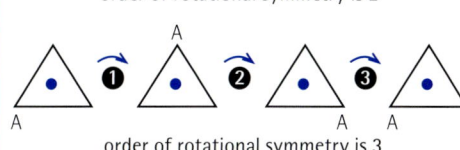

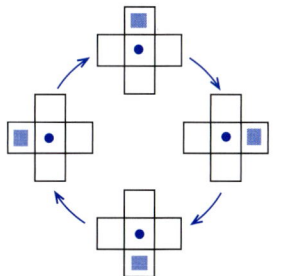

order of rotational symmetry is 1

round angle *see* angle

....

rounding

is done when a number is needed to a degree of accuracy. The closest number to that degree of accuracy is used in place of the original number.

SEE ALSO **decimal place, significant figure**

➤ **round (up/down)** to use the closest number to the required degree of accuracy above or below the original number. The digit after the required degree of accuracy is used as a signpost. If this is five or greater then the last digit must be rounded up by one. If it is less than five then the last digit remains the same.

EXAMPLE:

341 **rounded** to the nearest hundred is 300.

341 to the nearest hundred is **rounded down** to 300.

361 to the nearest hundred is **rounded up** to 400.

WORD BUILD

to the nearest ' ... '

indicates that an approximation has been made by rounding, so that the given value finishes on a digit whose place-value is stated in '...'. Usually this is done only with whole numbers, but it can be applied to decimal fractions (to the nearest tenth, etc.).

• *If the true attendance at a football match was 24,682, the attendance might be given as 24,680 (to the nearest 10) or 24,700 (to the nearest 100) or 25,000 (to the nearest 1,000).*

....

rounding error *see* error

....

row

A row of a matrix is the set of elements making up one complete line, reading across the matrix from left to right.

• *The matrix* $\begin{pmatrix} 1 & 7 \\ 8 & 5 \end{pmatrix}$ *has two* **rows**: *(1 7) and (8 5)*

SEE ALSO **column**

....

row matrix *see* **matrix**

....

row vector *see* **vector**

....

RPI *see* **Retail Prices Index**

....

ruled curve *see* **curve**

....

ruled surface *see* **surface**

....

rule of three *see* **unitary method**

....

ruler (*also* **rule**)

A ruler is a straight-edge with graduated markings along at least one of its edges so that lengths of a straight line can be measured.

---

parallel ruler

A parallel ruler or rulers is an instrument for drawing lines parallel to an existing line or direction.

scaled ruler

A scaled ruler is provided on maps and drawings which are drawn to scale. Lengths taken from the drawing can be measured on the ruler as actual sizes.

Ss

sample

❶ A sample is a set chosen from a population and used to represent that population in the statistical methods being applied. This is necessary where it is not possible to collect all the data from a very large population.

• *In conducting an opinion poll to see how people would vote in an election, it is only possible to ask a **sample** of the population about their intentions and predict a result for the whole population from that.*

❷ To sample a population is to take a sample from it.

SEE ALSO **population**

---

quota sampling

A quota sampling is done by deciding in advance how many of the population, in each of certain categories, are to be chosen. The quotas are often set to represent how many of each category are known to be present in the total population.

• *An example of **quota sampling**: A survey about attitudes among older persons might specify that, from the over-sixties, 100 men and 125 women are to be questioned.*

---

random sample

A random sample is a sample that has been chosen by a process of random selection from a population. Note that it is not certain that such a sample is properly representative of the whole population.

---

stratified sample

A stratified sample is created by dividing the population to be sampled into groups, or strata, according to some criterion, and taking appropriate samples (random or systematic) from each of those groups.

• *Age, sex, socioeconomic group, and occupation are commonly used criteria in **stratified sampling**.*

---

systematic sample

A systematic sample is one produced from a population which is arranged in some order.

The order might be actual or implied, as with birth dates.
• *From a list of thirty names, or a street of thirty houses, you are asked to choose one-third of them as a sample. Taking every third name or house would produce a **systematic sample** of ten.*

---

sampling error
is the difference between the mean of the sample and the mean of the population from which that sample was drawn.
• *It is important to have some idea of the probable size of the **sampling error** in order to assess how much confidence can be placed in any conclusions made, based on the sample.*

---

satisfy
A value is said to satisfy an equation if, when the value is substituted for a variable in the equation, it leaves the truth of the equation unchanged.
• *x = 2 **satisfies** the equation 3x + 7 = 13 since (3 × 2) + 7 = 13.*

---

scalar
❶ A scalar is a quantity which can be completely defined by a single number. It may or it may not have units attached.
• *Length, mass, speed, and numbers are all **scalar** quantities.*
❷ A scalar is any real number. It is often shown by the symbol λ.
❸ A scalar is a number which, when written in front (to the left) of a matrix, means that all the elements of that matrix have to be multiplied by that number.

EXAMPLE:

$$3\begin{pmatrix} 2 & 0 \\ 1 & 5 \end{pmatrix} \rightarrow \begin{pmatrix} 3 \times 2 & 3 \times 0 \\ 3 \times 1 & 5 \times 5 \end{pmatrix} = \begin{pmatrix} 6 & 0 \\ 3 & 15 \end{pmatrix}$$

---

scalar multiplication
Scalar multiplication of a vector is carried out by multiplying the size of a vector by a single number.

EXAMPLE:

The result of the multiplication of a vector v by a scalar λ (written λv) where $v = (x_1\ x_2\ x_3\ x_4$ etc.) is given by $λv = (λx_1\ λx_2\ λx_3\ λx_4$ etc.).

The result is a vector which is λ times the size of the original.

If λ is negative, the new vector will be in a reverse direction to the original.

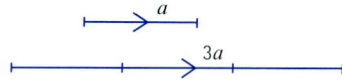

scalar multiplication of vector *a* by 3

---

scalar product (*also* inner product, dot product)
The scalar product of two vectors *a* and *b* (written *a.b*) is found by multiplying together their magnitudes and the cosine of the angle between them. The result is a scalar.

EXAMPLE:

$a.b = |a| \times |b| \times \cos θ$ more usually written as $|a|\,|b|\cos θ$

In the case where the vectors are given in terms of a coordinate system
where $a \equiv (x_1\ x_2\ x_3)$ and $b \equiv (y_1\ y_2\ y_3)$ then
$a.b = x_1 y_1 + x_2 y_2 + x_3 y_3$

Given $a \equiv (3, 6, 5)$ and $b \equiv (4, 7, 2)$ then
$a.b = 3 \times 4 + 6 \times 7 + 5 \times 2 = 64$

For unit vectors:
$i.j = j.k = k.i = 0$ and $i.i = j.j = k.k = 1$

⚠ WATCH OUT

Do not confuse a **scalar product** with **scalar multiplication**.

---

scale
When making a drawing of an object which is meant to be in proportion to the size of the object, and from which measurements can be taken, a scale is used to fix the ratio between the actual measurements on the object and those in the drawing. Scale is usually stated either as a ratio or as a statement of how one measurement is related to the other.
• *A **scale** of 1:1 means the drawing is the same size as the object, 1:10 means 1 cm on the drawing represents 10 cm on the object, 1:100 means 1 cm on the drawing represents 100 cm or 1 metre, and so on.*
• *In a **scale** of 1:25,000, 4 cm represents 1 km. This is a **scale** commonly used on maps.*

---

scaled ruler *see* **ruler**

-----

scale factor

A scale factor is the value of the multiplier used to make an enlargement.
• *The* ***scale factor*** *is a multiplier for changing lengths only.* • *The multiplier which affects the area will be the* ***scale factor*** *to the power of two.* • *For the change in volume of a 3D shape, the multiplier is the* ***scale factor*** *to the power of three.*

-----

scalene triangle *see* **triangle**

-----

scatter graph (*also* **scatter plot**) *see* **graph**

Schlegel diagram

A Schlegel diagram is a topological graph which represents a polyhedron. It is made by representing the polyhedron by its edges and deforming those, using only topological transformations, so that it lies flat. The edges, vertices, and faces of the polyhedron become those of the graph.

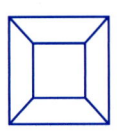

a cube   a tetrahedron

a triangular prism

-----

s'choty *see* **abacus**

-----

scientific calculator *see* **calculator**

-----

scientific notation *see* **standard form**

-----

seasonal variation *see* **variation**

-----

secant

❶ A secant is a line which cuts across a circle at two points. A tangent can be considered a special case of a secant in which the two points are coincident.

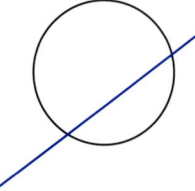

❷ A secant is one of the six trigonometric ratios.

SEE ALSO **trigonometric ratio**

-----

second

❶ The second is the unit of time in the SI.

SEE ALSO **SI**

❷ A second is the angle made by $\frac{1}{60}$ part of a minute.
• *Degrees and decimal fractions are most often used for angles, except in navigation, when minutes and* ***seconds*** *are used.* • *A double apostrophe " is the symbol used for a* ***second***.

SEE ALSO **degree**

-----

secondary data *see* **data**

-----

secondary diagonal *see* **diagonal**

-----

second quadrant *see* **quadrant**

-----

sector

❶ A sector of a circle is the shape enclosed between an arc and the two radii at either end of that arc.

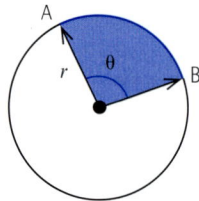

sector of a circle

FORMULA:

Area of sector $= \dfrac{\theta}{360} \times \pi r^2$

where

θ is the angle (in degrees) of the sector at the centre of the circle

r is the radius of the circle

❷ A sector of a sphere is a shape very similar to that of a right circular cone with its vertex at the centre of the sphere, and with its flat circular base replaced by the corresponding segment of the sphere.

FORMULA:

Volume of sector $= \dfrac{\pi d^2 h}{6}$

where

d is the diameter of the sphere

h is the height of the segment

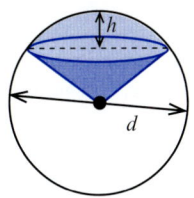

sector of a sphere

---

major sector

When a sector is made in a circle, the remainder of the circle makes another sector. The larger of the two is the major sector.

minor sector

When a sector is made in a circle, the remainder of the circle makes another sector. The smaller of the two is the minor sector.

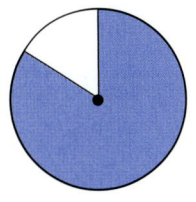

major sector   minor sector

. . . .

secular variation *see* **variation**

. . . .

---

segment

❶ A segment of a circle is the shape enclosed between a chord and one of the arcs joining the ends of that chord.

FORMULA:

Area of segment $= \left(\dfrac{\pi \times \theta}{360} - \dfrac{\sin \theta}{2} \right) \times r^2$

where

θ is the angle (in degrees) of the segment at the centre of the circle

r is the radius of the circle

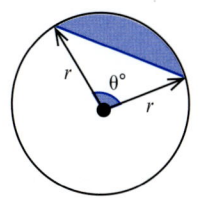

segment of a circle

❷ A segment of a sphere is the shape cut off by a single plane which passes through the sphere. The plane divides the sphere into two segments. A plane cutting through the centre of the sphere produces two identical segments which are hemispheres. A segment which is smaller than a hemisphere is also known as a cap.

FORMULA:

Volume of segment $= \dfrac{\pi d^2 h}{6}(3d - 2h)$

Area of curved surface only $= \pi dh$

where

d is the diameter of the sphere

h is the height of the segment

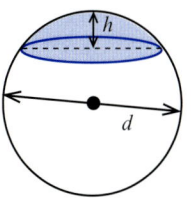

segment of a sphere   »

a
b
c
d
e
f
g
h
i
j
k
l
m
n
o
p
q
r
s
t
u
v
w
x
y
z

➤ **angle in a segment** The angle in a segment is the angle formed between the two lines drawn from the ends of the chord making the segment to any point on the circumference of that segment. It is the angle subtended at the point on the circumference by the chord. In any given segment all the subtended angles are the same size.

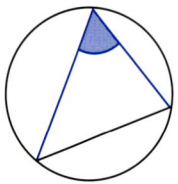 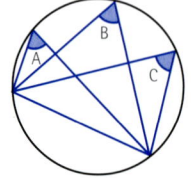

angle in a segment   All angles subtended in the same segment are equal.

alternate segment

Any chord drawn in a circle creates two segments, and one is said to be the alternate of the other. When a chord is drawn from the point of contact of a tangent then the angle between the tangent and the chord, measured on one side of the chord, is equal to the angle in the alternate segment, which lies on the other side of the chord.

major segment

When a segment is made in a circle, the remainder of the circle makes another segment. The larger of the two is the major segment.

minor segment

When a segment is made in a circle, the remainder of the circle makes another segment. The smaller of the two is the minor segment.

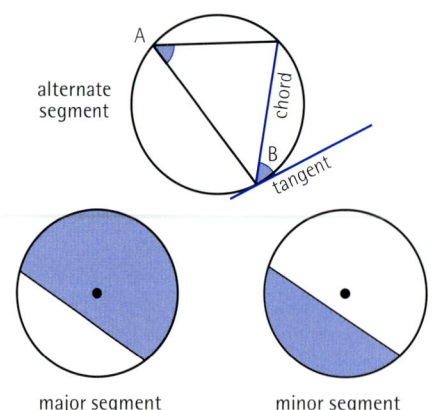

major segment   minor segment

self-evident

A statement is described as self-evident when it is thought that no reasoning is necessary to demonstrate that the statement is true. This is often used to describe the most basic ideas of a system which are generally 'known' but are impossible to define independently of the system.

• *The statement 'Any two things which are each equal to a third thing must be equal to each other' could be seen as being* **self-evident**.

selling price

The selling price of an article is the price at which that article is offered for sale.
SEE ALSO buying price, cost price

semicircle

A semicircle is one half of a circle made by cutting along a diameter.
➤ **angle in a semicircle** In any semicircle the angle subtended by the diameter at any point on the circumference is a right angle.

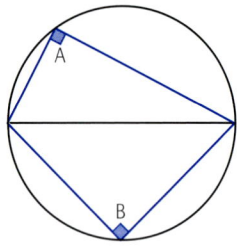

semi-interquartile range *see* quartile

semi-regular polyhedron *see* polyhedron

semi-regular tiling *see* tiling

sequence

A sequence is a set of numbers or objects made and written in order according to some mathematical rule.

doubling sequence

A doubling sequence is a sequence in which each term is twice (× 2) the value of the previous term.
• *A **doubling sequence** beginning with 1 has the next five terms: 2, 4, 8, 16, 32, ...*

Fibonacci sequence

The Fibonacci sequence is a recursive sequence where, starting with the first two terms as 1, 1, each new term is made by adding together the two previous terms.
• *The first ten terms of the **Fibonacci sequence** are: 1, 1, 2, 3, 5, 8, 13, 21, 34, 55, ...*

FORMULA:

Formally this is written as $F_n = F_{n-2} + F_{n-1}$

where

$F_1 = 1$ and $F_2 = 1$

The value of the nth term can be found from the formula:

$$F_n = \frac{1}{\sqrt{5}} \left(\frac{1 + \sqrt{5}}{2} \right)^n$$ rounded to the nearest

whole number.

Lucas sequence

The Lucas sequence is a recursive sequence where, starting with the first two terms as 1, 3, each new term is made by adding together the two previous terms.
• *The first ten terms of the **Lucas sequence** are: 1, 3, 4, 7, 11, 18, 29, 47, 76, 123, ...*

FORMULA:

Formally this is written as $L_n = L_{n-2} + L_{n-1}$

where

$L_1 = 1$ and $L_2 = 3$.

lucky number sequence

The lucky number sequence is made from the natural numbers by first deleting every second number
  – from those that are left delete every third number
  – from those delete every fourth number
  – then every fifth, sixth, seventh and so on until no more can be deleted
  – those remaining form the sequence.

• *The first ten terms of the **lucky number sequence** are: 1, 3, 7, 13, 19, 27, 39, 49, 63, 79, ...*

natural number sequence

The natural number sequence is that sequence which is used for counting.
• *The first ten terms of the **natural number sequence** are: 1, 2, 3, 4, 5, 6, 7, 8, 9, 10, ...*

random sequence

A random sequence is a set of numbers or objects made and written in order, according to no apparent rule and for which, no matter how many terms are known, the next cannot be predicted with certainty.

recursive sequence

A recursive sequence is a sequence in which each new term is defined in relation to some terms which have been made previously.

....

series

A series is made by placing addition or subtraction signs between the terms of a sequence.
• *Σ is the symbol used to show that a **series** is being given. The symbol is followed by an expression showing how each term in the **series** is made.*
SEE ALSO time series

alternating series

An alternating series is an infinite series in which the signs between the terms are alternately for addition (+) and subtraction (–).

EXAMPLE:

$$\frac{1}{1} + \frac{1}{2} - \frac{1}{3} + \frac{1}{4} - \frac{1}{5} + \frac{1}{6} - \frac{1}{7} + \frac{1}{8} - \text{...}$$ and so on

is an alternating series.

This series is convergent.

convergent series

A convergent series is an infinite series which, as more and more terms are used, moves towards some definite value.
• *An infinite geometric series is **convergent** if $|r| < 1$, otherwise it is divergent.* »

divergent series

A divergent series is an infinite series which is not convergent. Usually it means the value of the series grows as more terms are used.
• *An infinite geometric series is **divergent** if* $|r| \geq 1$.

harmonic series

The harmonic series is an infinite and divergent series $\Sigma \frac{1}{n}$.

EXAMPLE:

Written out, the **harmonic series** is

$$\frac{1}{1} + \frac{1}{2} + \frac{1}{3} + \frac{1}{4} + \frac{1}{5} + \frac{1}{6} + \frac{1}{7} + \frac{1}{8} + \dots$$

infinite series

An infinite series is a series whose terms are never-ending. There is no last term; it is always possible to write another one.

. . . .

set

A set is a collection of objects (letters, numbers, symbols, etc.) which is defined either by listing all the objects or by giving a rule that allows a decision to be made as to whether or not an object belongs in that set.
• *Before any operation can be used it is necessary to make clear on what **set** of objects it is to be used.*
• *The **set** might be 'all whole numbers' or 'only positive numbers' or 'real numbers' or 'quadratic equations', and so on.* • *Sets are usually shown listed or defined within curly brackets:* { }.
• $\in$ *is the symbol meaning 'is a member of' or 'belongs to'.*

EXAMPLE:

$\{a, e, i, o, u\}$ is a listed **set** that could also be described by the rule {the vowels}.
$a \in$ {the vowels}

$\{5, a \text{ person}, a \text{ table}, Z\}$ is a listed **set** for which a rule would be difficult to find.

{all the numbers} is a rule for a **set** that it is impossible to list. $12 \in$ {all the numbers}

denumerable set

A denumerable set is one for which a mapping can be established which puts all its members into a one-to-one correspondence with the positive integers.

disjoint set

Disjoint sets are those having no members in common.

empty set (*also* null set)

An empty set or a null set is a set which has no members.
• *The set {all odd numbers divisible by 2} is **empty**.*
• $\varnothing$ *is the symbol for the **empty set**.*

equivalent set

Sets are equivalent if they contain the same number of members as each other.

finite set

A finite set is a set whose members can be counted.

infinite set

An infinite set is a set whose members cannot be counted and the quantity stated in terms of any defined number.
• *The set of all real numbers is an **infinite set**.*

universal set (*also* universe)

A universal set or universe is a set which is first defined (by list or rule) and within which all the statements that follow must be interpreted.
• ξ *or* $\mathbb{U}$ *are symbols for the **universal set**, but others are used.*

EXAMPLE:

If the **universal set** is {positive numbers less than 10} then the set {even numbers} is only $\{0, 2, 4, 6, 8\}$.

If the **universal set** is {all positive numbers} then $x^2 = 4$ has only one solution $x = 2$ since -2 is not in the universal set.

. . . .

set square

Set squares are templates cut in the shape of a right-angled triangle whose two other angles are either both 45° or 30° and 60°.

• *Adjustable **set squares** are made with the hypotenuse hinged at one end so that it can be adjusted to form different angles.*

set theory

is the study of the properties and applications of sets.

sextant

A sextant is a hand-held instrument used to measure the subtended angle at the observer's position between two distant points. It uses a mirror so that the observer can see both points at the same time, and can move the mirror so as to bring them into line; the amount of movement needed to do this gives the size of the subtended angle.

• *A **sextant** is used mostly by navigators to find the elevation above the horizon (known as the altitude) of the Sun, the Moon or a star.* • *The **sextant** was invented in the 1730s, and the name comes from the fact that its calibrated scale is an arc which is one-sixth of a circle.*

sf *see* **significant figure**

shape

A shape is made by a line or lines drawn on a surface, or by putting surfaces together. It is usual in mathematics to require that the lines or surfaces are closed in such a way that an inside and an outside of the shape can be defined.

• *When a **shape** is named it needs a context to determine whether it is the enclosed space that is being referred to or its defining outline.* • *The word 'circle' may refer either to the line defining it, or to the **shape** enclosed by that line.*

---

composite shape

a two-dimensional shape made from a number of other two-dimensional shapes

plane shape

a shape which is contained entirely within a simple flat (two-dimensional) surface or plane

rectilinear shape

a shape whose edges are all straight lines. All polygons are rectilinear shapes.

---

shear

A shear is a transformation in which all the lines in the object parallel to some fixed line (usually referred to as the base line) are moved in a direction parallel to that line, and an amount which is proportional to their distance from that line.

• *A **shear** is not an isometry, but the areas of the object and image are the same.*

SEE ALSO isometry

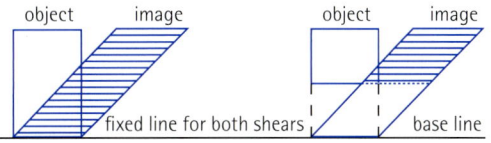

object image   object image

fixed line for both shears   base line

---

short division *see* **division**

SI

SI stands for Système International (d'Unités) or International System (of Units). It is a set of seven base units of measurements—metre, kilogram, second, kelvin, ampere, mole, and candela—from which all other measurement units can be derived. The definition of the SI units was most recently revised in 2019.

WORD BUILD
metre (*also* **m**)
The metre is the unit of length.
kilogram (*also* **kg**)
The kilogram is the unit of mass. »

second (also s)

The second is the unit of time.

kelvin (also K)

The kelvin is the unit of thermodynamic temperature.
• *The **kelvin** is named after the Scottish mathematician and physicist William Thomson, 1st Lord Kelvin (1824–1907).*

ampere (also A)

The ampere is the unit for measuring current.

mole (also mol)

The mole is the unit for measuring amounts of a substance.

candela (also cd)

The candela is the unit for measuring the intensity of light.

side

The word 'side' is used to refer to the edge of a two-dimensional shape.

sigmoid see ogee

signed number see number

significant figure (also sf)

Significant figures are used to express the relative importance of the digits in a number; the most important being the first digit, starting from the left-hand end of the number, which is not zero. Starting with the first non-zero digit, all digits are then counted as significant up to the last non-zero digit.
SEE ALSO rounding

4 sf	1,234	78,510	16.32	0.024 71	0.005 026
3 sf	1,230	78,500	16.3	0.024 7	0.005 03
2 sf	1,200	79,000	16	0.025	0.005 0
1 sf	1,000	80,000	20	0.02	0.005

➤ to '...' significant figures (also to '...' sf) indicates an approximation has been made by rounding to leave only the number of significant figures stated in '...'. Rounding off should be done.
• $\pi = 3.14$ *to 3* **sf** • $\pi = 3.14159$ *to 6* **sf**

similar

Geometrical figures are said to be similar if they are the same in shape but different in size.
• *If two shapes are **similar**, then one shape is an enlargement of another and corresponding angles in each shape will be the same size.* • *All the triangles illustrated below are **similar**.*
SEE ALSO congruent

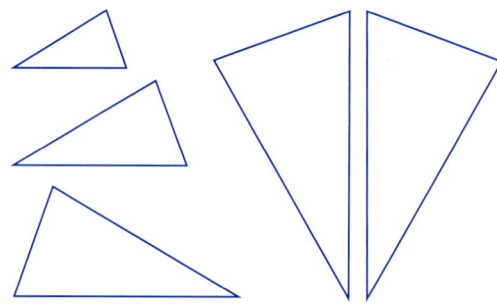

simple closed curve see curve

simple interest see interest

simplest form

When a fraction is written in its simplest form, the only common factor of the numerator and denominator is 1.
SEE ALSO lowest terms
EXAMPLE:

$\dfrac{9}{12}$ can be put in its **simplest form** by dividing the numerator and denominator by 3.

The fraction $\dfrac{3}{4}$ is then in its **simplest form**.

simplify

To simplify an algebraic expression, gather all like terms together into a single term.
- $2x^2 + 9 - 7x + 3xy + 5x + x^2 - 1$ **simplifies** to $3x^2 - 2x + 3xy + 8$.

Simpson's rule

is a method for finding the approximate area under a curve by dividing the space between the limiting ordinates into an even number of equal width strips.
- **Simpson's rule** *is usually more accurate than the mid-ordinate rule or trapezium rule. If the equation of the curve is known, the lengths of the ordinates (the y-values) can be calculated, rather than measured, for the greatest accuracy.*

SEE ALSO mid-ordinate rule

FORMULA:

With ordinates numbered from 1 to n, where n is odd, the area is given by:

area = width × [4 × sum of even ordinates + 2 × sum of odd ordinates − (first + last)] ÷ 3

simultaneous equations *see* **equation**

sin *see* **trigonometric ratio**

sin⁻¹ *see* **trigonometric ratio**

sine *see* **trigonometric ratio**

sine bar

A sine bar is a steel bar, made to a high degree of accuracy, which allows an angle to be set up by measuring lengths rather than by measuring the actual angle. The bar has two identical cylindrical pins fitted into its long surface, one at each end, with a known distance between their centres (typically 100, 200, or 300 mm).
- *Steel blocks of known thickness can be built up on which these pins rest, and so incline the* **sine bar** *at an angle to the base surface. Since all relevant measurements are known, the sine of the angle can be calculated, and thus the angle itself.*

- *In practice, it is usually the angle which has to be set up, and so the heights of the blocks have to be calculated.*

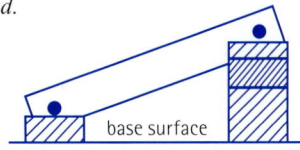

base surface

sine curve

A sine curve is the graph showing how the value of the sine of an angle changes with the size of the angle.
- *On a* **sine curve***, the values of the sine of an angle have an upper bound of 1 and a lower bound of −1.*

SEE ALSO cosine curve, tangent curve

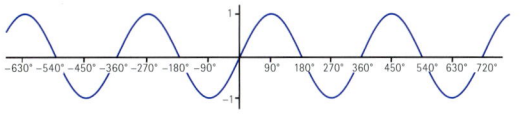

sine rule

The sine rule is based on the fact that in any triangle the length of any edge is proportional to the sine of the angle opposite to that edge.

SEE ALSO cosine rule

FORMULA:

$$\frac{a}{\sin A} = \frac{b}{\sin B} = \frac{c}{\sin C}$$

singular matrix *see* **matrix**

skewed distribution

A skewed distribution is one in which the frequency diagram, whilst having a single mode, is not symmetrical about the mean.

WORD BUILD

negatively skewed

A distribution is said to be negatively skewed if the mode lies to the right of the mean (mode > mean) in the frequency diagram.

»

A
B
C
D
E
F
G
H
I
J
K
L
M
N
O
P
Q
R
S
T
U
V
W
X
Y
Z

positively skewed

A distribution is said to be positively skewed if the mode lies to the left of the mean (mode < mean) in the frequency diagram.

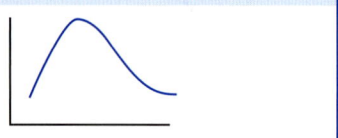

skew line

In 3D space, two lines that do not intersect and are not parallel are called skew lines.

slant edge

The slant edges of a pyramid are all those edges joined to the apex. The slant edges of a right pyramid are all the same length.

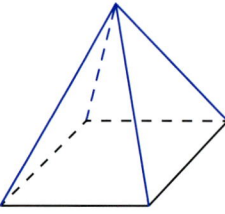

slant height

❶ The slant height of a right circular cone is the length of any straight line from the circumference of its base to the vertex.

FORMULA:

Slant height = $\sqrt{r^2 + h^2}$

where

r is the radius of the base of the cone

h is the perpendicular height of the cone

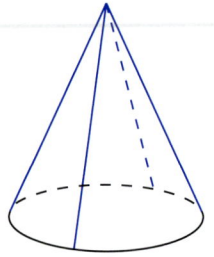

❷ The slant height of a pyramid is the length of a perpendicular from the mid-point of a base-edge to the apex. The slant heights of a right pyramid are all the same length.

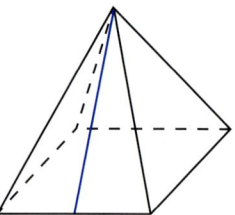

slide

When you slide a shape, you move it without turning it or flipping it over. You can slide horizontally, vertically, diagonally, or obliquely.

SEE ALSO transformation, translation

slide rule

A slide rule is a device for doing multiplication or division (and other similar operations) by means of two identically graduated strips positioned one beside the other.

EXAMPLE:

The illustration shows part of a very simplified **slide rule** set up to do 1.7 × 3.2, showing 5.44 as the answer.

Conversely this same setting of the slide rule is showing 5.44 ÷ 3.2 = 1.7 and, together with a knowledge of how to multiply and divide by 10, provides answers to:

17 × 320   0.17 × 32   544 ÷ 32   54.4 ÷ 0.32
for it or them.

small circle *see* great circle

solid

A solid is a shape formed in three-dimensional space. The most common of these are cube, cuboid, cyclinder, cone, pyramid, prism, and sphere.

Archimedean solid

a semi-regular polyhedron which is not a prism or antiprism. There are only 13 possible solids like this.

Platonic solid

a regular convex polyhedron. There are 5 possible solids like this.
• The **Platonic solids** are tetrahedron, cube, octahedron, dodecahedron, and icosahedron.
SEE ALSO **polyhedron**

solid angle

In three-dimensional space a solid angle is formed by all those lines which start at a common point and pass through a simple closed curve. Solid angles are to be found at the vertices of any three-dimensional shape.
SEE ALSO **steradian**

solution

A solution of an equation, or a set of equations, is a value of the variable or variables that will satisfy the equation.
• $4x - 5 = 7$ has the **solution** $x = 3$
since $(4 \times 3) - 5 = 7$.

trivial solution

A trivial solution is one which is obvious and of little interest.
• $x^n + y^n = z^n$ has a **trivial solution** $x = y = z = 0$.
It has other solutions.

unique solution

A unique solution is the only solution.
• $2x + 5 = 13$ has the **unique solution** $x = 4$.
• $x^2 = 9$ does not have a **unique solution**.
It has two: $x = 3$ and $x = -3$

solve

❶ To solve an equation or set of equations is to find a solution for it or them.
SEE ALSO **quadratic equation**

❷ To solve a triangle is to find the remainder of its dimensions, usually the lengths of its edges and the angles of the vertices, from a given (limited) amount of information about it.
SEE ALSO **ambiguous case**

Soma cube see **polycube**

soroban see **abacus**

sort

When a collection of objects or set of numbers is sorted into sets, they are put into groups according to given rules.
SEE ALSO **set**

space diagonal see **diagonal**

spatial pattern see **pattern**

Spearman's rank-order correlation coefficient

is used when two sets of data have each been ranked in order (or the same set ranked in two different orders) to give a measure of how well the two rankings agree.

FORMULA:

To calculate the value of Spearman's rank-order correlation coefficient:

Find the difference in value between each corresponding pair of rankings.

Square all the differences (this makes them all positive).

Add the squared values together and multiply by 6.

Divide the previous result by $n(n^2 - 1)$, where n is the number of pairs.

Subtract the result from 1.   »

speed

The speed of a moving object is a measure of the distance travelled by the object in a unit period of time.

SEE ALSO **acceleration, velocity**

⚠ **WATCH OUT**

Speed and **velocity** are very commonly used as having the same meaning, but there is a difference.

Velocity is a vector since it is described by giving both the speed of an object and the direction in which the object is moving.

Speed alone is not a vector.

average speed

When an object moves through some distance, its speed may vary as it travels, but its average speed is found by considering only the total time taken for the move and the total distance moved.

FORMULA:

The three equations used in working with average speed are:

speed = distance ÷ time
time = distance ÷ speed
distance = speed × time

EXAMPLE:

A car is driven from A to B, a distance of 780 km, and the journey takes 20 hours.

The **average speed** is $780 ÷ 20 = 39$ km per hour.

speed of light

The speed of light is 2.9979×10^8 metres per second.

sphere

A sphere is the shape of a surface in three dimensions which is everywhere the same distance from a single fixed point, or the solid shape enclosed by that surface.

• *The balls used to play most games are* **spheres**.

SEE ALSO **zone**

spherical trigonometry

is the study of the measurements, and relationships between those measurements, of the triangles which can be drawn upon the surface of a sphere. This is needed in making calculations relating to astronomical observations and navigation.

spherometer

A spherometer is an instrument for measuring the radius of curvature of a surface which is assumed to be part of a sphere. A spherometer consists of a base-plate on which three legs of equal length are fixed perpendicular to the base-plate. The points of these legs define an equilateral triangle.

• *The* **spherometer** *is placed on a curved surface and a screw in the middle of the base-plate adjusted until it just touches the surface. The radius of curvature can then be calculated, or read off on a suitably scaled dial.*

spiral

A spiral is the locus of a point moving in the plane of, and around, another (fixed) point while continuously increasing its distance from that fixed point.

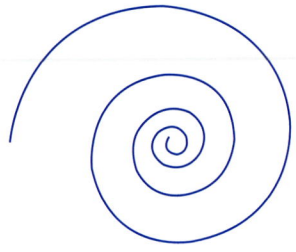

Archimedes' spiral

is a spiral where the locus of a point moves away from another fixed point at a constant speed.

EXAMPLE:

The equation for an **Archimedes' spiral** using polar coordinates is:

$r = a\theta$

where

a is a non-zero constant

θ is the angle

equiangular spiral

is a spiral where the locus of a point moves away from another fixed point at a geometric progression.

EXAMPLE:

The equation for an **equiangular spiral** using polar coordinates is:

$r = ae^{k\theta}$

where

a, k are non-zero constants

θ is the angle

e is the Euler number ≈ 2.7182818

hyperbolic spiral

is the inverse of the Archimedes' spiral.

EXAMPLE:

The equation for a **hyperbolic spiral** using polar coordinates is:

$r = a \div \theta$

where

a is a non-zero constant

θ is the angle

spread see **dispersion**

....

spreadsheet

A spreadsheet is a computer program which presents the user with a large number of cells, each of which can hold a piece of data, and these cells can be linked together in various ways so that a change of a piece of data in one cell produces a change in all those cells to whichit is connected. The data can be numbers or text. Spreadsheets can have several million cells and hundreds of different formulas to link them. They are capable of presenting the data in a wide variety of ways.

• *In the top left-hand corner of a* **spreadsheet***, cells are identified using the letters and numbers to get A1, C2, M15, etc.*

	A	B	C	D	E	F
1						
2						
3						
4						
5						
6						
7						
8						

....

square

❶ A square is a rectangle whose edges are all the same length. It has four lines of symmetry and rotational symmetry of order 4. Both diagonals are the same length and bisect each other at right angles.

SEE ALSO **magic square**

❷ The square of a number is the result of multiplying it by itself.

• *The* **square** *of 1 is 1.*

SEE ALSO **least squares**

❸ To square a number is to multiply it by itself.

• *x^2 is the symbol meaning '***square** *the number that appears in the place of x'. When x = 1.3, then x^2 means $1.3 \times 1.3 = 1.69$*

SEE ALSO **quadrature**

perfect square

A perfect square is a number whose square root is a whole number.

• *1, 4, 9, 16, 25, 36, and 289 are all* **perfect squares** *(with square roots of 1, 2, 3, 4, 5, 6, and 17 respectively).* »

WORD BUILD

difference of two squares rule

states that if an algebraic expression can be written in the form $a^2 - b^2$, then it can be factorized into $(a + b)(a - b)$.

EXAMPLE:

$x^2 - 9$ can be rewritten as $x^2 - 3^2$

Therefore $x^2 - 9 = (x + 3)(x - 3)$

square root

A square root of a number is another number which when squared will equal the first number.

EXAMPLE:

$\sqrt{}$ is the symbol meaning 'the **square root** of the number given'. For example:

$\sqrt{49} = 7$

and

$\sqrt{3.24} = 1.8$

The square roots of 16 are 4 and -4

....

square matrix see matrix

....

square number see polygon number

....

square root see square

....

standard deviation

The standard deviation of a set of data is a measure of its dispersion

• σ *(the Greek letter sigma) and s are symbols used for the standard deviation. σ is used when it is for the whole population; s is used for a sample*

• σ^2 *and s^2 are symbols used for the variance.*

SEE ALSO mean, mean deviation, variance

FORMULA:

To find the standard deviation of a set of data:

Find the difference in value between each piece of data and the mean of all the data.

Square all the differences (this makes them all positive).

Add them together and divide by how many there are.

Take the square root.

EXAMPLE:

This table shows the distribution of shoe sizes among 100 people and the weighted mean size has been calculated to be 4:

Shoe size	2	3	4	5	6	7
No. of people	15	19	35	18	8	5

Working from the mean of 4, the calculation is:

$[(-2^2 \times 15) + (-1^2 \times 19) + 0 + (1^2 \times 18) + (2^2 \times 8) + (3^2 \times 5)] \div 100 = 1.74$

So the standard deviation is $\sqrt{1.74} = 1.32$ (to 3 sf).

The variance in this example is $1.32^2 = 1.74$.

....

standard form (*also* scientific notation)

is a way of displaying a number in the form of a first number whose value lies between 1 and 10, and a second number which is always 10 with a suitable index, so that the two numbers multiplied together equal the value of the intended number.

• *143.6 is standard form is 1.436×10^2*

• *0.001436 in standard form is 1.436×10^{-3}*

....

star polygon (*also* n–gram)

A star polygon is made by joining every r th vertex of a polygon having n vertices ($1 < r < n - 1$); where n and r have no factors in common.

• *Star polygons are described using {n/r} notation.*

EXAMPLE:

A five pointed star can be drawn by joining alternate points together with a straight line.

That is, you draw a line from point 1 to point 3, then to point 5, then to point 2, then to point 4 and then back to point 1.

The resulting pentagon in the centre of the star is a {5/2} **star polygon** as the number of points of the star $n = 5$, and we join every second point in the star until we have joined all the points together, so $r = 2$.

A {5/2} and a {7/2} **star polygons** are illustrated.

A {5/2} star polygon

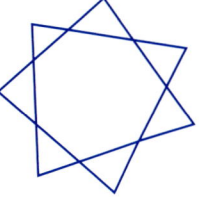

A {7/2} star polygon

statement
A statement made within a logical system is a form of words or symbols which carries information. The conventional way of representing statements is by using capital letters. The letters most often used are P and Q. P could represent the statement 'x is a prime number greater than 2'.
• *Within mathematics nearly everything is written in the form of **statements**. For example 'The length of the radius is 4 cm' or $3x + 2 = 7$*
SEE ALSO **P, Q**

stationary point
When the function $f(x)$ is drawn as a graph, stationary points on the curve occur against any x-values which produce a stationary value. That is, the curve will have zero gradient at that point (since the derivative is zero).
• *A **stationary point** is a maximum, a minimum or a point of inflection on a curve.*
SEE ALSO **point of inflection**

stationary value
A stationary value of a function $f(x)$, if it has one, is the value of that function at any point where the derivative is zero.

statistics
involves the collection, display, and analysis of information. Usually the information is numerical or changed into a numerical form.

stem and leaf plot
A stem and leaf plot is a frequency diagram which displays the actual data together with its frequency, by using a part of the value of each piece of data to fix the class or group (the stem), while the remainder of the value is actually listed (the leaves).
• *The **stem and leaf plot** shown uses the tens digit as the stem and the units as the leaves to show the data set:*
{1, 3, 12, 14, 14, 17, 20, 23, 25, 28, 29, 31, 36, 37}

stem (or class)						
3	1	6	7			
2	0	3	5	8	9	
1	2	4	4	7		
0	1	3				

$\quad$ 1 $\quad$ 2 $\quad$ 3 $\quad$ 4 $\quad$ 5
$\qquad$ frequency f

stencil *see* **template**

steradian
A steradian is the unit of measure of a solid angle. It is the size of the solid angle formed at the centre of a sphere of unit radius, by those lines radiating from the centre which cut off a segment whose curved surface is of unit area.
• *The maximum size of a solid angle is 4π **steradians**.*

straight angle *see* **angle**

straight edge

A straight edge is a plain unmarked flat bar (usually made of wood, plastic, or metal) that can be used to draw a straight line accurately. It has no markings and so cannot be used to make measurements.

straight line

A straight line is the line between two points having the least measurable size. Generally, the word 'line' used by itself means 'straight line' unless the context indicates otherwise.

stratified sampling see **sample**

strip pattern see **pattern**

structure

In mathematics, the structure of a system first defines the objects to be used and then the way in which they are to be used.

• *Arithmetic is an example of a system with a* **structure**, *in which the objects are numbers.*

suan pan see **abacus**

subject

The subject of a formula is the single variable, usually to the left of the = sign, that the rest of the formula is equal to.

• *In the formula $A = \pi r^2$, the* **subject** *is A.*

➤ **changing the subject** of a formula is rearranging it so that the value of a different quantity from that given can be worked out.

• *The* **subject** *of the formula $A = \pi r^2$ is changed to give*

$$r = \sqrt{\dfrac{A}{\pi}}\,.$$

subscript

A subscript is a letter or number written in small type placed to the right and at the bottom of a letter, number, or symbol written in full size.

• *In A_1, A_3, B_n, x_2, and x_r,*
1, 3, n, 2, and r are all **subscripts**.

SEE ALSO **superscript**

subset

A subset is a set which contains part of or all of another set.

• $\subset$ *is the symbol meaning 'is a* **subset** *of'.*
• *$\{2, 7, f, t, M, \phi\} \subset \{numbers, letters, symbols\}$*

proper subset

A proper subset is a subset which does not contain all the members of the other set and is not $\varnothing$.

WORD BUILD

superset

If A is a subset of B, then B is said to be a superset of A.

• $\supset$ *is the symbol meaning 'includes' or 'is a* **superset** *of'.* • *$A \supset B$ can be read as 'set A includes set B' or 'set A is a* **superset** *of set B' or 'set B is a subset of set A'.*

---

substitution

A substitution in algebra is done by replacing one expression, or part of an expression, by something of equivalent value so that the overall truth of the original expression is unchanged.

➤ **substitute** In algebra, to substitute an expression or part of an expression is to replace it by something of equivalent value.

EXAMPLE:

Given $4y + 3x = 22$ and $y = 2x$

Then $4(2x) + 3x = 22$

Which simplifies to $11x = 22$

---

subtended angle

Given three distinct points A, B and C (which are not in a straight line), the subtended angle of any two of the points at the third, is the angle formed between the lines drawn from the first two points to the third.

• *The angle* **subtended** *by the diameter of the Moon at any point on the Earth is about half a degree.* • *In the illustration, the* **subtended angle** *of points A and C at B would be the angle formed between the lines BA and BC.*

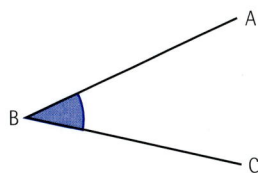

subtraction
is the operation of finding a number which gives a measure of the difference in size between two quantities or measures.
➤ **subtract** To subtract one quantity or measure from another is to find a number which gives a measure of the difference in size between them.
• ***Subtracting*** *nine people from a group of thirteen leaves four.* • $5°C - (-3°C) = 8°C$

subtrahend
In a subtraction sum the subtrahend is the number which must be subtracted from the other number.

SEE ALSO **minuend**

FORMULA:

minuend − subtrahend = difference

sufficient condition *see* condition

sum
❶ A sum is any process in arithmetic needed to solve a problem.
• *How many **sums** did you get right?*
❷ The sum of two or more specified numbers is the process of addition on those numbers.
• *Find the **sum** of all the numbers from 1 to 9.*

SEE ALSO **partial sum**

❸ The sum is the result produced by a process of addition. It is another word for total.
• *The **sum** of 8 and 4 is 12.*

summation sign
The summation sign is the symbol Σ, used to show that a series is being given.

SEE ALSO **series**

superscript
A superscript is a letter or number written in small type placed to the right and at the top of a letter, number, or symbol written full size.

SEE ALSO **subscript**
• *In* A^2, A^n, 5^2, 7^x, *and* y^3, *2, n, 2, x and 3 are all **superscripts**.*

superset *see* subset

supplement
The supplement of an angle is the amount needed to be added on to make 180°.
• *The **supplement** of 70° is 110°.*

SEE ALSO **angle**

⚠ **WATCH OUT**

Complement and **supplement** both relate to right angles.

To complement something is to complete it, so the **complement** is the angle needed to make one complete right angle.

To supplement something is to add something extra, so the **supplement** is the angle needed to be added in order to make two right angles or 180°.

supplementary angle *see* angle

surd
A surd is the square root of a whole number which produces an irrational number.
• *A **surd** can also be a cube (or other) root and is sometimes applied to an expression which contains a surd or surds.* • *The square root of any prime number is a **surd**.* • $\sqrt{2}$ *(≈ 1.414 ...),* $2\sqrt{3}$ *and* $\sqrt{19}$ *are all surds.*

a b c d e f g h i j k l m n o p q r s t u v w x y z

surface

A surface is the two-dimensional outer boundary (or skin) of a three-dimensional object.

EXAMPLE:

Surfaces combine with points and lines so sizes can be measured in two dimensions.

A **surface** is considered to have no thickness.

ruled surface

A ruled surface is a surface on which, at any point, at least one straight line can be drawn which lies entirely on that surface.

EXAMPLE:

A plane or flat surface is the simplest case of a **ruled surface**.

The curved surfaces of a cone and cylinder are also **ruled surfaces**, while a sphere is not.

surveying

is the science of measuring related to the Earth's surface and the presentation of those measurements in a suitable way.
• *Surveying is used in making maps, measuring fields, and in building roads, reservoirs, houses, etc.*

geodetic surveying

is surveying done over large areas where the curvature of the Earth must be considered.

plane surveying

is surveying done over small areas which can, without any serious errors, be treated as flat surfaces. The size limit for a 'small area' would depend on what degree of error is acceptable, but a square of edge-length less than 15 km would be regarded as 'small' for most practical work.

symmetric difference

The symmetric difference of two sets is the single set made which contains only members which were found only once in the original sets. A member found in both sets would not be included.
• Δ *(the Greek letter delta) is the symbol for the symmetric difference of two sets.*

EXAMPLE:

$\{2, 5, 8, 12\}$ Δ $\{1, 5, 12, 15\}$ is $\{1, 2, 8, 15\}$

symmetric expression

A symmetric expression is an algebraic expression using two or more variables whose value is unchanged if any two of the variables are interchanged.

EXAMPLE:

$x + y$

$x^2 + y^2$

$x^2 + y^2 + z^2 + xyz$

WORD BUILD

symmetric equation

A symmetric equation is an equation using a symmetric expression.

EXAMPLE:

$x + y = 6$

$x^2 + y^2 = 10$

$x^2 + y^2 + z^2 + xyz = 104$

symmetric function

A symmetric function is a function using a symmetric expression.
• *Symmetric functions, when drawn as graphs, will show some form of symmetry.*

EXAMPLE:

$f(x) = x + y$

$f(x) = x^2 + y^2$

$f(x) = x^2 + y^2 + z^2 + xyz$

symmetric relation

A symmetric relation is a relationship which is true (or false) whichever way it is read.

• *The most commonly encountered **symmetric relation** is the equals sign since, if x = y, then y = x.* • *Another **symmetric relation** is 'is parallel to' since, if AB is parallel to CD, then CD is parallel to AB.*

symmetry

The word symmetry applied to any object or situation means that parts of the object correspond to or match other parts in some way.

• *The **symmetry** of a shape describes how, under certain rules of movement, the shape fits exactly onto itself.* • *There are three types of shape **symmetry**: line, rotational and plane.*

SEE ALSO **axis of symmetry, line of symmetry, plane of symmetry, rotational symmetry**

line symmetry

is the symmetry of a plane shape which can be folded along a line so that one half of the shape fits exactly on the other half. The line is the axis of symmetry.

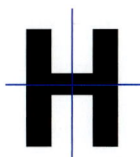 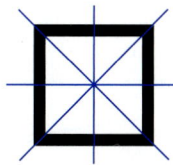

plane symmetry

is the symmetry of a three-dimensional shape in which a plane mirror could be placed so that the reflection looked exactly the same as the part of the shape being covered up by the mirror.

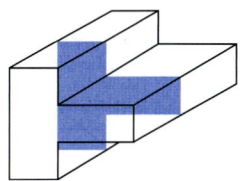

bilateral symmetry (*also* mirror symmetry, reflective symmetry)

is the same as line symmetry of a two-dimensional shape, or plane symmetry of a three-dimensional shape.

systematic sampling *see* **sample**

Tt

tacheometry
is the name of the method by which the distance from a theodolite to some distant point is calculated.

EXAMPLE:

The measurement of the angle subtended at the theodolite (T) by an object of known length placed at the distant point allows the distance to that point to be calculated.

tally
A tally is a physical record of an amount; usually applied to a system which records the amount as it is being counted.

EXAMPLE:

A classic example of a **tally** are marks made on paper, usually grouped in fives.

tan see **trigonometric ratio**

tan⁻¹ see **trigonometric ratio**

tangent
❶ A tangent to a circle is a line which, no matter how far it is extended, touches the circle at one point only.
• *From any one fixed point outside a circle two **tangents** can always be drawn to that circle.*
• *The radius drawn at the point where the **tangent** touches the circle is at right angles to the tangent.*

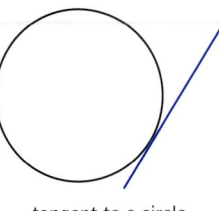

tangent to a circle

❷ A tangent to a curve is a straight line that touches the curve at a point. The tangent will have the same gradient as the curve at that point.

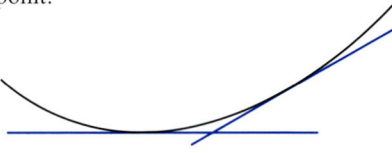

tangents to a curve

❸ A tangent of an angle is the trigonometric ratio between the adjacent side and the opposite side of that angle in a right-angled triangle.

SEE ALSO **trigonometric ratio**

common tangent
A common tangent is a tangent that touches two circles.

direct common tangent
A direct common tangent is a common tangent that does not pass between the centres of the two circles.

transverse common tangent
A transverse common tangent is a common tangent that does pass between the centres of the two circles.

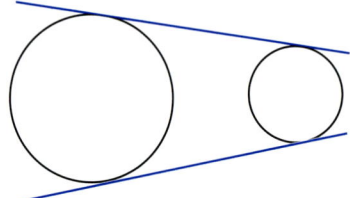

direct common tangents

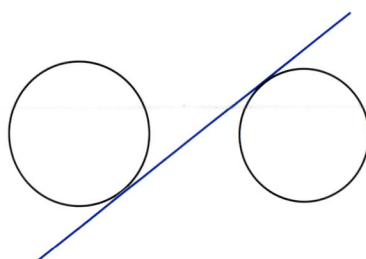

transverse common tangent

tangent curve

A tangent curve is the graph that shows how the value of the tangent of an angle changes with the size of the angle.

SEE ALSO cosine curve, sine curve

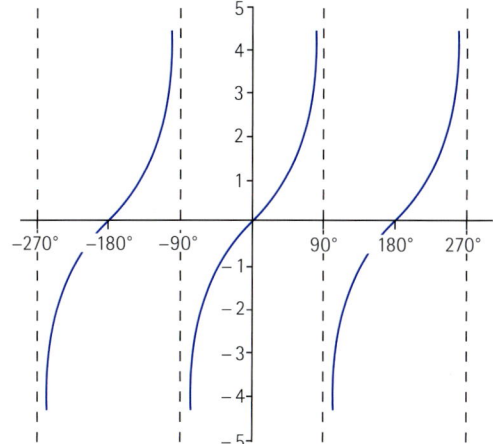

tangram

Tangram puzzles use a standard dissection of a square into seven pieces and require those pieces to be arranged to make up a given shape, which is shown only in outline.

  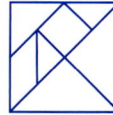

a tangram puzzle and its solution

temperature

The temperature of something is a measure of how hot it is according to a value given on a known scale.
• *When heat moves between objects, it always moves from an object at a higher* **temperature** *to an object at a lower one.* • **Temperature** *is measured by means of a thermometer or similar instrument.* • *There are three main scales used for measuring* **temperature***: Celsius, Fahrenheit, and Kelvin.*

SEE ALSO conversion graph

WORD BUILD

Celsius scale (*also* centigrade)

The Celsius scale sets the freezing point of water at zero degrees (0°C) and the boiling point at 100 degrees (100°C).

• *The* **Celsius scale** *was devised by Anders Celsius (1701–1744), a Swedish astronomer.* • *The* **Celsius scale** *was originally called centigrade but was then officially changed in 1948 because it could be confused with a system of angle measurement which used grades and* **centigrades***.*

FORMULA:

To change °F to °C, subtract 32 and multiply by $\frac{5}{9}$.

Fahrenheit scale

The Fahrenheit scale sets the freezing point of water at 32 degrees (32°F) and the boiling point at 212 degrees (212°F).
• *The* **Fahrenheit scale** *was devised by G D Fahrenheit (1686–1736), a German physicist.* • **Fahrenheit** *degrees are smaller than Celsius degrees.*

FORMULA:

To change °C to °F, multiply by $\frac{9}{5}$ and add 32.

Kelvin scale

The Kelvin scale starts at absolute zero and all temperatures are measured from that point in units called kelvins, where 1 kelvin is the same size as 1 degree on the Celsius scale. It sets the freezing point of water at 273.15 K and the boiling point at 485.15 K.
• *The* **Kelvin scale** *was devised by William Thomson, 1st Lord Kelvin (1824–1907), a Scottish physicist and mathematician.*
• *To change temperatures between the Celsius and Kelvin scales, use:*
Temperature in °C = Temperature in K − 273.15
Temperature in K = Temperature in °C + 273.15

FORMULA:

To change K to °C, subtract 273.15.

To change °C to K, add 273.15.

template (*also* stencil)

A template is a thin sheet of strong material (usually plastic) which is cut into a particular shape, or has shapes cut out of it, to provide outlines which can be drawn firmly and quickly.
• *The picture shows a template that might be used to draw some shapes, symbols, and letters.*

a b c d e f g h i j k l m n o p q r s t u v w x y z

tend see **infinity**

tercimal see **bicimal**

term
❶ The terms in a simple algebraic expression are the quantities that are linked to each other by means of + or − signs.
• *$5x^2 + 3x − xy + 7$ has four **terms***.
❷ A term of a sequence is one of its separate numbers or objects. The terms of a sequence are usually separated by a comma or a space.

---

constant term (*also* **constant**)

A constant term or constant in an expression or equation is any term, or terms, consisting only of a constant with no variables attached.
• *In $5x + y − 2$ the coefficients are 5 and 1; the **constant term** is −2.*

---

like term

Like terms are those terms that are completely identical in respect of their variables. They must contain exactly the same variables and each variable must be raised to the same power. The coefficients can be different.
• *The purpose of identifying **like terms** is that they may be collected together by addition or subtraction.*
• *Some pairs of **like terms** are 3x and 5x, and $7x^2y$ and x^2y.*

---

terminating decimal see **decimal fraction**

ternary see **number base**

tessellation
A tessellation is an arrangement of shapes which fit together to fill a space with no gaps or overlaps. Originally the word was only applied to two-dimensional space, but is now taken to apply to three-dimensional space as well.
• *In a **tessellation**, it must always be clear that the pattern used for filling can be continued indefinitely. It is usually assumed that the shapes used all have the same length of edge and touch each other along the full lengths of their adjoining edges.*
SEE ALSO **tiling**

theodolite
A theodolite is an instrument used by land-surveyors. It is usually mounted on a tripod and consists of a sighting-tube (like a telescope) which can be moved in both the horizontal and vertical planes, with these movements (measured in degrees) being shown on two suitable scales.

theorem
A theorem is a statement which has been proved to be true.
SEE ALSO **Fermat's last theorem, Pick's theorem, Ptolemy's theorem, Pythagoras' theorem**

theoretical probability see **probability**

thickness see **dimension**

third quadrant see **quadrant**

three-dimensional (*also* **3D**)
A space is described as being three-dimensional or 3D if, to give the position of any point in that space, three and only three measurements are necessary from three straight lines (no pair being parallel) fixed in that space.

three-dimensional coordinates
see **coordinate**

three-dimensional pattern see **pattern**

tile
A tile is an individual shape used in a tiling.
• ***Tiles** are usually polygons, but curved shapes can also be used.* • *Some of the more unusual shapes that work as **tiles** are pentominos, hexominos, and any polyiamonds made from six or eight triangles.*

tiling (also **mosaic**)

A tiling is a tessellation in two-dimensional space.
• *Additional requirements are sometimes applied to a **tiling**, such as: all the shapes must be identical; shapes may not be turned over; shapes may not be rotated, and so on.*

➤ **notation for tilings** In a tiling where three or more vertices meet at a common point, each separate vertex is given a series of numbers reflecting how many edges each shape meeting at that vertex has.

• *At the common point marked in the centre of the diagram, the numbers 3, 3, 4, 3, 4 would indicate that a triangle, a triangle, a square, a triangle, and a square meet at that point. This is usually abbreviated to 3^2, 4, 3, 4.*

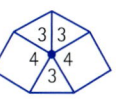

non-periodic tiling (also **aperiodic tiling**)

A tiling which is not periodic is described as non-periodic or aperiodic.

periodic tiling

A tiling is said to be periodic if a section of it can be identified which will itself do the tiling by means of a translation only. In effect, the section becomes the shape which is used to do the tiling.

EXAMPLE:

Most tilings which are seen are **periodic**.

regular tiling

Regular tilings are those tilings made by using only a single shape which is a regular polygon.
• *There are only three possible shapes that can be used in a **regular tiling**: an equilateral triangle, a square, or a regular hexagon.*

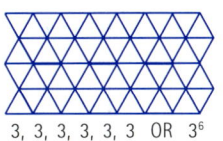

3, 3, 3, 3, 3, 3 OR 3^6

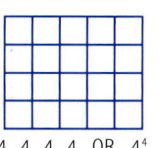

4, 4, 4, 4 OR 4^4

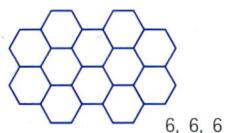

6, 6, 6 OR 6^3

semi-regular tiling

Semi-regular tilings are those tilings which use more than one shape, but all the shapes are regular polygons and the notation at every point where vertices meet is the same.
• *There are only eight possible shapes that can be used in a **semi-regular tiling**, although one of them can exist in two forms with one being a mirror image of the other. The only regular polygons used are the triangle, square, hexagon, octagon, and dodecagon.*

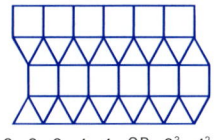

3, 3, 3, 4, 4 OR 3^3, 4^2

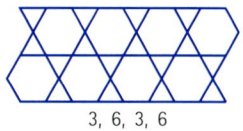

3, 6, 3, 6

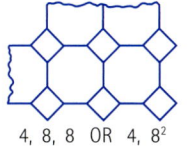

4, 8, 8 OR 4, 8^2

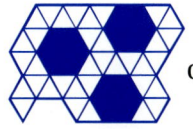 **OR**

3, 3, 3, 3, 6 OR 3^4, 6
(which allows two mirror image forms)

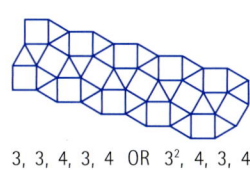

3, 3, 4, 3, 4 OR 3^2, 4, 3, 4

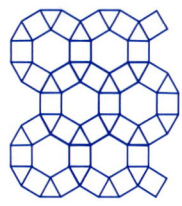

3, 4, 6, 4

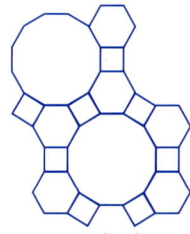

4, 6, 12

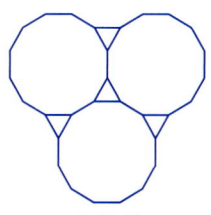

3, 12, 12

a b c d e f g h i j k l m n o p q r s t u v w x y z

time series

A time series is one of the most commonly seen types of graph in everyday use. It gives several values of a measurement taken at different times, shows how the measurement varies with time, and is often used to make predictions about what will happen.

SEE ALSO **trend, variation**

EXAMPLE:

The graph shows a possible set of values for a **time series**. No scales are marked. It could show the amount of radioactivity in a certain spot against time measured in nanoseconds, or the amount of movement of a glacier (in metres) against time measured in centuries.

This graph shows an upward trend.

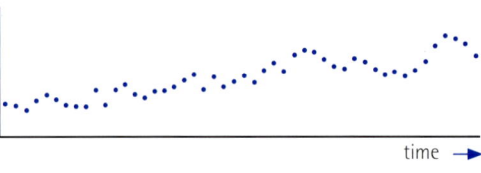

time →

tolerance

is the amount by which a nominal value may vary.

• *Tolerance is commonly used as a measure in the manufacturing industry.*

EXAMPLE:

A piston diameter is given as 65 mm ± 0.015 mm, so it has a nominal diameter of 65 mm but could be as small as 64.985 mm or as big as 65.015 mm.

The error allowed is not always evenly spread, as in $76^{+0.023}_{-0.037}$ mm.

topological graph *see* **graph**

topology

is the study of shapes and their properties which are not changed by transformations of a particular type.

• *Topology is popularly known as 'rubber-sheet' geometry because of the way shapes can be deformed, but it is also possible to move lines from 'inside' a space to 'outside', working within the allowed rules.*

topological transformation

Topological transformations allow a shape to be deformed in almost any way provided that it always retains:

- the same number of vertices, edges and faces
- the same order for all the vertices
- the points along each edge following in the same relative positions.
- Length and direction do not matter.

• *The illustration shows a* **topological transformation** *of a railway map from an actual layout to a topologically equivalent diagram.*

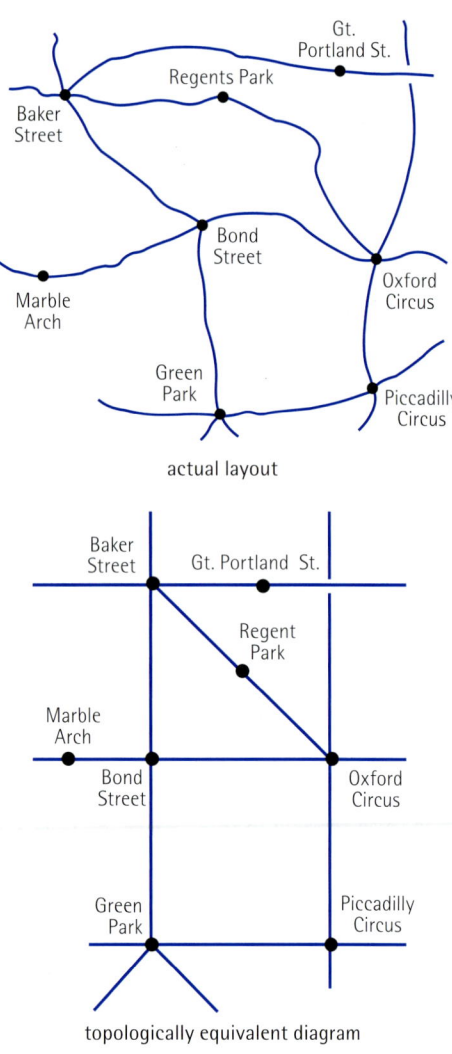

actual layout

topologically equivalent diagram

topologically equivalent

Two shapes are said to be topologically equivalent if, using only topological transformations, one can be deformed in such a way as to become identical to the other.
• *Bus and rail organizations often use diagrams that are **topologically equivalent** to the real layout of the roads and rails, to simplify them.* • *No measurements can be made on such diagrams.*

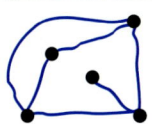

topologically equivalent graphs

torus

A torus is a solid ring, in which the 'band' making the ring has a circular cross-section.
• *The minor radius of a **torus** is the radius of the circular band.* • *The major radius of a **torus** is the distance between the centre of the **torus** and the centre of its circular band.*

FORMULA:

Volume = $(2\pi R)(\pi r^2)$

Surface Area = $(2\pi R)(2\pi r)$

where

R is the major radius of the torus

r is the minor radius of the torus

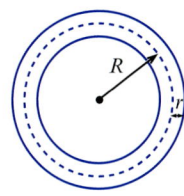

major and minor radii of a torus

total (*also* aggregate, sum)

A total is the final number produced by the process of addition. It is also called the aggregate or the sum.
• *In 9 + 4 = 13 the number 13 is the **total**.*

trace

The trace of a square matrix is the sum of the elements in the main diagonal.

SEE ALSO matrix

EXAMPLE:

In $\begin{pmatrix} -6 & 10 \\ 14 & 18 \end{pmatrix}$ the trace is $-6 + 18 = 12$.

trailing diagonal *see* diagonal

trammel compass *see* compass

transcendental number *see* number

transformation

A transformation is a change carried out under specific rules, especially the operations that may be used on a figure to affect its position, shape, or size.
• *In a **transformation**, the figure being transformed may be as small as a single point, and anything larger may be thought of as being made up of many points.* • *If a circle is drawn on a coordinate grid, then a **transformation** can be applied to all the points which define that circle to produce a new shape. This is usually done using matrices.*

SEE ALSO image, object, translation

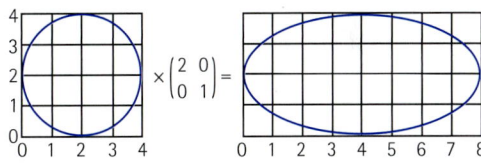

▶ **transform** To transform something such as a figure is to carry out a change to it under specific rules.
• *A circle can be **transformed** into an ellipse by means of a one-way stretch.*

transformation geometry

deals with the operations that may be used on a figure to affect its position, shape, or size; or any combination of those.

a b c d e f g h i j k l m n o p q r s t u v w x y z

translation

A translation is a transformation such that every point in the object can be joined to its corresponding point in the image by a set of straight lines which are all parallel and of equal length.

• *A **translation** is described by the direction and length of the movement.*

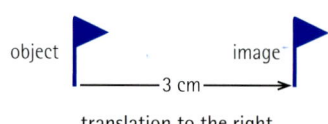

translation to the right

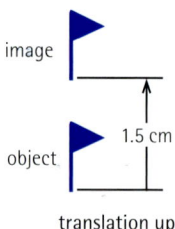

translation up

. . . .

transpose

❶ To transpose an equation or formula is to rearrange it.
• *The equation $4x + y = 5$ can be **transposed** to $y = 5 - 4x$.*
❷ The transpose of a matrix is made by rewriting the rows of the matrix as columns.
• *In the **transpose** of a square matrix, the leading diagonal will be unchanged.*

EXAMPLE:

For $\begin{pmatrix} a & b & c \\ d & e & f \end{pmatrix}$ the transpose is $\begin{pmatrix} a & d \\ b & e \\ c & f \end{pmatrix}$

. . . .

transversal

A transversal is a straight line that cuts across other straight lines. The other lines are usually parallel.

. . . .

transverse common tangent *see* tangent

. . . .

trapezium *plural* trapezia, trapeziums

A trapezium is a quadrilateral with only one pair of parallel edges.

FORMULA:

Area of a trapezium $= \dfrac{(b + p)}{2} \times h$

where

b is the length of the base

p is the length of the edge parallel to the base

h is the perpendicular height of the trapezium

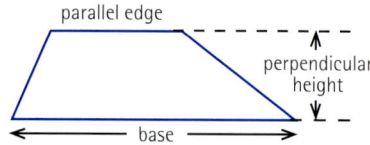

isosceles trapezium

An isosceles trapezium is a trapezium in which the two opposite edges, which are not parallel, are the same length. It has one line of symmetry and both diagonals are the same length.

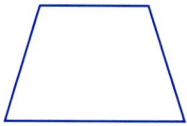

. . . .

trapezium rule *see* mid-ordinate rule

. . . .

trapezoid

❶ In UK usage, a trapezoid is a quadrilateral in which no two opposite edges are parallel.
❷ In US usage, a trapezoid is another word for a trapezium.

. . . .

trapezoidal rule *see* mid-ordinate rule

. . . .

travel graph *see* distance-time graph

. . . .

traversable

A topological graph is said to be traversable if it can be drawn as one continuous line without going over any edge more than once. Such a graph must have either zero or two vertices with an odd number of edges joined to them. i.e. a traversable graph must have zero or two odd vertices.

SEE ALSO **vertex**

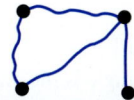

WORD BUILD

unicursal

A topological graph is said to be unicursal if it is traversable and any start and finish are at the same point. It will have no odd vertices.

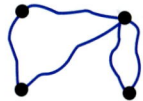

---

traverse

A traverse is a line which forms part of a survey.
• *Usually the length of the **traverse** is known. Sometimes the direction is also known.*

---

tree diagram

A tree diagram is drawn to find and display all possible results when several outcomes are being combined.
• *When three coins are tossed, all possible results can be found and displayed by using a **tree diagram**. In this **tree diagram**, H stands for head and T stands for tail.*

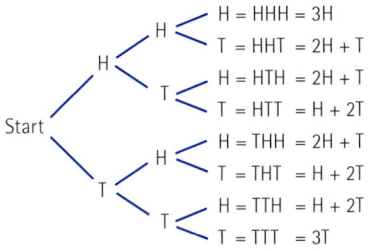

---

trend

The trend of a time series is an indication of the general direction of its movement over the period of time for which the measurements were made.

SEE ALSO **time series**

---

trend line

A trend line is the single line that best represents the general direction of a set of points.
• *A **trend line** is especially useful when some observed data has been plotted that does not lie on a straight line, but estimates are required to be made based on that data.*

WORD BUILD

line of best fit

The line of best fit is the trend line drawn on a scatter graph.
• *The higher the correlation, the easier it is to draw the **line of best fit**.*

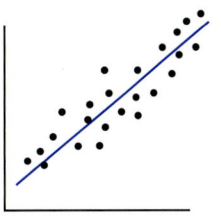

---

trial

A trial is an experiment, for example rolling a dice or tossing a coin to discover the outcome.

SEE ALSO **event, probability, random**

---

trial and improvement (*also* trial and error)

is a method of looking for a solution in which a guessed-at value is put into a problem then the consequences are followed through, and, on the basis of any error found, a better guess-value is made.
• ***Trial and improvement** is a very powerful method and capable of solving almost any kind of problem, provided that it is solvable.*

EXAMPLE:

To find a root of $2x^3 + 4x - 5 = 0$, first try $x = 1$ in the expression. This gives a value of 1.

Trying $x = 1.1$ gives a value of 2.062, so try $x = 0.9$ to get 0.058.

In this way, we can find ever closer answers to the expression for x.

triangle

A triangle is a polygon which has three edges. Its three interior angles add up to 180 degrees. Triangles are usually described by reference to their edges or their vertices (or both).

SEE ALSO trigonometric ratio

FORMULA:

Area = (base × perpendicular height) ÷ 2

➤ **notation for triangles** Triangles are usually identified by three capital letters placed at each vertex (like ABC).
• *There are two methods for referring to the edges and the angles of triangles.* • *One identifies edges by the two letters of the vertices at each end of that edge (AB, BC, AC) and the vertex angles by the three letters of the vertices to be taken in order as they trace out that angle (ABC, BCA, CAB).*
• *The other method, used in formulas, is to identify edges by a single small letter (a, b, c) corresponding to the letter of the opposite vertex, and the vertex angles either by the single capital letter of that vertex (A, B, C) or by the corresponding greek letter (α, β, γ).*

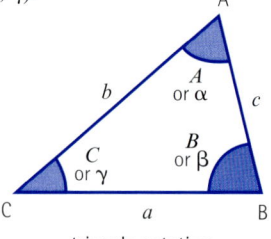

triangle notation

acute triangle

An acute triangle has no angle greater than 90°. It must also be either a scalene triangle, an isosceles triangle, or an equilateral triangle.

equilateral triangle

An equilateral triangle has all of its edges of the same length. All its angles are of the same size and equal to 60°. It has three lines of symmetry and rotational symmetry of order 3.

Heronian triangle

A Heronian triangle is a triangle whose three edge lengths and its area are all rational numbers.

isosceles triangle

An isosceles triangle has two edges of the same length. Two of its angles must also be of the same size. It has one line of symmetry.

median triangle

The median triangle is the one formed by drawing straight lines between the mid-points of the three edges of another triangle.
• *A **median triangle** divides the original triangle into four congruent triangles.*

obtuse triangle

An obtuse triangle has one angle greater than 90°. It is also either an isosceles or a scalene triangle.

pedal triangle

The pedal triangle of a given triangle is the triangle formed by drawing straight lines between the points at the feet of the three altitudes of the original triangle. It is also the triangle having the smallest possible perimeter that can be inscribed in the given triangle and touches all its edges.

right-angled triangle

A right-angled triangle has one angle equal to 90°. It is also either an isosceles or a scalene triangle.

scalene triangle

A scalene triangle has all its edges of different lengths. All of its angles must also be of different sizes. It has no symmetry.

vector triangle

A vector triangle is made when three vectors are added together to form a triangle whose resultant is zero.

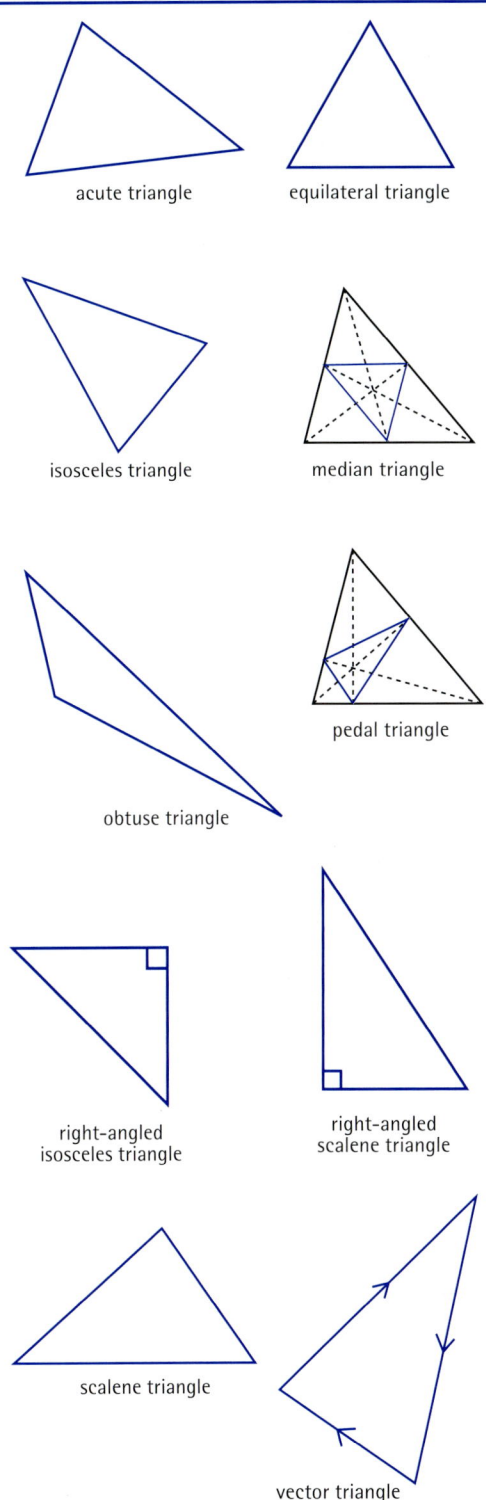

acute triangle

equilateral triangle

isosceles triangle

median triangle

pedal triangle

obtuse triangle

right-angled
isosceles triangle

right-angled
scalene triangle

scalene triangle

vector triangle

triangle number *see* polygon number

triangulation

is the method of dividing up the surface which has to be measured into a set of triangles, so that each triangle is joined to at least two other triangles. Triangulation is useful because, from knowing only one edge-length, and most (but not all) of the angles involved, all the other edge-lengths can be calculated. Angles can be measured more accurately and more easily than lengths.

• *In the diagram, the black outline marks the edges of the shape being surveyed and the blue lines give the **triangulation**. If the length of the thick (blue) line is known, together with the sizes of all the angles at each of the five marked (black) points, then the lengths of all the other lines can be calculated.*

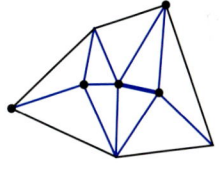

trick

There are many tricks involving the manipulation of numbers (often using cards, dice, and dominoes) which seem to produce 'magical' results but which depend on elementary principles of arithmetic.

EXAMPLE:

A number **trick** with dice: Ask someone to roll two dice without revealing the results.

Then to multiply one of them by 5, add 7, double the result and add the other number, and give the result.

From the two digit answer, subtract 14 and the two digits remaining will give the numbers showing on the dice.

a
b
c
d
e
f
g
h
i
j
k
l
m
n
o
p
q
r
s
t
u
v
w
x
y
z

trigonometric function

The trigonometric functions are the group of functions (linked to the trigonometric ratios) which map the size of any angle to a real number. This is done by expressing each of the functions as an infinite series.

• *The series for the sine, cosine, and tangent functions are given below where the angle x has to be expressed in radians.* • *The coefficients needed for sin x and cos x follow an obvious pattern. This is not so for tan x where they are generated by a more complex relationship.*

FORMULA:

$$\sin x = x - \frac{x^3}{3!} + \frac{x^5}{5!} - \frac{x^7}{7!} + \frac{x^9}{9!} - \cdots$$

$$\cos x = 1 - \frac{x^2}{2!} + \frac{x^4}{4!} - \frac{x^6}{6!} + \frac{x^8}{8!} - \cdots$$

$$\tan x = x + \frac{x^3}{3} + \frac{2x^5}{15} + \frac{17x^7}{315} + \frac{62x^9}{2,835} + \cdots$$

trigonometric ratio

Trigonometric ratios express the relationship which exists between the size of one angle and the lengths of two edges in a right-angled triangle.

• *These trigonometric ratios can be defined in relation to the triangle shown, where A, B, and C are the three angles, and a, b, and c are the lengths of the three corresponding edges.*

SEE ALSO cosine curve, cosine rule, sine curve, sine rule, tangent curve

FORMULA:

There are six trigonometric ratios:

sine A (sin A) = $\frac{a}{c}$

cosine A (cos A) = $\frac{b}{c}$

tangent A (tan A) = $\frac{a}{b}$

cosecant A (cosec A) = $\frac{c}{a}$

secant A (sec A) = $\frac{c}{b}$

cotangent A (cot A) = $\frac{b}{a}$

Some relationships between these ratios are:

$\sin^2 A + \cos^2 A = 1$

$\tan A = \dfrac{\sin A}{\cos A}$

$\operatorname{cosec} A = \dfrac{1}{\sin A}$

$\sec A = \dfrac{1}{\cos A}$

$\cot A = \dfrac{1}{\tan A}$

In any of the fractions given above, none of the bottom values can be zero.

The trigonometric ratios of negative angles can be found using:

$\sin(-\theta) = -\sin \theta$

$\cos(-\theta) = \cos \theta$

$\tan(-\theta) = -\tan \theta$

For example: $\sin(-30°) = -\sin 30° = -0.5$

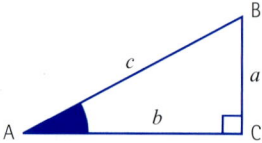

inverse trigonometric ratio

is the inverse function of a trigonometric ratio.
• *Each inverse function has two notations.*
For example, the inverse of sin A can be written as arcsin A or sin⁻¹ A. • *The table shows the possible values for the inverse trigonometric ratios.*

		Possible x	Possible y
$y = \arcsin(x)$	$x = \sin(y)$	$-1 \le x \le 1$	$-90° \le y \le 90°$
$y = \arccos(x)$	$x = \cos(y)$	$-1 \le x \le 1$	$0° \le y \le 180°$
$y = \arctan(x)$	$x = \tan(y)$	all real numbers	$-90° < y < 90°$
$y = \operatorname{arccot}(x)$	$x = \cot(y)$	all real numbers	$0° < y < 180°$
$y = \operatorname{arcsec}(x)$	$x = \sec(y)$	$x \le -1$ or $1 \le x$	$0° \le y < 90°$ or $90° \le y < 180°$
$y = \operatorname{arccsc}(x)$	$x = \csc(y)$	$x \le -1$ or $1 \le x$	$-90° \le y < 0°$ or $0° < y \le 90°$

trigonometry

is the study of triangles with regard to their measurements and the relationships between those measurements using trigonometric ratios. It also deals with trigonometric functions.

SEE ALSO **spherical trigonometry, trigonometric function, trigonometric ratio**

trinomial see **multinomial**

triplet see **Pythagorean triplet**

trisect

To trisect an object is to cut or divide it into three parts which are equal in size and shape.

SEE ALSO **geometrical construction**

trivial solution see **solution**

trivium

In the Middle Ages the trivium was the three subjects grammar, rhetoric, and logic. Combined with the quadrivium (the four subjects arithmetic, geometry, astronomy, and music), they formed the seven liberal arts, the basis of most university educations at that time.

troy ounce

The troy ounce is an old measure still used for precious metals and stones.

• *1 troy ounce = 31.103 476 8 grams.*

true

Within a system, a statement is said to be true when it is a known fact, or follows from some other true statement by means of a valid argument, or is considered to be self-evident.

truncate

To truncate something is to cut it short without rounding up.

• *In order to work with π in a calculation we always have to **truncate** the true value because it is a never-ending decimal.*

truncation error see **error**

T–square

A T-square is an instrument in the shape of the capital letter T which is used on a drawing board for drawing parallel lines. Professionals today usually use a drawing board which incorporates a parallel-motion mechanism.

• *The drawing shows a **T-square** on a drawing board with some lines drawn.*

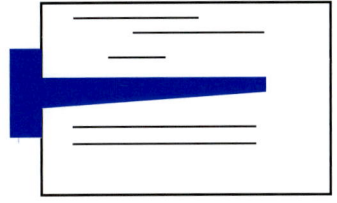

turn

When something turns it spins, rotates, revolves, or whirls.

SEE ALSO **anticlockwise, clockwise, revolve, rotate, transformation**

two–dimensional (*also* **2D**)

A space is described as being two-dimensional or 2D if, to give the position of any point in that space, two and only two measurements are necessary from a pair of non-parallel straight lines fixed in that space.

two–dimensional pattern see **pattern**

a
b
c
d
e
f
g
h
i
j
k
l
m
n
o
p
q
r
s
t
u
v
w
x
y
z

two-way table

A two-way table is a table of data which shows the combined effect of two separate happenings.

EXAMPLE:

The diagram is a **two-way table** which shows (in blue) the combined total scores possible when two dice are rolled.

From this table it can be seen that, with two dice, a score of 7 can happen in more ways than any other score, while 2 and 12 can happen in only one way.

+	Second die					
	1	**2**	**3**	**4**	**5**	**6**
1	2	3	4	5	6	7
2	3	4	5	6	7	8
3	4	5	6	7	8	9
4	5	6	7	8	9	10
5	6	7	8	9	10	11
6	7	8	9	10	11	12

(rows labelled: First die)

Uu

unary operation *see* operation

. . . .

undecidable

Within a system, a statement is said to be undecidable when it cannot be shown to be either true or false.

. . . .

unicursal *see* traversable

. . . .

uniform *see* constant

. . . .

union

The union of two (or more) sets is their combination into a single set containing all the members of the original sets. A member found in more than one of the original sets need only be shown once in the union.

• U *is the symbol for the* **union** *of sets.*
• *{4, 7, 13, 20}* ∪ *{2, 7, 10} is*
{2, 4, 7, 10, 13, 20}

. . . .

unique solution *see* solution

. . . .

unit

❶ Unit is a name for 'one'. Hundreds, tens, and units or ones are used in place value.
• *In the decimal number 143, 3 is in the position of* **units**.

SEE ALSO place value, base

❷ Units are used in measuring.
• *Litre is a* **unit** *of capacity.*
• *Kilogram is a* **unit** *of mass.*
• *Metre is a* **unit** *of length.*

SEE ALSO SI

. . . .

unitary method

The unitary method can be used when the relationship between two quantities is fixed, the value of a third quantity is given, and the value of a fourth quantity has to be found having the same relationship to the third as the first pair have to each other.

• The **unitary method** is based on making one of the first pair of quantities of unit value.

EXAMPLE:

How much petrol will be needed for a journey of 1,000 km if a car goes 480 km on 30 litres of petrol?

Divide both sides by 480. A car will go 1 km on 0.0625 litres of petrol.

So a car will go 1,000 km on 62.5 litres of petrol.

WORD BUILD

rule of three

The rule of three applies to the same type of problems as described in unitary method, but solves them by writing the given quantities down in a prescribed order, multiplying together the third and the second and dividing by the first.

EXAMPLE:

How much petrol will be needed for a journey of 1,000 km if a car goes 480 km on 30 litres of petrol?

$480 : 30 :: 1,000 : ?$

$1,000 \times 30 \div 480 = 62.5$

unit vector

A unit vector is a vector which is considered to be the unit of size from which other vectors are made by scalar multiplication.

➤ **unit vectors i, j, k** In a three-dimensional vector system, with the axes perpendicular to each other, the three unit vectors (length = 1) lie on the main axes (x, y, z) and are identified as i, j, and k respectively.

• *Expressed numerically, $i = (1, 0, 0)$, $j = (0, 1, 0)$ and $k = (0, 0, 1)$.* • *All the other vectors can then be written in terms of the 3 **unit vectors**. For example $(4, 17, 9) \equiv (4i, 17j, 9k)$.*

EXAMPLE:

For **unit vectors**

$i \times j = k$

$j \times k = i$

$k \times i = j$

$i \times i = j \times j = k \times k = 0$

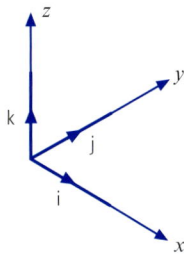

unity

the number one

universal set *see* set

universe *see* set

upper quartile *see* quartile

 Vv

valid

A valid proof (or statement) is one in which all the arguments leading up to it are correct within the logic of the system being used.

WORD BUILD
invalid

An invalid proof (or statement) is one which is not valid.

....

value

A value is the amount or quantity denoted by a symbol or letter.
• Find the **value** of x.

SEE ALSO **absolute value, place value, stationary value**

nominal value

The nominal value of a number is the 'named' amount or, in the case of a measurement, the size it is intended to be.

....

Value Added Tax *see* VAT

....

variable

A variable is a symbol (usually a letter such as x, y, z) that may take any value from a given range of values. Unless the range of possible values is stated, then the variable can be any real number.

dependent variable

In a mapping, the dependent variable is the element or number to which the mapping goes.
• *The usual symbol is y or f(x).* • *The example shows the mapping for $f::x \rightarrow x^2 - 1$.*
*The values of the **dependent variable** are $\{0, 8, 15, 24, 35, 48, 63\}$.*

independent variable

In a mapping, the independent variable (usually x) is the element or number from which the mapping starts.
• *The example shows the mapping for $f::x \rightarrow x^2 - 1$.*
*The values of the **independent variable** are $\{1, 3, 4, 5, 6, 7, 8\}$.*

EXAMPLE:
$1 \rightarrow 0$
$3 \rightarrow 8$
$4 \rightarrow 15$
$5 \rightarrow 24$
$6 \rightarrow 35$
$7 \rightarrow 48$
$8 \rightarrow 63$

real variable

A real variable is a variable whose values must be real numbers.

....

variance

The variance of a set of data is a measure of its dispersion. Its value is given by the square of the standard deviation.
• *It can also be said that the standard deviation is the square root of the **variance**.* • *σ^2 and s^2 are symbols used for the **variance**.*

SEE ALSO **standard deviation**

....

variation

All measurements taken for a time series show variations for many reasons, not all of which can be identified.

SEE ALSO **time series**

cyclical variation

If a time series has a cyclical variation, the general shape of the graph has a tendency to repeat over time.

periodic variation

A periodic variation is a cyclical variation which happens at identifiable intervals over time.

random variation

A random variation is one which happens in an uncontrollable and unpredictable way throughout.

• *Random variations may be assumed to be present in any time series in addition to any known types.*

seasonal variation

A periodic variation where the intervals can be matched to the seasons of the year.

secular variation

A secular variation is one which can only be observed after long periods of time. A long period of time is usually taken to be greater than 2 years, and may be several thousands of years.

VAT (*also* Value Added Tax)

is a tax paid on the goods or services bought by a customer, which is then paid by the supplier of those goods or services to the government.

• *The rate at which VAT is charged is given as a percentage, and varies with different goods and in different countries.*

vector

❶ A vector is something which can be defined by two quantities: its size and its direction.

• *Velocity is a **vector** since it is described by giving both the speed of an object and the direction in which the object is moving. Speed alone is not a **vector**.*

• *Force is also a **vector**.*

SEE ALSO absolute value, dimension, magnitude

❷ A vector is a set of numbers which can be represented in an appropriate space by a line to show both its length and its direction. The line may be actual or imagined. A vector having *n* numbers needs an *n*-dimensional space for its representation.

• *The **vector** (2, 3) could be shown by an actual line drawn in a two-dimensional space, while (1, 7, 5) would require a three-dimensional space.*

• *With a **vector** having four numbers (6, 3, 8, 2) the space needed would be four-dimensional and its representation could only be imagined.*

SEE ALSO unit vector

➤ **addition of vectors** Two or more vectors can be added by joining them together end to end, always so that their directions 'follow on' from each other, and the answer is the single vector which can be drawn from the 'start' point to the 'finish' point of the vectors. The order in which they are joined does not matter.

• *The diagrams show that when adding two vectors a and b, the results are the same for a + b or b + a. When subtracting one from the other, the results are the same in size but opposite in direction.*

adding vectors

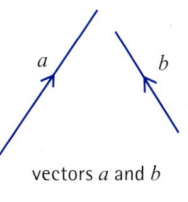

vectors *a* and *b*

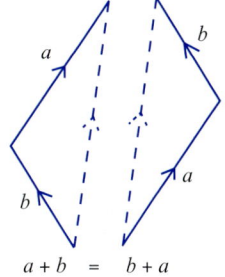

$$a + b \quad = \quad b + a$$

subtracting vectors

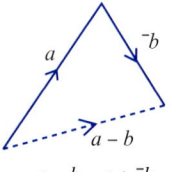

$$a - b = a + {}^-b$$

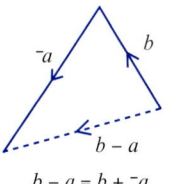

$$b - a = b + {}^-a$$

➤ **notation for vectors** The most commonly used way of showing that vectors are being referred to in printed work is by using bold-face lower-case letters. Vectors are often written using angle brackets: ⟨7, 3, 14⟩. Commas are not always used. $\overrightarrow{AB}$ and AB are used in diagrammatic and written work to refer to a vector whose size is represented by the distance between A and B and whose direction is from A to B. The size is often referred to some scale. A single letter is also used (A or **a** or A, etc) but only after the vector has been defined in some way. In written work $\underset{\sim}{A}$ and $\underset{\sim}{a}$ is also used.

• *Given **a** ≡ (7, 4, 12) and **b** ≡ (6, 0, 5) it is much easier to write 3**a** + **b** than to write the vectors out in full.*   »

column vector

A column vector is a vector in which the set of numbers is written in a vertical line.

SEE ALSO matrix

free vector

A free vector is a vector which does not have a defined starting point and so can be placed anywhere in space.

negative vector

The negative of a given vector is another vector that is the same in size but opposite in direction to the given vector.

null vector (also zero vector)

A null vector or zero vector is a vector which, when represented by a line, has no length and no direction; in its numerical form all the numbers will be 0.

orthogonal vector (also perpendicular vector)

Orthogonal or perpendicular vectors are vectors whose directions are at right angles to each other.
• *Two vectors whose scalar product is zero are said to be* **orthogonal vectors** *or perpendicular vectors.*
• *This can happen because cos θ = 0 or the product of their magnitudes is 0.*

EXAMPLE:

Given $\mathbf{a} \equiv (2, 7, 3)$ and $\mathbf{b} \equiv (4, 1, -5)$ then since $(2 \times 4 + 7 \times 1 + 3 \times -5) = 0$, they must be perpendicular to each other.

parallel vector

Two vectors (neither of which is a zero vector) must be parallel to each other if their vector product is zero.

plane vector

A plane vector is a vector whose direction can be given solely by reference to two-dimensional space.
• *The direction of a* **plane vector** *might be given by using coordinates such as (x, y), or by using an angle such as a compass direction.*

position vector

A position vector is a vector which starts at some known point, and its finishing point gives a position relative to that starting point.
• *Any coordinate system may be thought of as a vector system, where the origin is the starting point of a* **position vector** *which goes to or finishes at the given position.*

row vector

A row vector is a vector in which the set of numbers is written in a horizontal line.
• *(3, 5) (4, 0, 2) (15, −6, 11, 28) are all* **row vectors**. *Without the commas, each can also be considered to be a row matrix.*

SEE ALSO matrix

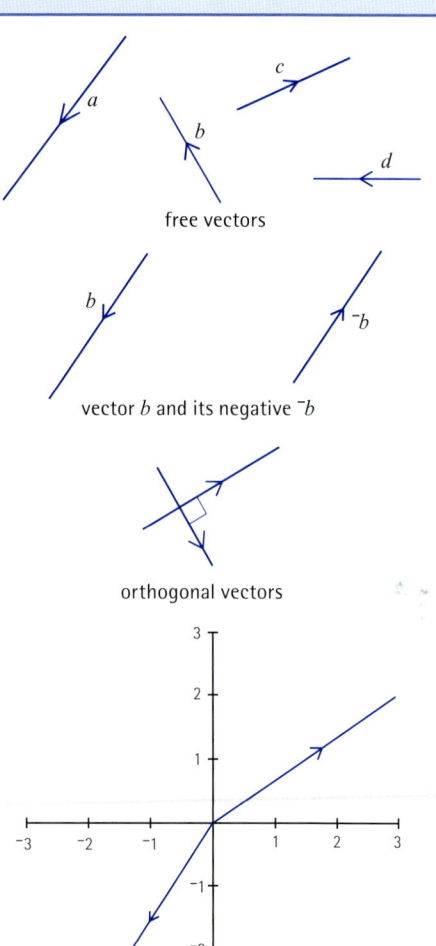

free vectors

vector b and its negative ⁻b

orthogonal vectors

position vectors
(3, 2) and (⁻3, ⁻2)

vector product

The vector product of two vectors *a* and *b* (written $a \times b$ or $a \wedge b$) with an angle between them of θ ($0 < \theta < 180°$) is vector *c* whose magnitude is the product of the magnitudes of *a*, *b*, and $\sin \theta$ and is perpendicular to both *a* and *b* in a direction that makes *a*, *b*, *c* a right-handed system.

SEE ALSO **unit vector**

EXAMPLE:

$a \times b = |a| \times |b| \times \sin \theta$ is more usually written as $|a|\, |b|\, \sin \theta$

....

vector triangle *see* **triangle**

....

velocity

The velocity of a moving object is given by stating both its speed and the direction in which the object is moving. It is a vector quantity. If the velocity is stated without reference to any direction, it must be assumed that the object is travelling in a straight line and that the overall direction of that line does not matter.

• *The SI unit of velocity is metres per second, abbreviated to m/s or ms⁻¹.*

SEE ALSO **acceleration, distance-time graph, speed**

⚠ **WATCH OUT**

Speed and **velocity** are very commonly used as having the same meaning, but there is a difference.

Velocity is a vector since it is described by giving both the speed of an object and the direction in which the object is moving.

Speed alone is not a vector.

....

velocity-time graph

A velocity-time graph is a graph that shows the relationship between the velocity of an object in relation to time.

• *The gradient of a line drawn on a **velocity-time graph** is a measure of acceleration.* • *If the line of the relationship is curved, the particular acceleration at some moment in time can only be found by drawing a tangent to the curve at that point and measuring its gradient.* • *The area under the curve (or the line of relationship) between two ordinates drawn from the time scale measures the distance travelled in that time interval*

SEE ALSO **distance-time graph**

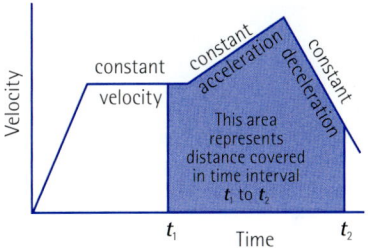

Venn diagram

Venn diagrams are used to give a pictorial view of the relationships of sets and subsets within a universal set; the universal set is shown enclosed by a rectangle, and all others by circles or simple closed curves.

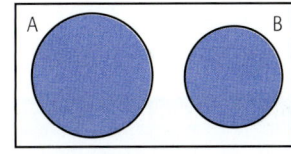

2 subsets (A and B) within a universal set
A and B are disjoint

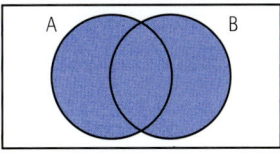

A ∪ B = union of A and B

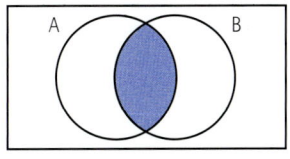

A ∩ B = intersection of A and B　　》

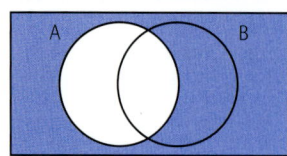

A' = complement of A

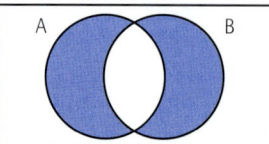

A Δ B = symmetric difference of A and B

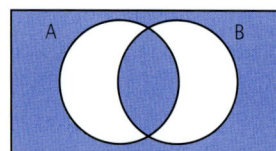

(A Δ B)' = complement of symmetric
difference of A and B

. . . .

versine
is a function is used in calculations in spherical trigonometry. It is an abbreviation of versed sine.

FORMULA:

versine θ (where θ is any angle) = 1 − cos θ

versine 30° = 1 − cos 30° = 1 − 0.866 = 0.134
(to 3 dp)

WORD BUILD

haversine

is an abbreviation of half-versine.

SEE ALSO **spherical trigonometry**

FORMULA:

haversine θ = (versine θ) ÷ 2 or 0.5 × (1 − cos θ)

. . . .

vertex *plural* vertices
❶ A vertex is a point where two edges of a polygon meet to form a corner.
❷ A vertex of a polyhedron is the angular point where three or more edges meet.
❸ The vertex of a cone is the fixed point used in making it.

❹ Vertex is sometimes used to mean the apex of a pyramid.
❺ (*also* **node**) A vertex or node in a topological graph is one of the points which make the graph.

even vertex

An even vertex is a vertex whose order (the number of edges attached to that vertex) is an even number.

odd vertex

An odd vertex is a vertex whose order (the number of edges attached to that vertex) is an odd number.

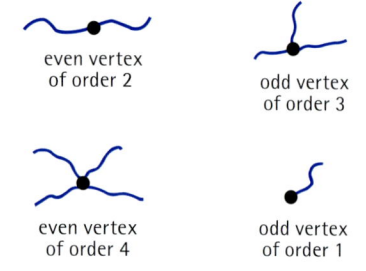

even vertex
of order 2

odd vertex
of order 3

even vertex
of order 4

odd vertex
of order 1

. . . .

vertical
A vertical line at any point on the Earth is the straight line which would join that point to the centre of the Earth.
• *Usually, in drawings, a **vertical** line means one which goes in the top-to-bottom direction of the page.*
SEE ALSO **horizontal**

. . . .

vertically opposite angle *see* angle

. . . .

vinculum
A vinculum is a horizontal bar placed over the top of a mathematical expression to indicate that it is to be treated together as one unit.
• *The **vinculum** is rarely seen now, having been replaced by the use of brackets.*
• *$3x + 5\overline{x − y}$ would now be written as $3x + 5(x − y)$.*
• *It still appears as part of the square root symbol:*
$\sqrt{}\overline{8x + y}$ is now written as $\sqrt{(8x + y)}$ or $\sqrt{8x + y}$.

. . . .

visual proof *see* **proof**

....

volume

The volume of a three-dimensional shape is a measure of how much space is contained within, or occupied by, that shape.
• *Volume is usually measured in terms of how many cubes of some unit size (cubic inches, cubic metres, etc.) would fill an equivalent amount of space.*
SEE ALSO **capacity**

....

volume of revolution

is the volume of a 3D solid which is formed by rotating the graph of a function in the Cartesian plane about a line in the plane. The volume may be calculated by integration.

....

vulgar fraction *see* **fraction**

....

Ww

wallpaper pattern *see* **pattern**

....

weight

❶ The weight of a body is a measure of how much it weighs (how much force the body produces when in a gravitational field). Weight is a vector quantity.
SEE ALSO **mass**
❷ In statistics, a weight is a value given to one of a set of items to indicate its relative importance.
SEE ALSO **mean**

....

weighted mean *see* **mean**

....

whole number *see* **number**

....

width *see* **dimension**

....

working mean *see* **mean**

....

world coordinate system *see* **coordinate**

....

a b c d e f g h i j k l m n o p q r s t u v w x y z

X x

x-axis *see* **axis**

x-coordinate *see* **coordinate**

Y y

y-axis *see* **axis**

y-coordinate *see* **coordinate**

Z z

z-angle *see* **angle**

Zeno's paradoxes

are concerned with motion and some apparent impossibilities. They were important in the development of mathematical thinking.

EXAMPLE:

There are four of **Zeno's paradoxes**, but the best known is that of Achilles and the tortoise.

Achilles races against a tortoise and, since Achilles is clearly the faster of the two, gives the tortoise a good start. By the time Achilles gets to the point at which the tortoise started, the tortoise has moved, and this is repeated over and over.

Can Achilles ever catch up with the tortoise?

zero *see* **place-holder**

zero index *see* **index**

zero vector *see* **vector**

zone

A zone of a sphere is the shape contained between the sphere itself and two parallel planes which cut across the sphere.

EXAMPLE:

The area of the curved surface around the outside of the **zone** is equal to the curved surface area of a cylinder the same diameter as the sphere, and same height as the **zone**.

The volume of a **zone** can be found by considering it as one segment minus another.

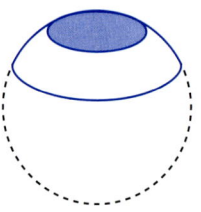

zone of a sphere

What have customers been saying about the *Oxford Student's Mathematics Dictionary?*

Choose Oxford Maths for revision support that counts

Browse our range of Revision Guides, Homework Books, and Exam Practice Workbooks at

www.oxfordsecondary.com/revision

ISBN: 978-0-19-835168-9

ISBN: 978-0-19-835170-2

ISBN: 978-0-19-835152-8

ISBN: 978-0-19-835154-2